Inventing the New Negro

Inventing the New Negro

Narrative, Culture, and Ethnography

Daphne Lamothe

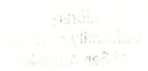

PENN

University of Pennsylvania Press
Philadelphia

Published by
University of Pennsylvania Press
Philadelphia, Pennsylvania 19104-4112

Printed in the United States of America on acid-free paper

10   9   8   7   6   5   4   3   2   1

Library of Congress Cataloging-in-Publication Data

Lamothe, Daphne Mary
  Inventing the new Negro : narrative, culture, and ethnography / Daphne Lamothe.
    p. cm.
  Includes bibliographical references and index.
  ISBN 978-0-8122-4093-1 (alk. paper)
    1. Blacks. 2. Ethnology—United States. 3. African American intellectuals.
4. African American anthropologists. 5. American literature—African American authors.
6. African Americans in literature. 7. Anthropology in literature. 8. Harlem Renaissance.
I. Title.

GN645.L36 2008
305.896—dc22

2008007777

Contents

Chapter 1
Ethnography and the New Negro Imagination

In 1925, after having won second prize in an *Opportunity* magazine contest for her short story "Drenched in Light," the intrepid Zora Neale Hurston made her way from Eatonville, Florida, to the crowded streets of New York City in search, like so many other Southern migrants, of education and opportunity. Soon after her arrival in the city, she enrolled at Barnard College, where she studied anthropology with Franz Boas. It did not take long for Hurston to become a vital member of Harlem's social and literary scene, even as she gained credentials as an anthropologist. In 1927, and again in 1934 after having been awarded a Guggenheim fellowship to study folklore, she took the education and cultural capital that she had accumulated in New York with her on her fieldwork in the South. She was intent on documenting the particular contributions of Southern Blacks to American society, but consequently, she found that the return to the South demanded that she negotiate the spaces—both real and rhetorical—between the familiar and the strange, the insides and the outside of a culture that she knew so well yet learned to value only once she moved away and saw it through the eyes of a stranger.

Hurston, like so many of her New Negro peers, would build a career at the borders of American interracial and cross-cultural encounters. *Inventing the New Negro: Narrative, Culture, and Ethnography* represents one attempt to examine the geographical locations identified by, and socially mediated gazes used by, Black intellectuals in the early decades of the twentieth century. These writers and artists adopted and adapted anthropology, folklore, and sociological discourses to name and create a cohesive, collective, and modern Black identity. I refer to the texts they produced as "sites of culture" in order to underscore the attempts of writers like Hurston to create counternarratives to American society's racist discourse on blackness by mapping African American culture across particular geographical spaces, while viewing it from their socially mediated "sights," or perspectives.

For Hurston, making visible the process of collecting folklore and writing culture was the counter-narrative, the alternative to totalizing, simplistic, and dehumanizing representations of blackness found in so much of popular American culture. This is a project she will continue to develop in her second ethnography, *Tell My Horse* (1938), but even in *Mules and Men* (1935) she felt compelled to dissect the complicated work of collecting, transcribing, and translating cultures. She writes, for example:

Folk-lore is not as easy to collect as it sounds. The best source is where there are the least outside influences and these people, being usually under-privileged, are the shyest. They are the most reluctant at times to reveal that which the soul lives by. And the Negro, in spite of his open-faced laughter, his seeming acquiescence, is particularly evasive. You see we are a polite people and we do not say to our questioner, "Get out of here!" We smile and tell him or her something that satisfies the white person because, knowing so little about us, he doesn't know what he is missing. The Indian resists curiosity by a stony silence. The Negro offers a feather-bed resistance. That is, we let the probe enter, but it never comes out. It gets smothered under a lot of laughter and pleasantries.

The theory behind our tactics: "The white man is always trying to know into somebody else's business. All right, I'll set something outside the door of my mind for him to play with and handle. He can read my writing but he sho' can't read my mind."[1]

Hurston's shift from third-person ("they") to first-person plural ("we") takes place at the precise moment when the subject of evasiveness—the "featherbed of resistance"—arises. It underscores her duality as both the looker and a subject under scrutiny, as does her slippage from writing about listening to folktales, to writing about her audience reading her narrative. By linking her text so closely with a community that is never willing to completely expose itself to scrutiny, Hurston subtly challenges the assumption that one can attain complete, unmediated access to this culture by reading the ethnographic narrative. "He can read my writing but he sho' can't read my mind," she insists and the reader wonders if the speaker is the informant or the ethnographer.

The answer, of course, is that Hurston is both native informant, by virtue of her racial identity and place of origin, and ethnographer, by virtue of her training. This duality, resulting in a subject I call the native ethnographer, is common to all New Negro writers who delved into anthropology and ethnography, even those not as intimately familiar with Southern culture and mores as Hurston. Thus, the focus of any critique of this body of literature is always, inescapably, on narrative, positionality, and the relation between the two. New Negro artists and writers looked to ethnography for strategies for representing their cultural identity and combating racist preconceptions at the same time that they maintained a firm grasp of themselves as culture-workers and creative individuals. Therefore, even as I foreground the influential role played by ethnography in African American artistic expression, I caution against ethnographic readings of literary texts that look for signs of authenticity and bind the narrative by expectations of the "real." As Hurston's commentary suggests, such expectations—even in supposedly straightforward ethnographies—are bound to be confounded.[2]

The Spy-Glass of Anthropology and the Black Modernist Gaze

By examining the New Negroes' strategies for self-examination, I am suggesting a new way to think about their modernity. One aspect of New Negro modernity is the insistence on a way of seeing that dislocates ways of knowing especially visible in their literature's engagement with anthropology. Their writing shows how a culture can be perceived in multiple, sometimes conflicting, ways, inviting, like Ludwig Wittgenstein's duck-rabbit, the possibility of the "dawning of a [different] aspect" each time an object is encountered. Wittgenstein writes, "If you search in a figure (1) for another figure (2), and then you find it, you see (1) in a new way. Not only can you give a new kind of description of it, but noticing the second figure was a new visual experience."[3] New Negro literature is equally disorienting (or, more accurately, multiply oriented) in that its creators produce multiple, fluid, and dynamic portraits of African America, depictions that resist absolutist thinking about the other. Thus, even as they respond to and challenge stereotypical representations of African Americans as subhuman and inferior, they resist questions of truth and illusion, authenticity and falsity, and turn our attention to a redefinition of truth as multiply unfolding and composed of a constellation of interconnected concepts and experiences.

New Negroes were modernists because of their willingness to grapple with the uncertainty of knowing and to use this in self-reflection. In this way, Black modernism echoes the larger sense of instability and uncertainty in the face of multiple and rapid social change that characterized U.S. society in the interwar years. Although Houston Baker distinguishes Black modernist preoccupations from "high" modernist unease, common ground can be found in both groups' narrative explorations of modern instability that center on the gaze.[4] Baker identifies high modernist preoccupations as centering around a kind of "civilization and its discontents" that not only excludes the contributions of African American modernists but also situates Black people as the polar opposite of a "civilization" in decline and mourned for by Elliot, Joyce, Fitzgerald, and the rest. While I agree with his contention that Black modernists had concerns that differed from those of some of their Anglo-American peers, my point here is that they jumped right into the discursive fray and challenged on its own terms the colonizing gaze that would render them unspeakably and monstrously other.

One example of this modern and modernist unease has been examined by Mitchell Breitwieser.[5] Breitwieser cites as evidence of the trauma brought about by shifting racial and social hierarchies various instances in which F. Scott Fitzgerald proposes and then rapidly shuts down the possibility of Negro subjectivity, figured through the image of a "fugitive" gaze (23). Fitzgerald describes one such incident when Nick and Gatsby, riding in Gatsby's car, witness another vehicle: "As we crossed Blackwell's Island a limousine passed us, driven by a white chauffeur, in which sat three modish negroes, two bucks and a girl. I laughed aloud as the yolks of their eyeballs rolled toward us in haughty rivalry."[6] Breitwieser offers a number of insightful observations about this scene, including the foreclosed possibility of cross-racial identification as the pair of socially ambitious, upwardly mobile White men pass by and then rebuff a group of equally ambitious African Americans whom they dismiss as upstarts. What I want to focus on here, however, is the significance he reads into the series of looks and counter-looks that pass between them. Breitwieser states:

Deprived of a look that supplied a way of being seen to which we have grown accustomed and with which we have merged ourselves, we are suddenly captured in another look that does *not* see us as we are—or rather, that does not see us as we wish to be seen, but sees instead what we have secretly feared to be the case about ourselves, squalid, peculiar attributes and motives over which dead love had urged us not to worry, but now, incited by this novel gaze, escape the restraint of a reassuring normality, insist upon themselves, itch at us. (19)

The gaze, from the perspective of Anglo-American modernism, is an attribute that connotes consciousness and the powers to reason, universalize, and objectify that which the viewer surveys. The modernist anxiety arises when Gatsby and Nick become aware of an other, presumed to lack these attributes, witnessing their activities. They experience something very similar to what W. E. B. Du Bois labeled double-consciousness, the awareness that another's perception of one's self differs radically from one's own self-understanding. Nick and Gatsby immediately displace the anxiety and confusion that it generates by reasserting their dominance by objectifying the "Negroes," invoking the minstrel image of rolling eyes, and equating them with food, capable of being consumed but never having the power or capacity to "consume" another.

While the Anglo-modernist gaze in this instance is characterized by its dislocation and anxious restoration of a previous sense of order, we see in New Negro ethnography and ethnography-inspired writing an engagement with modernity that insists on displacement and resists the reassertion of racial and social hierarchies exemplified by Gatsby and Nick's colonizing looks. I do not mean to elide the differences between the modernist's will to not see and modern anthropology's establishment of a tradition of gazing on the other from a position of objectivity and with a commitment to ideas of cultural relativism. But what links these different ways of looking (one racist and one progressive) is the colonizing impulse to construct and contain through observation and narration. What I argue is that New Negro writers interrogate and ultimately critique the colonizing gaze on the racialized subject, intersecting and shifting the presuppositions of both literary modernism and modernist anthropology by making their narratives as much about epistemology as they are about objectivity.

In *Mules and Men*, Hurston never positions herself as an all-seeing and transcendent anthropologist. Instead her mentor, Franz Boas, suggests in his preface to this collection of folklore that she garners her authority from her likeness to her informants, who are assumed to be open to and available for examination. Hurston's visibility in the narrative is reinforced by the dual roles she performed as both social scientist and raced individual. Boas validates this duality in the preface when he writes, "the great merit of Miss Hurston's work [is] that she entered into the homely life of the southern Negro as one of them and was fully accepted as such by the companions of her childhood" (x). Boas expected that sharing racial and cultural traits with Eatonville's inhabitants would facilitate Hurston's identification with "the folk" and her participation in communal rituals, presumably making more "authentic" her representation of Black folk life. He also expected and assumed that she would maintain her objectivity and scientific detachment, another precondition of producing a cultural portrait that would be regarded as authentic.

Hurston seconds these assumptions in her introduction to the collection and then later undercuts them. She states, for example, "I didn't go back there [to Eatonville] so that the home folks could make admiration over me because I had been up North to college and come back with a diploma and a Chevrolet. I knew they were not going to pay either one of these items too much mind. I was just Lucy Hurston's daughter, Zora" (3). Nonetheless several chapters later, kinship ties prove useless when she has to explain away her difference, signified in one case by her "shiny gray Chevrolet," by concocting a story about being a bootlegger (66). In other venues, Hurston's accounts of her work's reception suggest that this duality is in fact a double bind. One example can be found in an anecdote she recounts in her autobiography, *Dust Tracks on a Road* (1942), in a chapter devoted to research. In it, her patron requests that she entertain visitors with folktales and songs: "There she was sitting up there at the table over capon, caviar and gleaming silver, eager to hear every word on every phase of life on a saw-mill job. 'I must tell the tales, sing the songs, do the dances, and repeat the raucous sayings and doings of the Negro farthest down.'"[7] Hurston's stature as social scientist diminishes—although esteem in her storytelling prowess may escalate—as she launches into a performance of race and culture designed to reaffirm the dominant culture's sense of itself as superior. The chapter proceeds with tales of her misadventures in the field, and snatches of folktales and songs accumulated during her years spent studying the folk of Polk County, Florida (177–205). The image of Charlotte Osgood Mason enjoying capon and caviar as Hurston regales her with stories of chain gangs and knife fights offers an unsettling portrait of the native ethnographer assuming the guise of the native informant and distorting it to the point of ridiculousness. Hurston does not question or problematize this moment in the autobiography. Yet in her ethnographic texts, her physical, Western, gendered, intrusive body is insistently present in the field, and her equally problematic self is evident at home, forcing the reader to question at all times the autonomy and authenticity of the self being represented at any given moment. In the previous example, for instance, Hurston appears to perform for Mason an image expressly designed to meet the dominating patron's desires for exotic entertainment.

Hurston was not unaware of the complexity of her situation. In fact, she is unique among her contemporaries in the extent to which she theorizes specularity, linking ways of seeing to ways of knowing, and calling into question absolutist claims to authenticity, truth, and meaning. She links perception and knowledge in her introduction to *Mules and Men*:

When I pitched headforemost into the world I landed in the crib of negroism. From the earliest rocking of my cradle, I had known about the capers Brer Rabbit is apt to cut and what the Squinch Owl says from the house top. But it was fitting me like a tight chemise. I couldn't see it for wearing it. It was only when I was off in college, away from my native surroundings, that I could see myself like somebody else and stand off and look at my garment. Then I had to have the spy-glass of Anthropology to look through that. (3)

On one hand, Hurston narrates what Joanne Passaro has called "the epistemology of distance," suggesting that social distance and greater degrees of "otherness" between ethnographer and informants are necessary to ensure the appropriate level of objectivity.[8] Hurston makes clear her inability to appreciate and even see the distinctiveness of her culture until she acquires a geographical, educational, social, and perhaps emotional distance from her home. On the other hand, her notion of culture shifts from a description of it as a kind of material environment to one as a garment, something layered onto yet also difficult to separate from her physical being because it fits so "tightly." The idea of culture as garment implicitly challenges the more commonly held belief that race and culture were synonymous. In its place, Hurston suggests that culture is something acquired through proximity to a particular environment; and she sets the stage for a consideration of the sophistication and beauty of African American culture that would contest widely held assumptions of racial inferiority. Living a culture, Hurston suggests, is a markedly different experience from seeing and thereby claiming to know it. During her Southern girlhood, she suggests, she lived Negro culture unreflexively. It took leaving that culture for her to recognize its unique attributes and its value. Anthropological methods provided Hurston with the tools with which to experience the double-consciousness that characterizes the modernist gaze–"see[ing] myself like somebody else"—and to experience that condition as self-awareness as opposed to the lack of self-knowledge that Du Bois ascribes to the African American's doubled-consciousness in *The Souls of Black Folk*. And finally, Hurston inscribes Black communities' orally conveyed tales and songs in order to allow them to present their own notions of social reality. Yet Hurston equates proximity, sight, and insight in a letter to Langston Hughes, dated March 8, 1928, in which she describes with excitement the success of her fieldwork: "I am getting inside of Negro art and lore. I am beginning to *see* really and when you join me I shall point things out and see if you see them as I do."[9] As in the previous example, seeing and knowing are virtually synonymous. But in contrast to her statements in *Mules and Men*, here Hurston stresses the importance of "getting inside" Negro culture in order to be able to see it clearly.

Not only does Hurston consistently equate looking and knowledge; she also links language and knowledge in her narratives. The John-Massa stories recorded in *Mules and Men*, for example, illustrate this point. John, described by Hurston as "the great human culture hero in Negro folk-lore," is a trickster figure whose opposition to authority figures such as the master, God, and the Devil make him a cultural hero to the people who invented him (253). John, like Hurston, does not often make explicit his strategies of resistance, but he relies on duplicity and verbal dexterity to cover for his oppositional behaviors and consciousness. The John stories function as personal and collective allegories, resonating with the situations of African-descended peoples who transform displacement and disempowerment into a tenacious will to survive, and even thrive, in a hostile environment through sheer creativity and (self-) invention.

Described as "de first colored man what was brought to dis country," who "doesn't know nothin' mo' than you told him," John, in one folktale, is taken by his master around the house and told fantastical names for the objects that fill it (85). The master tells him, for example, that the fireplace is a "flame 'vaperator," the stairs are his "jacob ladder," and the bed is the "flowery-bed-of-ease," and so on. The tale of an individual stripped of knowledge and language alludes to slavery and the erasure of an African cultural heritage. It reminds us, Robert Hemenway argues, "that whoever attempts to control language, the naming process, attempts to control our understanding of who we are, our definition of reality."[10] This allegory of language acquisition, power, and control takes a hairpin turn when John sets fire to the master's barn and attempts to explain the sequence of events that have led to the disaster. First he speaks in sentences that string together the master's neologisms with astonishing facility; second, the master is completely incapable of understanding him when the language game goes beyond the pointing and naming he has instigated; and lastly John drops the pretense and uses direct, plainspoken language that has a more immediate and forceful impact than the more rarified language of the master. This tale speaks to African Americans' acquisition, mastery, and negotiation of foreign languages and cultures upon enslavement. It can also be read as a self-referential narrative that celebrates Hurston, the native ethnographer's polyvocality, and her ability to slip between, around, and within multiple modes of narration.

Hurston's ethnography enacts a paradoxical Black modernist gaze that looks at Black culture and looks back at the dominant culture with which the anthropologist is identified. Shamoon Zamir argues that W. E. B. Du Bois, another subject of this study, merits "a place in the history of American literary modernism . . . not because the work transcends the particulars of race.

It deserves this kind of reassessment precisely because [they] can use the history of race in America as an entrance into issues of modernity."[11] Like Du Bois (and Hurston), other ethnographically inclined New Negroes consistently questioned the ways and means of knowing. Their work may not often conform to the formalistic experimentalism of high modernism, but their immersion into the murky terrain of knowledge and knowledge production is an intrinsic part of the modernist project. Working with and through ethnographic conventions—indeed, by transforming ethnographic paradigms—these artists and intellectuals carve open spaces from which Black people's experiences and desires seep out, refusing the social scientist and the larger society's attempts at cultural acquisition, mastery, and containment.[12]

Encounters in the Field: Anthropological Methods and Literary Symbols

Ethnographic literature of the Harlem Renaissance shares many of the defining characteristics of ethnography, a genre that depends on a method, namely fieldwork, to produce a narrative that simultaneously invents and documents a culture. New Negro encounters with the ethnographic imagination resulted in, for example, literature that attends to the Black intellectual's travel to, participation in, and observation of folk communities. Although most of the artists I focus on were closely identified with the Harlem Renaissance, it is important to note that their interest in ethnography, anthropology, and folklore took them to places outside of New York City, such as the rural South and the Caribbean, and that such locations played a central role in their creative work. The trope of travel to bounded, symbolic sites of Black culture (for example, the South and Haiti) is indebted to an ethnographic method, established by anthropologist Bronislaw Malinowski, which privileges the immersion of the participant-observer in the "field."[13] Sterling Brown, who, by virtue of his youth and residence in the South during the twenties, is least identified with the Harlem Renaissance, articulates the centrality of traveling to the South to his poetry in a 1974 interview in which he declared, "when they were down there [in Harlem] flirting with Carl Van Vechten, I was down south talking to Big Boy."[14] The point I want to make is that each of the writers examined in this book spent time down South (or in other culturally identified spaces) talking to their own trusted informants, and went on to incorporate those fieldwork-like journeys into their fiction, essays, anthologies, and theories of blackness.

New Negro ethnographic literature, produced after fieldwork and/or folklore collecting endeavors, was not exclusively ethnographic. While some of the texts I discuss were produced explicitly to describe the defining attributes of cultures perceived as exotic or primitive, others describe in fictional or nonfiction forms the contact between ethnographer-like observers and peoples indigenous to a location, and still other texts present themselves as nothing more than works of art (whether dance, fiction, or poetry) and only the works' symbolism hold the signs of their ethnographic origins. Narratives of ethnographic encounters allowed Black intellectuals to explore "native" encounters not only with ethnographers but also with other figures who represent literate, dominant society. These representations offer their authors the chance to stage the complex dynamics between center and periphery in narratives that may feature not only anthropologists but also Black teachers, community leaders, and other members of the professional classes who often returned to and interacted with their communities as liminal figures, participant-observers who are modeled, at least in part, on the fieldworker so central to the ethnographic method.

This book is also about generic encounters between ethnography and other, primarily literary, genres and the cultural productions that emerge as a result. Ethnographic literature (a form related to but distinct from ethnography) is typically understood as conforming to the formal constraints of literary realism, offering empirical representations of a community's social, economic, and political life.[15] Without diminishing the intellectual and artistic merit of such works, I focus primarily on texts that are not explicitly ethnographic in intent, but that use ethnography to trouble or expand the conventional limits of particular artistic forms (such as Sterling Brown's poetry and Katherine Dunham's choreography), or that use literary form and conventions to problematize and render more complex the conceptual frames of ethnography (such as Hurston's *Tell My Horse* and Du Bois's *The Souls of Black Folk*). Many of these authors systematically wrote against the grain of ethnographic conventions that insisted on a "scientific" presentation of folkloric materials at the same time that they challenged literary conventions. Their work compels us to question equally what attributes of a narrative cause it to merit the labels, "ethnographic" or "literary" because these authors refused to be limited by convention or orthodoxy.

Hurston, for example, was thrilled at the possibility that literature and folklore could not only interact, but also intermingle. She wrote to Langston Hughes, for example, about her efforts to promote his poetry in the Florida communities to which she traveled:

In every town I hold 1 or 2 story-telling contests, and at each I begin by telling them who you are and all, then I read poems from "Fine Clothes." Boy! They eat it up. Two or three of them are too subtle and they don't get it . . . but the others they *just eat up*. You are being quoted in R. R. camps, phosphate mines, Turpentine stills, etc. . . . So you see they are making it so much a part of themselves they go to improvising on it.[16]

Hurston pushed the boundaries more than others in that she was able to imagine a world not only in which literate society developed the capacity to appreciate and appropriate folk communities, but also in which folk communities could appropriate and appreciate "mainstream" art and culture and use it to their own ends. While she represents an extreme in the array of authors I examine in this book, she is not unique because they all consider the fertile possibilities of creative and conceptual cross-fertilization between ethnography and other genres. For the most part, I restrict my focus primarily to figures that have produced a wide and deep *narrative* body on the multiple experiences of encountering ethnography, including narratives by the dancer-choreographer Katherine Dunham, who also wrote about the paradoxes and peculiarities of fieldwork.

Genres such as fiction and memoir may enable the kind of self-reflection that I view as a central and inherent element of this tradition. But I find equally compelling texts that combine ethnography with a range of other genres because generic hybridity is a mode of representation central to the Black modernist imagination. By juxtaposing radically different narratives within the same text, African American intellectuals developed a critical strategy for writing about the multiple factors that contributed to representations of "other" cultures. The hybrid narrative in and of itself is a theoretical site in which knowledge production can be queried and staged. Juxtaposing different modes of representation compels the reader to question how we know what we know. Zora Neale Hurston and W. E. B. Du Bois will be emblematic of this rhetorical stance because they, more than the other authors in this study, use different forms of address within the same texts to open up a space of critical inquiry about the social position of the knower.[17]

In *Inventing the New Negro*, I focus on the art and/or ethnographies produced by Katherine Dunham, Zora Neale Hurston, W. E. B. Du Bois, James Weldon Johnson, and Sterling Brown. The ethnographic novel has traditionally held an appeal for marginalized individuals, habitually excluded from academic positions and seeking a wider audience for their work; and ethnography has always been influenced by literature.[18] By focusing on these individuals, I am able to examine the processes by which artists and intellectuals used ethnography to self-reflexively assume the roles of translators and explicators of African American and African Diasporic folk cultures to West-ern audiences.

A large number of Renaissance-era writers, because of the movement's focus on cross-cultural translation, saw in ethnography, which entered its "classical period" at the turn of the twentieth century, both a mode that fa-cilitated this representational endeavor and a discursive framework that brought into relief the vexed interplay between dominant and marginalized groups.[19] New Negro writers provide complex portraits of ethnography as instrument of colonialism *and* heroic venture.[20] On the one hand, they seized hold of ethnography's claim to be able to translate seemingly incomprehen-sible actions into "meaningful" behavior.[21] On the other hand, all of these writers, to varying degrees, recognized the epistemological constraints of an academic discipline rooted, as anthropology was, in conditions of colonial conquest and domination.

Du Bois, Johnson, Brown, Dunham, and Hurston wrote during a time when White Americans' fascination with African and African-derived cul-tures provided a receptive climate and ready audience for the work of writ-ers and ethnographers who documented and explicated the language, culture, religion, and philosophy of "primitive" Black cultures.[22] They did so at a point when anthropologists began to rework the discipline, institution-alizing and encoding its methods and procedures so as to distance itself from a previous generation who, as David Levering Lewis notes, "located Negroes somewhere on the frontier between the great apes and hominids" and pro-vided the ideological rationale for racial subjugation.[23] Black intellectuals found that appropriating the authority of science in the service of battling these stereotypical notions was far from simple. In fact, those who worked overtly as folklorists and ethnographers had to repeatedly assert their suit-ability for the job. Du Bois struggled, for example, to find a professional placement that matched the prestige of his academic training and impress-iveness of his accomplishments. And Hurston repeatedly stressed that her work was scientifically sound, not only to satisfy her own ambitions but also to answer the doubts of her professors, mentors, and grant administrators, who often expressed concern that she lacked the discipline to succeed as an anthropologist.[24]

Although these writers worked in a number of genres and fields outside of the social sciences, including dance, education, and politics, they used ethnography in some of their most important works of fiction and nonfic-tion because it provided a clear, powerful, and socially accepted language with which to observe and document a folk culture that many Americans were convinced was populated by dark and primitive others. As W. E. B. Du Bois writes in "Of the Quest of the Golden Fleece," one of the chapters focusing on Dougherty County, Georgia, in *The Souls of Black Folk*, "And yet how little we really know of these millions, of their daily lives and longings, of their homely joys and sorrows, of their real shortcomings and the meaning of their crimes! All this we can only learn by intimate contact with the masses, and not by wholesale arguments covering millions separate in time and space, and differing widely in training and culture."[25]

In his biography of Du Bois, Lewis notes that the culture and institutions of the rural South "were as mysterious to most early twentieth-century readers as Livingstone's Africa" (285). So Du Bois is prominent among the many African American writers who assumed the responsibility of explicating a culture and landscape viewed by their audience as mysterious, foreign, exotic, or strange. These efforts to affirm the value of African American culture took place within a climate in which perceptions of racial difference were intertwined with assumptions of White racial superiority and Black inferiority and that saw little significance in class or regional differences among African Americans. The social consequences of the migration of thousands of Blacks from the rural South to New York City between 1894 and 1915 made such biases all the more acute, fueling the efforts of Black intellectuals, anthropologist Franz Boas, and other racially progressive individuals to develop a persuasive, scientific, and activist response to the totalizing and absolutist discourses of race and racism.[26]

Du Bois's image of the Black intellectual lifting the veil and moving back and forth across a racial divide is useful in imagining what most hoped to achieve in their representations of poor and working-class Black cultures to White America. It provides a visual analogue to the ethnographic project, which emphasized, particularly after the 1920s and 1930s, the movement between cultures. In the 1920s, ethnographers were increasingly expected to employ their skills as "trained onlooker[s]" to record and explain the "characteristic behaviors" and rituals of a particular group (Clifford 31). This purportedly objective perspective carried far more weight for readers of ethnographic accounts than did the views of indigenous people on their own lives, much less their opinions about "first world" nations. The materiality of the veil indicates the acceptance of the notion that Black and White societies were clearly distinct from each other, and could be contained and framed by the ethnographer's gaze. Du Bois's shifting position behind, above, and across the veil signifies his ability to see both Black and White worlds with an insight that is unique to the Black subject, and perhaps even more presciently, to the Black or native ethnographer. The veil can function as a metaphor for the native ethnographers' privileged perspective, but their doubled-consciousness also offered them the ideal vantage point from which to survey, critique, and complicate the terms used to categorize humans and the societies they lived in.

Even as New Negro intellectuals appropriated new anthropological theories of race and culture to further their anti-racist agendas, they often revealed a wariness of and confrontation with the discipline's own absolutist assumptions. They recognized, for example, that scientific detachment could be not only the root of authority for the marginalized subject but also a source of conflict because the scientific imperative encouraged a separation between ethnographers and the subjects of their study.[27] Their narratives illustrate the inherent tensions in the notion that "the scientific position of speech is that of an observer fixed on the edge of a space, looking in and/or down upon what is other."[28] Contemporary theorists and cultural critics have recognized that empiricism can result in epistemic violence because "in trying to become 'objective,' Western culture made 'objects of things and people when it distanced itself from them, thereby losing 'touch' with them." "This dichotomy," Gloria Anzaldùa has argued, "is the root of all violence."[29] New Negro intellectuals may have adopted and adapted anthropology to challenge the dichotomy of White humanity and non-Whites' presumed subhumanity, but they found the discipline lacking because of its continued reification of a Western subject/non-Western object dichotomy under a different guise.[30] They saw literature and art as performing the same work as anthropology, adding rhetorical fuel to the fire of rehabilitating the image of Blacks; nonetheless, their engagement with the social sciences was not uncritical and even as they applied social science methods and theories, they continued to identify and challenge practices—including their own—that risked maintaining the subordination of Black peoples.

The paradoxes, ironies, conflicts, and tensions experienced by native ethnographers of the Harlem Renaissance are typical for anthropologists who share the same identities as the subjects of their study. Kath Weston employs the term "virtual anthropologist" to describe such individuals. Weston argues that academia continues to presume the virtual anthropologist's familiarity and identification with the cultural, racial, and gendered others upon which anthropology is predicated, rendering them incapable of assuming the full authority of the scientist who is imagined as white and male in his "ideal" form.[31] She argues that despite this supposition, the virtual anthropologist offers a subject position that problematizes and even collapses the subject/object dichotomy on which conventional ethnographies rely by continually questioning the terms that are used to define her.[32] Certainly, this questioning stance can be discerned in the work of these first- and second-generation modern ethnographers whose works are characterized by a dialectical exchange between themselves and the communities they enter, and their queries into the tensions and contradictions between their rhetoric and actions. The deconstruction of binaristic logic, we will see, is a central aim of many of these texts. Rational/irrational, civilized/primitive, modern/traditional, and cosmopolitan/tribal are all oppositions that these writers investigate for their racial, cultural, and even political significance.

The difference between the native ethnographers' relatively privileged social positions and the subjugation experienced by so many of the "folk" they set out to celebrate could be as much of a source of unease as was their status in the view of the dominant culture. Ethnographic discourse may have had its rhetorical place, but it also had its pitfalls because it emphasized the Black intellectual's position of superiority and detachment in relation to people who suffered the same political disenfranchisement as they and to whom they thus felt politically and culturally allied. African American documenters of Black culture were in the position to demonstrate both detachment from the culture and an authentic identification with it. A shared racial identity provided them with easier access to their subjects, and gave them an affinity with the experiences and feelings of those they observed, apparently allowing them to render folk culture more realistically and truthfully to their audience. At the same time, class, regional, and national differences could result in mutual incomprehension and distrust. Detached observation pushed and pulled against racial, political, and cultural solidarity in much of their writing, and the native ethnographer's simultaneous position as both outsider and insider to Black cultures imbue the texts with a strong measure of self-consciousness, ambivalence, and irony.

Anthropologist James Clifford calls participant-observation "shorthand for a continuous tacking between the 'inside' and 'outside' of events: on the one hand grasping the sense of specific occurrences and gestures empathetically, on the other stepping back to situate these meanings in wider contexts" (34). This stance, which he deems inevitably ironic, proved both cumbersome and enabling for the writers I examine in this study. They shuttle continually between the inside and outside of the cultures they observed. Their resistance to an ethnographic authority based solely on scientific detachment and an absolute assurance of the boundaries between the observer and the observed anticipates poststructuralist critiques of such anthropological conventions, making these individuals—who are to this day frequently dismissed as amateur or failed anthropologists—innovators in the field.[33]

The ethnography—produced explicitly by Hurston, Dunham, and Du Bois and implicitly by Johnson and Brown-which is characterized by its blurring of inside and outside and its writer's mobile subject position, has found fuller articulation in the work of contemporary theorists such as George Marcus and James Clifford. Their works' openness to confronting the politics and poetics of representation anticipates the postmodern era's "crisis of representation."[34] The native ethnographer privileged the blurring of boundaries between social categories and challenged the belief that one could possess absolute knowledge of a world tenuously holding onto its sense of internal order and meaning. While the writers I examine found the presence of chaos and excess unsettling, they also implicitly recognized such epistemological instability as inevitable conditions of the modern world.

In this chapter, I have argued for the literary and discursive innovation made possible by the New Negro encounter with the social sciences. In the second chapter, I explore the historical and disciplinary conditions from which this literary school emerged. The reliance of U.S. racial discourse on sociological and anthropological narratives, and the racially progressive interventions made by disciplinary forefathers, Boas and Du Bois, all prove pivotal to understanding the choices made and challenges faced by New Negro intellectuals.

In the third chapter, I interrogate the ethnographic distance and simultaneous closeness with the subject that Renaissance figure struggled with in their art by focusing on W. E. B. Du Bois's *The Souls of Black Folk*. In it I argue that if Du Bois's image of the veil in *The Souls of Black Folk* is a potent figure for racial divisions and inequality, then the act of raising the veil signals the ethnographer's skill in cross-cultural transit and translation. In taking on such a project, however, Du Bois struggles with binaries often employed to explain Black/White difference, including subject/object, high culture/low culture, and modernity/tradition—binaries that habitually place African Americans in the position of inferiority. *Souls* disrupts these binaries, however, through its author's use of a liminal language to capture his liminal status as native ethnographer. Du Bois moves, in other words, between the detached, empirical language of sociology and the invested, emotional rhetoric of a subject who shares a bond with and the fate of his fellow African Americans. Du Bois's situatedness, the ways in which he finds himself enmeshed between languages, communities, indeed even identities, enables him to interrogate the terms used to identify him.

Like liminality, hybridity is a central and focalizing concept in this chapter, for I argue that Du Bois employs a generic hybridity, merging different genres into a single and singular text, in order to explore different ways of viewing, and hence knowing, Black culture. For example, he uses fiction—the short story "Of the Coming of John"—to stage and theorize his ambivalence about the Negro intellectual's relations with the folk he means to represent. This story's presentation near the end of a series of sociological, philosophical, and autobiographical essays compels the reader to think anew about the relations between and locations of author and subjects, factors that inform the shaping of the narratives that precede the story. Ultimately, I argue that Du Bois is a central figure whose role in the intersection of Harlem Renaissance literature and anthropology has been overlooked and inadequately analyzed. Ethnography, the narrative mode and method shared by sociologists and anthropologists, proves the link between Du Bois and Boas. These two figures' great influence can be seen in their combined work on cultural relativism and pluralism. But it is also Du Bois's willingness to depart from social science conventions that made a mark on the next generation of authors.

That questioning is immediately evident in Chapter 4, which focuses on James Weldon Johnson's use and critique of fieldwork as a model for the "talented tenth's" engagement with folk communities. Johnson metaphorizes the protagonist's travels through the South as a kind of anthropological exercise in participant-observation. He condemns the protagonist's detached analysis of folk communities as indicative of his alienation and imperialistic motives, characteristics that disqualify him from assuming the category of race leader to which he aspires.

Chapter 5 demonstrates how another author uses fieldwork as a trope for the encounter between dominant and marginalized groups. My reading of Sterling Brown's poetry situates it in relation to his statements vis-à-vis the differences between sociological narratives and true literature. Brown argued that literature transcends the sociological because of its capacity to convey characters' humanity and individuality. Nonetheless, I insist on the importance of considering that the store of images he draws from is indebted at least in part to the ethnographic imagination and his folklore collecting expeditions. Brown explicitly and implicitly reinscribes the notion of the rural South as cultural center for Black America. He privileges the field, the South, as locus of African American culture. Yet he resists isolating Black culture in that location by emphasizing travel and migration, resisting the depiction of Black culture as static, pre-modern, and fixed in the Southern landscape.

Brown's blues poems, and the figure of the Southern road, meditate on the influences of place *and* travel in the production of African American culture.

The sixth and seventh chapters, on Katherine Dunham's *Island Possessed* and Zora Neale Hurston's *Tell My Horse*, respectively, move away from male writers' depictions of Southern Black culture to female anthropologists' analyses of Jamaican and Haitian cultures. As the gender shift alters the terms and implications of the ethnographer's embodiment, so does the change from regional to international travel alter the meaning of the ethnographer's "native" status. Hurston and Dunham's texts fall more clearly than any other texts I discuss under the rubric of ethnography. Although neither narrative is typically considered part of the Harlem Renaissance canon (particularly Dunham's memoir/ethnography which was published in 1969), both authors conducted their fieldwork in the mid-thirties at the tail end of the Renaissance period and were heavily influenced by *and* helped to inform modernist notions of cross-cultural translation. Both Hurston and Dunham wrote self-reflexive ethnographies that place the ethnographer and her colonialist enterprise under as much if not more scrutiny as the cultures that they observed. In this sense, their texts clear the space to interrogate how social science methods and discourse endow cultural patterns and social behaviors with meaning.

Dunham's writing in the memoirist mode, one might argue, facilitates the kind of self-reflection that I view as a central element of this tradition. Although Hurston employs a strikingly different kind of narration, self-reflection proves to be a central element in her narrative as well. Typical readings of *Tell My Horse* diminish the significance of the travel narrative and social commentary that frame the Vodou ethnography because of its impressionistic, ethnocentric, and amateurish tone. I insist, however, that a reading of the "frame" is absolutely necessary because it deconstructs the ethnographic project through proximity. The text lays bare the yoking of imperialist and ethnographic ventures through its multiple modes of representation (travelogue, memoir, ethnography), opening the narrative and its author up to the reader's scrutiny. It is, in other words, another example of the kind of generic hybridity that Du Bois employed in *Souls* and that underscores for readers the social position of the "knower."

By turning to Hurston's *Their Eyes Were Watching God* in the eighth and final chapter, I investigate the diasporic relations in this text in relation to the center-periphery model of exchange presented by ethnography. In comparison to *Tell My Horse*, which heavily emphasizes transnational politics and imperialist encounters between Americans and Haitians, *Their Eyes*, written during Hurston's stay in Haiti, minimizes colonizer-colonized dynamics and instead foregrounds the shared social and political concerns of African Diasporic communities (specifically Haiti, Harlem, and Eatonville). *Their Eyes* has typically been understood in local/regional terms, but I place it within a global context of African Diaspora writing.

In contrast to scholars who argue that the narrative's turn to the rural South and to the Caribbean displaces African Americans' increasing movement to urban, Northern centers in the twenties, I argue that Hurston sought to explore through metaphor and symbolism the social and political concerns of African Americans in the North, South, and throughout the Caribbean. In other words, where some might argue that Hurston was stuck in the proverbial village at precisely the moment when significant numbers of African Americans were striking out for the city, I counter with the notion that Hurston found in the village many of the same conflicts, desires, and aspirations as her more urban-identified peers around the Diaspora. By symbolically associating her protagonist, Janie, with the Haitian *lwa* (goddess) Ezili, Hurston was able to explore those elements that enabled or hindered a collective self-expression and self-determination, the very characteristics that Alain Locke identified with the modern, urban New Negro.[35] Haitian Vodou provided Hurston with the ideal vehicle to voice African Diasporic peoples' (especially women's) views on their social status and experiences, demonstrating that "primitive" peoples and their traditions had something to say about the modern world.

Renaissance writers accepted social science discourse, assuming a stance in their fiction, memoirs, and ethnographies that questions an intellectual legacy of objectifying cultural and racial others in ways that are both indebted to the disciplines of sociology and anthropology and that break with the disciplines' methods of writing culture. For example, while modern anthropologists were trained to guard against their own subjective interpretations of other cultures by immersing themselves in the subject's milieu through participant-observation fieldwork, the New Negro writers I investigate represent their encounters in the "field" as full of ambivalence and conflict. In other words, they depict fieldwork as a power-inflected site of social conflict and negotiation as opposed to a setting in which to view "primitive" cultures in their natural settings. Where Franz Boas recognized that the social sciences could be used to critique and radically rethink the status quo, the African American writers I discuss *wrote into their narratives* their perception that the ethnographic endeavor could also reflect rather than transcend the status quo. Their writing and reflections reveal their awareness of the social and political reform that could be achieved through the practice of a progressive anthropology, what Walter Jackson calls an "applied anthropology."[36] Yet they also reveal their awareness of ethnography's inherently political nature, casting doubt on the orthodoxy of their time, which contended that anthropology could and should be a "politically neutral quest for objective knowledge and truth about the human condition."[37]

A paradigmatic example of how this neutrality was maintained can be seen in the juxtaposition of Bronislaw Malinowski's ethnography *Argonauts of the Western Pacific*, published in 1922, which according to James Clifford creates "the fashioned wholes of a self and of a culture,"[38] and his diaries published in 1967, which take advantage of the genre's "tendency toward self-scrutiny" to reflect on his self-doubt and sexual fantasies about and exasperation with the inhabitants of the Trobriand Islands, whom he viewed as brutes.[39] The important point here is that Malinowski considered it an imperative to keep private reflection and interpersonal conflict from his ethnographic depiction because to meld the two would disrupt his representation of the culture (and his relationship to it) as whole. In their overtly ethnographic narratives, New Negro ethnographers/writers move habitually between introspection and representation of the other, between subjective analysis and clinical detachment.[40] In doing so, they highlight the possibility of scientific objectivity to slip into objectification, anticipating by decades the kinds of questions about knowledge production being asked by current anthropologists. In critiquing the ethnographic framework within which they worked, they confront the classist, racist, and cultural biases of the dominant society and challenge their readers to imagine a different set of relations between the powerful and the oppressed.

Chapter 2
Men of Science in the Post-Slavery Era

Evolutionists to Environmentalists: The Development of Modern Anthropology and Constructions of Race

In choosing to appropriate classical anthropology's cultural pluralist, anti-racist agenda, New Negro intellectuals intervened on a long history of anti-Black and anti-African rhetoric and practices that extended back before the nineteenth century, when the notion of a Great Chain of Being provided one measure of human civilization. This human taxonomy positioned Africans near or at the bottom of the social hierarchy and Europeans at the top, linking the status of the "lesser" races with their presumed fall from grace. When in the nineteenth century scientific rationales for theories of racial inferiority supplanted the theological frame that had previously been used to validate these ideas of social order, the scientific literature was often heavily intertwined with religious arguments to the extent "that it was hard to tell where one ended and the other began."[1] The sense that Africans and their New World descendants deserved in some way their own subordination by virtue of divine ordination persisted even as scientific discourse began to supplant religious ideologies of social formations. The most popular explanation in the nineteenth century for the existence of racial stratification was social Darwinism, a theory that used biological evolution as a metaphor for social development. Lewis Henry Morgan, a New York lawyer who became an ethnologist, proved highly influential in this development because he "adapted Darwinian natural selection to a [Herbert] Spencerian notion of absolute cultural progress. Morgan concluded that the races were in different stages of physical and cultural evolution that could be linked to three stages of cultural achievement: savagery, barbarism, and civilization Not surprisingly, he positioned the Aryan race at the apex of civilization and Africans "in the middle stage of barbarism" (Hovenkamp 654). By 1908, most American experts on race were evolutionists who theorized that racial characteristics were biologically determined, but the racist ideologies of the previous era remained fixed in the nation's consciousness.

Anthropology gained a prominent role in the construction of racial ideologies and, thus, underwent a significant shift in status at this historical juncture. The discipline situated itself as a science at a time when the sciences were preoccupied with new biological theories; as a result Darwinist analogies dominated the field for almost a century. This generation of anthropologists believed that "to explain man's physical structure was to explain mankind" (Hovenkamp 652). Consequently race experts, led in the social sciences by ethnologists such as the Briton Edward Tylor and the American Lewis Henry Morgan, argued that some characteristics, such as intelligence, do evolve. Some even professed that Blacks might eventually develop an intelligence equal to Caucasians, but even these more progressive thinkers concluded that Africans' cultural and intellectual development would take so long to evolve that racial differences were virtually permanent.[2]

Modern anthropology has left a mixed legacy in that it reinforced racialist discourses while also sowing the seeds for a more progressive and relativistic view of cultures. For example, although Tylor followed an evolutionary model of culture that prompted him to study "primitive" cultures as "exempla of the lower rungs of the human evolutionary scale," succeeding generations of anthropologists were indebted to his definition of culture as a "complex whole which includes knowledge, belief, art, morals, law, custom, and any other capabilities and habits acquired by man as a member of society." Ironically, Tylor's notion of culture as a complex whole comprised of "functional and integral parts" undercut the Victorian ethnologists' belief that culture could be attained or exhibited through great works of art or displays of intellect.[3] Moreover, the idea of culture as a "complex whole" would eventually lead the way to the cultural relativism proposed by Franz Boas in the early decades of the twentieth century.

Even as evolutionary ideas about race were gaining prominence, by 1880 another group of scientists was developing yet another theory of racial formation. This group, the environmentalists, argued for the influence of historical, geographic, and social factors in determining racial patterns and cultural behaviors. A generation after the abolition of slavery, African Americans were considered to be a national problem, and while the environmentalists might have shared with evolutionists the idea that Black communities fostered severe pathologies, they differed from them in that they considered their weaknesses to be caused by environmental factors.[4]

As these theories were being debated, anthropology was transformed from a field populated by individuals interested in natural history but trained in other fields such as medicine to, by the 1880s, a professionalized discipline with the standard characteristics of a specialized field, such as a national organization, a professional journal, and an institutional base in universities and museums. The 1880s saw a number of important developments in the history of modern anthropology, from the professionalization and institutionalization of the discipline, the popularization of anthropological ideas on race at Worlds Fairs, the entry of Franz Boas—who would become a major shaping force in the discipline within the next twenty years—into the field as an assistant to Francis Ward Putnam, and the introduction of African Americans, for the first time in significant numbers, working as ethnologists and folklorists.

These changes coincided with, and indeed facilitated, the formation of an organization dedicated to the collection and study of folklore at the Hampton Normal Institute, an industrial school for Blacks founded after the end of the Civil War to help rehabilitate former slaves and prepare them for the new societal and civic roles they were on the cusp of assuming. An examination of the Hampton Folklore Society (HFS) will give us a glimpse into the uses to which the environmentalists were putting their work, and it will also anticipate some of the goals and complications faced by Black ethnologists, who, in the 1920s, formed the next significant body of African American individuals loosely organized around their mutual interest in collecting and representing African American folk culture.

The Hampton Idea of Folklore Collection

The Hampton Institute, founded in 1868 in Virginia by the American Missionary Society, was designed to educate the state's population of newly emancipated slaves. Its founder, Samuel Chapman Armstrong, anticipated that Hampton students would fan across the South to teach the members of their communities still mired in the legacy of slavery, manual skills, and rudimentary letters in order to render them useful members of Southern society. The "Hampton Idea," first articulated by Armstrong and later popularized by Hampton graduate Booker T. Washington, who went on to found Tuskegee Institute in 1881 and become a national spokesman for the race, was that an industrial education would elevate the station of Blacks by giving them the manual skills and the moral character that would make them fit for civil society. Armstrong faulted slavery and its negative effects rather than any inherent inferiority in African Americans for the moral, intellectual, and political inadequacies he identified in their communities. Understanding the word "industry" to mean broadly "diligence in the pursuit of a goal" and more narrowly to mean "the application of manual skills in the production of some agricultural or mechanical object," he considered the school's emphasis on an industrial education in preference of schooling in a classical education the key to saving Black people from the primitive conditions in which slavery and impoverishment kept them mired.[5]

It was under this premise that Alice Bacon, a Hampton teacher, founded the Hampton Folklore Society (HFS) in 1893. The society, whose members were composed of students, alumni, and some teachers, worked until they disbanded six years later to collect data gathered from the communities in which they lived and worked.[6] Students brought with them to the Hampton campus knowledge of folklore from their Southern homes. Non-resident members of the Society (many, but not all, of them Institute graduates), known as "correspondents," often worked as teachers in other parts of the South (for example, South Carolina, Florida and Alabama), and probably obtained folklore from their own students (Waters 8). The organizational efforts of the Hampton Folklore Society were new and untested, for folklore groups were just beginning to be organized in the 1890s. The group's emphasis on scholarly presentation and scientific investigation departed from prior methods because up to that point individuals interested in African American folklore, like Joel Chandler Harris, moved between "disciplined presentation of data and literary adornment of it" (Waters 37). HFS members understood folklore to be the repository of cultural memory and communal values, and yet they worked within an institution that saw little value in African American culture if it deviated from hegemonic norms that were associated with progress.[7] The question arises, then, what did the HFS members have in mind when they went out to collect folklore?

Hampton's commitment to putting its students on the road to economic and social progress compelled them to choose from several options vis-à-vis their relation to folk culture and communities. They could express an uncritical belief in folklore (a perspective which was discouraged by their instructors and benefactors); they could disavow Black folk traditions as backward and see themselves bringing progress and civilization to their people; or they could choose, as Donald Waters maintains members of the Hampton society did, to commit themselves to protecting Black folklore from contempt and ridicule by submitting it to careful and respectful study and presentation (Waters 46–47).

The second choice—the idea of racial uplift through cultural assimilation—proved equally compelling according to Lee Baker, who stresses that the founders and members of the Hampton Folklore society saw their attempts to record the cultural practices of rural Blacks as a contribution to the larger institution's mission. They could show that industrial education accomplished its goal of "fostering the so-called Christian civilization of its graduates," he argues, by using folklore to underscore how much of these people's African traditions remained entrenched and in need of uprooting.[8] Certainly Bacon aspired to have HFS members bridge and show the divide between their own literate, upwardly mobile existences and the illiterate and impoverished lives of most Black folk. But the Hampton community's shared goal of closing that gap was deeply invested in removing any remaining traces of African heritage and African American slave culture.[9]

Armstrong and Bacon's goals were virtually indistinguishable, with the exception of Bacon adding an interest in historical preservation to Armstrong's "civilizing mission" (Baker, "Research" 55). Bacon's interest in conservation and her belief in modernity's inevitable advancement is evident in an 1893 letter she circulated to Hampton graduates and interested parties:

The American Negroes are rising so rapidly from the condition of ignorance and poverty in which slavery left them, to a position among the cultivated and civilized people of the earth, that the time seems not far distant when they shall have cast off their past entirely, and stand an anomaly among civilized races, as a people having no distinct tradition, beliefs or ideas from which a history of their growth may be traced. If within the next few years care is not taken to collect and preserve all traditions and customs peculiar to the Negroes, there will be little to reward the search of the future historian who would trace the history of the African continent through the years of slavery to the position which they will hold a few generations hence.[10]

Bacon imagined progress for the Negro to be synonymous not only with economic upward mobility but also with assimilation to Euro-American cultural norms. Many adherents to the Hampton philosophy associated backwardness and primitivity with any traits that deviated from a White social norm, as well as with anything identified or identifiable as African in origins. Blackness and impurity are linked in the minds of Booker T. Washington's readers when he provocatively declared that his most pressing aspiration as a teacher was to introduce Tuskegee students to the uses of a toothbrush because he and his teachers noted "the effect that the use of the toothbrush has had in bringing about a higher degree of civilization among the students."[11] Washington's emphasis on hygiene throughout his autobiography indicates his shared understanding with Bacon and Armstrong that the goal of an industrial education should be the figurative "whitening" of the school's Black students, both morally and socially.

Nonetheless, Bacon's letter also makes it clear that she considers it regrettable if progress were achieved at the expense of Negro cultural heritage. Hampton officials' belief in African Americans' cultural assimilability was progressive for its time, but Bacon understood that it might not be completely positive to the future development of the race if the consequence of assimilation was the loss of identity. Bacon's hesitation at the idea of fully erasing Negro cultural heritage even as Black communities modernized becomes more palpable when we consider the statements of HFS's Black membership. Their reflections on their relation to the uplift work in which they engaged points to issues that are both complex and fascinating.

Their letters and essays emphasize in part the connection between educators and their not so distant past, between teachers and their illiterate, less acculturated pupils. HFS members, like other students, faculty, and graduates of the school were committed to a project of racial uplift that strove to address economic and racial inequality. Rather than framing their descriptions of their "less civilized" peers in terms of class, they did so in terms of culture (Baker, "Research" 51).[12] And as a consequence, their shared definitions of social mobility exerted a pressure on cultural formations, resulting in the stigmatization of traits typically associated with African or African American communities. Baker writes that in this earlier period:

Uncivilized Blacks were the ones who believed in conjure doctors, told the animal stories, sang the work songs, and gyrated their bodies in the ring shouts and jook joints. They were also the field hands, manual laborers, domestics, and washer women who never had the opportunity to attend one of the normal schools in which strict discipline and obsession with proper behavior convinced students they had become civilized. And it was the uneducated and less refined souls who were held responsible for the vice, promiscuity, and debauchery associated with all black Americans. Moreover, many Negro elites found the main culprit of their neighbors' cultural degradation in African cultural patterns. ("Research" 52)

Nonetheless, despite the potency of the Hampton Ideology, which emphasized racial "cleansing," its folklorists retained a sense of connection to the traditions their teachers encouraged them to leave behind in pursuit of mainstream notions of progress. For example, Daniel Webster Davis wrote in a correspondence to Robert Russa Moton (both were elected officers of the organization, and Moton went on to succeed Booker T. Washington as president of Tuskegee) that he found folk games such as ring plays to be "sweet" and "fair" like a dream. He also described taking pleasure in the memory of participating in these games. Waters argues that equating "expressions of Negro folklore" with a dream underscores the strangeness of these traditions to the "normal conscious activity of proper black educators or, more generally, of properly educated black people." Yet he also astutely notes that the educators' expressions of sympathy and memory "emphasized the broad continuities between unlettered folk and educators" (Waters 50).[13]

Some African American members and supporters of the society emphasized more than disdain, ambivalence, or nostalgia in the researcher's approach to the collection of Negro folklore. Educator Alexander Crummel, for example, cautioned HFS members to "offer a positive and not a negative interpretation of their African heritage" (Baker, "Research" 57). And activist and writer Anna Julia Cooper cautioned society members not to lose sight of their people's genius in the face of what must have seemed to be an "overpowering" model of civilization. Cooper warned against a definition of achievement and success that would compel the Negro to accept the notion that "Anglo Saxon ideas, Anglo Saxon standards, Anglo Saxon art, [etc.] must be to him the measure of perfection," and reminded her audience that "the American Negro cannot produce an original utterance until he realizes the sanctity of his homely inheritance."[14] These statements, resonating with cultural pride, clearly anticipate the thinking of New Negro intellectuals who would follow a generation later.

Hampton Folklore Society scholars thought deeply about the value of African American folklore and their work as collectors, and they also considered the uses to which that work would be put. In fact, the group's origins were based on an article linking science and the study of race, published in *The Atlantic Monthly* by Nathaniel Shaler, a Harvard professor of paleontology and geology. Despite the intrinsic racism of Shaler's essay, "Science and the African Problem" (1890), it suggested to Alice Bacon the idea of starting a society of folklorists. Shaler argued that the transplantation of Africans to the New World constituted "a most remarkable experiment," which offered the opportunity to study the "improvability of the lower races of mankind" (cited in Waters 10). He proposed that a systematic study of Negro "improvability" be taken from three methods of inquiry: one, a historical investigation that would examine the slave trade to ascertain the African origins of slaves; two, an anthropological study to assess the physical and mental characteristics of Blacks in the United States and to compare those traits to those of Africans; and three, a study of "the social and civic quality of the race" to determine how to secure its advancement (Waters 10–11). Although Shaler accepted many of the crudest stereotypes of the African American character (he believed, for example that Blacks were promiscuous, were naturally rhythmic, and were in need of supervision), he did believe that Whites' assumptions about Black folk were formed in "the midst of a great darkness" and scientific inquiry was necessary for their enlightenment (Waters 12). The Hampton folklorists, recognizing the severity of America's race problems, must have desired to participate in an organized, collective scientific inquiry of these issues (Waters 12). At the same time, the Society departed from Shaler's belief in genetically based racial difference by embracing the Hampton ethos of environmentalism, which argued that Blacks had an innate capacity for social and intellectual improvement.[15]

Like participants in the related disciplines of anthropology and sociology, by this time in the 1890s, folklorists viewed themselves as participating in a "scientific" endeavor, and they considered their professionalism evident in the objectivity and thoroughness of their studies. In underscoring the precision of folklore collection as science, Hampton folklorists were indebted to the influence of William Wells Newell, Franz Boas, and their colleagues who founded the American Folklore Society (AFLS) in 1888.[16] The founders of the AFLS sought to describe the concept of folklore with a precision that it had lacked up to this point. Its founders considered the then popular definition of folklore—"a particular kind of mental and cultural expression with its 'own set of facts'"—to be unnecessarily vague. So they shifted definitions of and added nuance to the term by having it refer to "oral transmission and its traditional, or conventional character" (Waters 23–25). Newell also insisted on the importance of methodological rigor in the study of folklore. He recognized that folklore needed to be written down in order for it to be studied systematically, but he also considered it essential that the collector refrain from adding to, "adorning" to render more literary, or otherwise tampering with the "evidence" (Waters 27). Newell argued that folklore was entirely different from literature although both made use of figurative devices. Where literature was "systematic" in its application of such devices, folklore used them as a matter of convention and not aesthetic judgment. Newell concluded that the addition of aesthetic principles to conventional materials was the equivalent of falsifying the material; it would fundamentally change the data. "Folklore, in other words, is a separate and independent subject, not a subset of literature" (Waters 28). The AFLS founders established folklore's suitability for scientific inquiry by locating it under the rubric of anthropology as part of culture, namely the oral tradition. They considered any similarities between literature and folklore to be coincidental, occurring merely because both are modes of communication.[17]

Boas and Newell rejected evolutionary ideas of racial and cultural development, as did Armstrong, Bacon, and the other Hamptonites. Instead, they focused on analyses of the historical, geographic, and social factors that determined the development of oral traditions; these analyses were facilitated by scrupulous methods of collection. AFLS founders discovered that their agenda intersected with that of the Hampton Folklore Society, so much so that Newell, acting as secretary of the AFLS, traveled to Hampton in May 1894 in order to personally address the group at one of its first meetings and to recruit its members for his organization's membership.[18] Newell's address, which was later published in the *Southern Workman* in July 1894, covered familiar rhetorical ground, including remarks on the importance of recording cultural traditions that were in the process of disappearing. Newell defined folklore as "the learning or knowledge peculiar to the Negro race. It is that mass of information which they brought with them from Africa, and which has subsequently been increased, remodeled, and Anglicized by their contact with the whites" (Waters 186). Calling folklore a "body of thought [that] belongs to the past," that was vanishing under the march of African Americans' educational progress, he asked the society members to consider what purpose was served by their turning their attention to "these out-grown notions and usages" (Waters 186).

Newell's answers to that question diverged. On the one hand, he professed a humanistic vision, claiming membership in no race other than the human race and declaring that races existed "to be merged in the unity of races, as rivers flow to disappear in the ocean."[19] Yet he also suggested that folklore reveals that "each [race] has its distinctive customs, ideas, and manners." Newell expressed ambivalence over the impending erasure of "racial memory" and suggested that only folklore (defined as race-knowledge) could preserve it. Thus, he declared, it was the responsibility of the individual to preserve the "memory of his race" in order to "to tell of the height to which they rose, the depth through which they have passed." Finally, Newell also touched on the mobility and dynamism of African traditions, a subject that Black scholars like Du Bois and Locke would remark on to much greater effect in their own writings. Newell stated that Negro folktales were cosmopolitan by virtue of the ground they had traversed: "These tales are by no means solely the possession of Negroes; on the contrary, a good many are nearly cosmopolitan. Proceeding from some common center, they have traveled about the world, and that by several different routes, meeting in America by the way of Africa, by that of Europe, and it may be, also by that of Asia. So extraordinary a phenomenon in itself excites curiosity to a high degree" (Waters 187–89). Newell's remarks underscore the ambivalence that many felt about the value of African American folklore, suggesting that it preserves the race's "depths," but that it also embodies a cultural dynamism that could edify the race. These remarks, mere drops of enlightenment in a sea of negative racial constructs, would take on new and previously unimagined manifestations in the hands of New Negro intellectuals who found inspiration and insight in the proponents of this emerging science.

Heartening as Newell's support proved to be, Lee Baker's descriptions of HFS members' participation in the national meetings of the AFLS illustrate some of the complexities faced by African American scholars who were sometimes treated as native informants as often as they were considered ethnologists. For example, when a Hampton delegation, consisting of Robert Moton, F. D. Banks, William Daggs, and J. H. Wainwright, attended the December 1894 meeting in Washington, D.C., they were well received by well-known scholars of ethnological research like Boas, Frank Hamilton Cushing, J. Walter Fewkes, and Newell. Here, Moton challenged the deformation of African American music by minstrels and categorized "Negro Folk Songs" into secular and spiritual music. He and his colleagues then formed a quartet and performed samples of the music to illustrate Moton's descriptions. The reaction of the audience while positive and enthusiastic, was telling. Newell and Thomas Wilson's proposal that they record the performance on phonograph suggests the wall between scientist and informant had been breeched with the introduction of the phonographic equipment.[20] Their enthusiasm for the equipment's ability to reproduce sound with "exactness" would seem to suggest that they believed themselves to be witnessing a moment of cultural authenticity as opposed to a demonstration that might approximate the music in its indigenous setting (Baker, "Research" 64–65). Moton and colleagues were not alone in finding their academic personae stripped away. For example, on another occasion, while waiting for the arrival of a graphophone when preparing to travel to the AFLS's annual meeting, Bacon realized it would not arrive in time for her group's presentation. In its stead she proposed, as Baker puts it, "the real thing":

a most delightful paper by Prof. D. W. Davis of Richmond, on 'Echoes from a Plantation Party,' which may be worth studying up on. Davis is a full blooded Negro, a teacher in Richmond and the authority of a number of dialect processes. He takes a real interest in the old customs of his own people, and has been at considerable pains to collect all he can. . . . I asked him if he would be willing to describe it [his paper] in New York at the annual meeting and he says that he can. . . . The songs are a great part of it. It is rather better than a phonographic reprint as he gives it.[21]

Davis's "full blooded" Black body wedged him into a paradoxical corner, rendering him simultaneously more fit (because there was ocular proof of his cultural authenticity) and less fit (because he troubled the line between scientist and subject) to assume the ethnologist's identity.

Despite the obvious difficulties of the Hampton folklorists' attempts to establish their scientific credentials, obvious links can be made between their groundbreaking work and the more radical work and politics of the New Negro intellectuals. But first, significant changes had to be made in the social and historical landscape before American society could see an upsurge of interest in African American folklore in the twentieth century. Waters notes that folklore studies at Hampton slowed to a "standstill" after 1900 because Bacon moved to Japan, weakening the links with Shaler, Newell, and Boas, and more importantly because funding from philanthropists dried up. In that time between 1900 and 1920s, however, Black activists mounted "a major political and organizational effort to balance the influence of the Hampton idea [of African American inferiority]." This shift in thinking accompanied a change in anthropological studies, which did not focus on African American culture until well into the twentieth century.[22]

Only after the emergence of influential groups like the National Association for the Advancement of Colored People in the twenties, Waters argues, "were the educational forces sufficiently balanced that room again appeared for the academic study of Negro folklore" (Waters 51–52). In the intervening years, moreover, Franz Boas became a major force in the shaping of the American school of anthropology, introducing new ideas about cultural relativism that would transform social constructions of race. He also trained or worked with a generation of students and scholars who would go on to make a deep impression on the American consciousness including, among many others, Melville Herskovits, Elsie Clews Parsons, and Zora Neale Hurston. Finally, the ethic of the Black intellectual shifts from this period in the late 1890s. Where, for example, Armstrong sought to train and morally elevate Black teachers, who would then go on to instill "character" in other Blacks at the elementary level, the next generation of Black intellectuals, who often repeated or represented the schoolteacher's trajectory southward into Black rural communities, were less interested in the transference of character and far more interested in the translation of culture across geographic, historical, and social boundaries.[23] They strove, in other words, to articulate a cohesive idea of Negro culture that would be recognized as a valid part of American national identity. These ideas did not come to fruition until a generation of folklorists and ethnologists, following in the footsteps of the HFS members, had been trained to regard folklore as the fullest expression of a people's lived experiences, as opposed to evidence of a community's quaintness or backwardness.[24]

Franz Boas and the Attack on Scientific Racism

Lee Baker has argued that in examining New Negro representations of Black culture, it is crucial to consider the geographic proximity of the movement to Columbia University at the precise moment that Franz Boas was spearheading new anthropological approaches to race and culture through his theories of racial equality and cultural relativity.[25] New York's density and compactness made it an ideal setting for fostering bohemian, intellectual communities that strived to overturn convention; the cultural innovators of the Harlem Renaissance could easily find affinity with the academic advances taking place on Columbia's campus.[26] Boas began teaching at Columbia in 1896 as a lecturer in physical anthropology, and was promoted to professor in 1899. The position became permanent in 1901. He would usher in a sea change in the field from his perch at Columbia, transforming anthropology from a discipline that constructed and affirmed racist constructs to one that bolstered egalitarian notions, anti-racist activism and legislation, and integrationist social policies.[27] The American school of anthropology, under Boas's leadership, favored meticulous descriptions of cultures that represented the circulation of cultural traits among bordering groups through the exhaustive comparison of evidence from "material culture, ceremonial, social organization, recorded history, language, mythology, and folklore" (Deacon 149). In order to understand any culture, Boas argued, it had to be situated within its historical and geographic context, and its particular traditions had to be taken into consideration. This approach to understanding culture, he argued, challenged the idea that any culture possessed a higher or lower value than another.

Boas, born in Minden, Germany in 1858, was educated at the Universities of Heidelberg, Bonn, and Kiel, where he was trained in conducting empiricist and positivist research, methods that influenced his future scholarship.[28] He retained throughout his career a commitment to empirical research. Boas rarely proposed grand theories and he rejected the notion that the social sciences should be used to engineer social policies or relations. Nonetheless, his progressive views on race and immigration were well known and his theories were enthusiastically taken up and appropriated by racial vindicationists[29] like the New Negro intellectuals. Most likely, Boas's radical racial politics arose from his personal struggles with anti-Semitism. Although born into middle-class privilege, as a Jew he suffered from political persecution, which caused him to migrate to the United States in 1886.[30] Once in the States, Boas continued to experience anti-Semitic discrimination. For example after serving as assistant chief to Frederick Ward Putnam at the World Columbian Exposition in 1893, despite his impressive credentials, he had difficulty securing a permanent position in an American university until his appointment at Columbia.

From that point on he would begin to teach and extend his influence over an impressive range of individuals, many of whom gained stellar national reputations, including Alexander Goldenweiser, Robert Lowie, Paul Radin, Alfred Kroeber, Edward Sapir, Melville Herskovits, Ruth Benedict, and Margaret Mead. Particularly during World War I, when the numbers of male graduate students were depleted by the demands of the war, Boas took an active role in educating and mentoring women in anthropology. His support of women's participation in the field went against the much more common social opposition to women's professional goals. By 1912, when he published *The Mind of Primitive Man*, Boas had achieved his highest standing within the profession.

In addition to teaching at Columbia, Boas also assumed a position as assistant curator at the American Museum of Natural History (AMNH), again in 1896; in 1901 he was promoted to curator. During this period, anthropology was primarily a museum-based profession. At the AMNH Boas undertook major research expeditions, including the Jesup North Pacific Expedition. He struggled to exhibit the material procured during these expeditions at the museum in a way that challenged ideas of racial inferiority, but he met resistance from the evolutionists who dominated the field. Baker describes the debates, ostensibly over exhibition styles, but really over the merits of scientific racism, that were conducted through letters to the editor of *Science* that Boas exchanged with Otis T. Mason, president of the Anthropological Society of Washington, and John Wesley Powell, director of the Bureau of American Ethnology. In one letter Boas argued, "It is my opinion that the main object of ethnological collections should be the dissemination of the fact that civilization is not something absolute, but that it is relative, and that our ideas and conceptions are true only so far as our civilization goes. I believe that this object can be accomplished only by the tribal arrangement of collections" (Baker, *From Savage to Negro* 104).

Boas mounted challenges to evolutionary anthropology and other forms of scientific racism like eugenics in a variety of venues, such as essays, editorials, and speeches. Giving his first public address in 1894 at the American Association of Anthropological Societies, he delineated the racism that governed anthropological discourse. He laid out the fundamental principles of the environmentalists by warning against evolutionary theories that tended to view certain traits as expressions of racial character rather than as an effect of social surroundings.[31] Although he deferred to physical anthropologists who maintained that their findings proved racial inferiority, Boas contended that there was an overlap of supposedly racial traits among various groups. He concluded:

the fundamental difficulty of collecting satisfactory observations lies in the fact that no large groups of primitive man are brought nowadays into conditions of real equality with whites. The gap between our society and theirs always remains open and for this reason their mind cannot be expected to work in the same manner as ours. The same phenomenon which led us to the conclusion that primitive races of our times are not given an opportunity to develop their abilities prevents us from judging their innate faculty. (234)

Boas used arguments like this to contest methods of research that emphasized the comparison of cultures while refusing to study them holistically, and in relation to the total culture.

Boas viewed anthropological investigation, founded on empirical research and taking into consideration historical and social contexts, as a tool for proving the equal potential of the races. This approach, he argued, would demonstrate that societies, regardless of their racial makeup, all revealed cultural and artistic accomplishments. In an address delivered at the Second National Negro Conference in May 1910 called "The Real Race Problem," Boas took up the fallacy of presumptions of racial inferiority, focused on the inevitable mingling of Black and White races in American society, and introduced some preliminary thoughts on solving the race problem.[32] He began by acknowledging the "fact" of racial difference, announcing that "the anthropologist recognizes that the Negro and the white represent the two most divergent types of mankind" (22). Boas pointed to differences in color, hair, and facial features as easily recognizable. Yet despite these biological differences, he disputed the rationale for assigning superiority or inferiority to either race. "When we consider inferiority and superiority from a general biological point of view, it must be interpreted as meaning that one type is nearer to certain ancestral forms than another. In this sense, the anthropologist must say that in certain respects the Negro resembles the hypothetical ancestral forms of man more than does the European; while in other respects the European shows greater similarity to the supposed ancestral form. . . . On the whole, the morphological characteristics of the two races show rather a specialized development in different directions than a higher development in one race as compared with the other" (22). On the question of mental capacity, Boas again invoked a theory of diffusion arguing that differences in brain size and capacity between the two races "is exceedingly small" compared to the "range of variability" of brain size and form in either race (22).

Boas's rejection of scientific racism was based on the strict application of anthropometrical statistics used to support his claims, or to refute the validity of others' claims. But he also argued that any interpretation must take into consideration as well a "painstaking investigation of the social conditions with which the phenomenon is correlated" (22). Thus, an examination of the period of development of Black and White children must take into account the more favorable social situation of Whites. Boas concluded that between Whites and Blacks, "The existing differences are differences in kind, not in value" (23). In another essay, "The Negro and the Demands of Modern Life," he cited similar statistics to argue that there is no proof that licentiousness, laziness, or lack of initiative are intrinsic characteristics of the race.[33]

Just as Boas argued that perceptions of African American inferiority were based on fallacious assumptions, so did he find that views of Africa frequently betrayed the biases of its commentators. Too often, he argued, Whites' perception of Africa "is based altogether too much upon the condition of the uneducated descendant of the American Negro slave" whose collective achievement was stunted by his or her participation in forced labor, the absolute break from African traditions, and the difficulties of assimilation into the dominant group ("Real Race Problem" 23). In reality Boas argued, indigenous African societies, albeit "primitive," had developed flourishing and complex agricultural, industrial, and political organizations.

Finally Boas disputed the notion that mulattoes had "inherit[ed] all the vile characteristics of both parental races, and none of their good qualities" by attacking contradictions in anti-miscegenation rhetoric. He reiterated the argument that those making claims of hereditary causes for racial inferiority had to also take social factors into account and by comparing interbreeding among animals and across a wide range of cultures, he demonstrated that hybridity has consistently resulted in positive outcomes for many species and societies ("Real Race Problem" 23–24). In the case of sub-Saharan Africa and

Northern Africa, for example, he stated, "The development of culture, and the degree of assimilation of foreign elements, depend in the whole area, not upon the purity of the race, but upon the stability of political conditions, which during long periods have been characterized by alternation of peaceful development and of warlike conquest" (24).

The status of the mulatto was important to consider because, as Boas astutely pointed out, with the lack of immigration from Africa, the likelihood of the Negro race remaining "pure" was unlikely. "The gradual process of elimination of the full-blooded Negro may be retarded by legislation, but it cannot possibly be avoided," he claimed (25). Boas strongly believed in the likelihood and value of African American assimilation into the dominant culture. Working from the assumption that miscegenation would continue to take place primarily between White men and Black women, he suggests that the "relative proportion of Negro blood in the following mixed generation" will decrease and similarities between Whites and Blacks will develop. He viewed this as a positive development, one that would minimize racial animosity stemming from what he called "racial feeling." Racial feeling, Boas argued, depended on two causes: one, contact between two races that were relatively proportionate in number (because social divisions could arise when the numbers of each were sufficient to enable the development of a strong economic presence and habits particular to each race), and two, the "amount of difference of type" (25). Boas argued that the race problem would be alleviated "the less the difference in type between the different groups of our people, and the less the isolation of certain social groups" (25). He therefore concluded that at least part of the solution "lies entirely in the hands of the Negro himself." The less the Negro represented his culture as distinct from that of the White race, "the more satisfactory will be the relation between the races" (25).

It may seem contradictory, given these beliefs, that Boas publicly urged African Americans to recognize and harness the greatness of their African past. But the vindication of that heritage was necessary for the cultivation of ideas of social equality between the races which might then lead to the wholesale assimilation that Boas predicted. In "Industries of the African Negro," he asserted, "this loss of connection with the historic past is without doubt one of the most degrading influences in human culture."[34] The argument was accompanied by numerous illustrations of African artistic and industrial achievement culled from the African and South Pacific Collections of the Royal Ethnographical Museum of Berlin, such as pottery, ornately decorated weapons, and elaborate wood carvings. If American Negroes failed to achieve similar accomplishments, their social and cultural disintegration could be attributed to European influences. "Their former activities disappeared, and a new kind of work was forced upon them that had no relation to their inner life" (222). Boas, using a vocabulary that would resonate with an audience conditioned by the industrial school system to appreciate the improvability of the African American, asserts, "industrious life reigns throughout the [typical African] village" (224). A deeper awareness of African industriousness would reveal various African societies' concern with the manufacture of useful goods and textiles, with a social cohesion and organization that were dependent on the equitable dispensation of justice, and with beauty, among other laudable qualities.

In a May 30, 1906 commencement address at Atlanta University entitled "The Outlook of the American Negro," delivered at the invitation of W. E. B. Du Bois, Boas encouraged the gathered students to strive for a level of achievement similar to that reached by their African ancestors:

If, therefore, it is claimed that your race is doomed to economic inferiority, you may confidently look to the home of your ancestors and say, that you have set out to recover for the colored people the strength that was their own before they set foot on the shores of this continent. You may say that you go to work with bright hopes, and that you will not be discouraged by the slowness of your progress; for you have to recover not only what has been lost in transplanting the Negro race from its native soil to this continent, but you must reach higher levels than your ancestors had ever attained.[35]

Critics frequently cite Du Bois's reference to this address in *Black Folks Then and Now* (1939) as evidence of Boas's influence on him. Du Bois wrote, "Franz Boas came to Atlanta University where I was teaching history in 1906 and said to a graduating class: 'You need not be ashamed of your African past'; and then he recounted the history of the Black kingdoms south of the Sahara for a thousand years. I was too astonished to speak. All of this I had never heard and I came then and afterwards to realize how silence and neglect of science can let truth utterly disappear or even be consciously distorted."[36] George Hutchinson cites this as one example of the existence of often overlooked interracial networks of American modernist intellectual exchange during the first decades of the twentieth century, arguing that the connections between Boasian anthropology, pragmatism, and the Harlem Renaissance illustrate a "confluence of [these] 'communities of interpretation' [that offer] a model of the sort of effective interdisciplinary and intercultural exchange to which many academic intellectuals today aspire."[37] Moreover, he makes a case for

Boas's influence in establishing the institutional and intellectual context in which the Renaissance imagination flourished.[38] In a similar vein, Vernon Williams argues that Black intellectuals found affinity with the anthropological principle that social differences had cultural and not racial explanations; and as they adapted this theory to their own work, they passed on Boas's legacy of progressive, egalitarian politics (4).

The Politics of Influence

Boas and his students mounted an assault on racism by articulating a theory of multiple "cultures" in place of a unified, vertically stratified "Culture," and by insisting that cultures be judged from within their own relative value systems.[39] This "culture concept" contributed to an ideology of cultural pluralism to which Harlem Renaissance figures found themselves drawn.[40] Boasian anthropology's presence can also be felt in the self-reflexivity of New Negro literature, in the writers' assumptions that tradition is dynamic and that culture is always changing and adapting to circumstance, and in the assumption that indigenous peoples are subjects and collaborators, not mere objects for study.[41] It is a common feature of Harlem Renaissance criticism to note that writers worked from the assumption that Southern slave culture was dying due to the post-emancipation period's growing modernization and urbanization.[42] Hurston, for example, writing to Franz Boas in 1927, emphasized the urgency of collecting folklore at that historical juncture, telling him, "It is fortunate that it is being collected now, for a great many people say, 'I used to know some of that old stuff, but I done forgot it all.' You see, the negro is not living his lore to the extent of the Indian. He is not on a reservation, being kept pure. His negroness is being rubbed off by close contact with white culture."[43] Even this ethic was informed by what Marc Manganaro, referencing James Clifford, calls the anthropological "allegory of salvage."[44]

This allegory of salvage lies in tension with the simultaneous awareness that culture persists in mutable and adaptable forms. Both Du Bois and Hurston, for example, represent Southern communities as heterogeneous and fluid in some instances, while in others they ascribe to a depiction of the Black Southern culture as a relic of the past, or in Hurston's case, privilege ideas of Negro culture that stress its authenticity and purity from outside contract. Paying sustained attention to these emphases cultivates in their readers an acute awareness of the discursive and symbolic *uses* to which the New Negro put constructions of the South. For example, in "The New

Negro," Alain Locke described the migration of African Americans from the rural South to the urban North as a "deliberate flight not only from country-side to city, but from medieval America to modern" (6). By relegating the South to medieval times, Locke signals its ultimate demise, a figuration that, one could argue, is necessary for the very constitution of a Harlem Renaissance. In other words, it is through the identification of "there and then" as backward that New Negro intellectuals could establish their "here and now" as progressive and forward-looking. Consequently, they took on a multilayered project: to document the cultural transformation that was occurring at the turn of the century, to preserve the remnants of what they perceived as a dying slave culture, and to interrogate the dynamics between the New Negro intellectual, the dominant culture, and the Black subjects of their art. Boasian anthropology—and by this I mean the intellectual tradition produced and practiced by Boas and his students—played an important role in this social and intellectual movement.

Because of their enthusiastic reception of social science theories, Black intellectuals played an active role in the *Journal of American Folklore* (JAFL) during the Renaissance years. For example, between 1917 and 1937, the JAFL dedicated fourteen issues, known as the "Negro Numbers," to African American folklore. JAFL editors actively courted New Negro intellectuals like Arthur Huff Fauset, Zora Neale Hurston, Alain Locke, Arthur Schomburg, and Carter G. Woodson, who all contributed to the journal (Baker, *From Savage to Negro* 144). From its inception in 1888, Baker argues, the JAFL was committed to making African American folklore a central component of the society and its journal. Its initial organization included a department of Negro folklore and its editorial policy dedicated a quarter of the journal's space to the subject. Newell, the JAFL's first editor from 1888 to 1900, recruited Alice Bacon and the Hampton Folklore Society in order to get around the blatant racism and unprofessionalism of AFLS's White southern members (Baker, *From Savage to Negro* 146). The society's interest in African American folklore waned after Newell's departure from his editorial post, but was revived in 1920 when Boas made a determined effort to develop the program in African American folklore and to train Black graduate students.[45]

The influence of social sciences was widely recognized by Black scholars during the early decades of the twentieth century. For example, Alain Locke, in two 1935 book reviews for the journal *Opportunity* (both entitled "The Eleventh Hour of Nordicism"), links art and the social sciences in their abilities to end ideologies of White supremacy. In the January "retrospective review of the Literature of the Negro for 1934," Locke praises Nancy

Cunard's *Negro, An Anthology*, among other literary works produced that year for hurling "shell, bomb and shrapnel at the citadel of Nordicism."[46] The second of this two-part article was published a month later, and in it Locke argues that sociology and, even more importantly, anthropology have set their sights on "Nordicism" through "scientific encirclement and bombardment."[47] The appeal of Boas's assault on scientific racism is clearly articulated by Locke, but his review also makes clear the point at which the New Negro agenda began to diverge from that of Boas's own, namely in Locke's unabashed enthusiasm for the notion that the social sciences might be used as an instrument in the service of social reform, as a weapon to combat White supremacy. Boas's anti-racist, liberal politics were certainly well known, as he did not hesitate to voice them in conversations, letters, and essays written for popular publication. Yet he also resisted the politicization of scholarship such as that suggested by Locke in "The Eleventh Hour of Nordicism." Boas considered objectivity a necessary prerequisite for academics to maintain their integrity. Baker astutely notes, however, that New Negro intellectuals' keen awareness of the "racial politics of culture" made them less wary than Boas of using anthropology to try to reform social attitudes about race:

Schomburg, Fauset, Hurston, Woodson, and to a certain extent Locke pressed into service the liberal politics, relativistic orientation, and credentials of anthropologists who limited their exploration of African American culture to research and academic journals. Although the intellectuals of the movement were always careful scientists and historians or creative artists and performers, they were clear that scholarship and performance by and about black people involved political stakes that were entwined and woven into the very fabric of the movement to transform race relations and the meaning of being black in America. (Baker, "Research" 74)

The New Negro intellectuals' investment in a collective project of social reform, their exploration of the limits and possibilities in racial solidarity, and their celebration of "race consciousness" are all areas where they diverge from Boas's application of his theories on race and culture; yet, they were indebted to Boasian anthropology for the concepts, vocabulary, and the modes of representation that they used to advance their agenda of racial reform and uplift through artistic achievement.[48]

This agenda led Arthur Fauset (novelist Jessie Fauset's brother), for example, to underscore the African origins of Negro folklore, and to argue that both varieties of tales were endowed with the same fundamental traits of "human kinship and universality."[49] The building blocks of race pride can be ascertained in his declaration that, alluding to Aesop's fabled African origins,

"Africa in a sense is the home of the fable; the African tales are its classics" (243). Fauset was a highly trained and rigorous folklorist whose orientation reflected the ideology of the American Folklore Society's leaders. He shunned literary embellishment of folk materials, for example, and privileged authentic recreation as opposed to interpretation. Thus Fauset minimized the role of the storyteller in his presentation of the folktale, arguing, "as in the case of all true folk tales, the story teller himself was inconsequential; he did not figure at all—a talking machine might serve the purpose just as well" (240). Certainly, there are differences that can be ascertained among the stances and approaches taken by the various New Negro intellectuals. A figure like Hurston was supremely unconcerned with the blurring of disciplinary and generic boundaries, whereas Sterling Brown can be aligned with Fauset because he too, insisted (this time from a poet's point of view) that literature not be confused with sociological materials.

Writers and intellectuals like these found numerous points of engagement with folklore, anthropology, and ethnography, yet they did not always feel compelled to follow the proscribed methods of these disciplines because their aims differed from that of Boas and his students, who set out to redefine culture. As Lee Baker astutely observes, the New Negro intellectuals emphasized, in addition, the racial politics of culture (*From Savage to Negro* 168–87). Boas viewed relativism, for example, as a means of enhancing the fieldworker's objectivity while conducting research, not as an instrument for promoting racial or cultural pride. But Black intellectuals used the nonhierarchical, relativistic view of culture to formulate and articulate a discrete "race consciousness" that bound Black people together through their common heritage in Africa and shared goals of social advancement and emancipation. According to Baker, "Artists and intellectuals turned to the blues and spirituals, holiness churches and ring shouts, as well as other traditional cultural practices to offer an empowering way to transform segregation into a form of congregation by challenging the derogatory assessments that the culture of rural Negroes was backward and inferior" ("Research" 73). But in "The Mind of Primitive Man," published in the *Journal of American Folk-Lore*, Boas explained how a relativist orientation was best suited for use *in the field*: "the student must endeavor to divest himself entirely of opinions and emotions based upon the peculiar social environment into which he is born. He must adapt his own mind, so far as feasible, to that of the people whom he is studying. The more successful he is in freeing himself from the bias based on the group of ideas that constituted the civilization in which he lives, the more successful he will be in interpreting the beliefs and actions of man."[50] The connections between Boas's theories and his desire for social justice are obvious. Nonetheless, he treated with suspicion attempts at merging scholarship with social reform because he feared losing his objectivity. Thus he preferred to write dispassionate reports on fieldwork to anything that suggested propaganda.[51]

Because Boas believed that African American's cultural assimilation would contribute to the resolution of the race problem in the United States, he was "absolutely opposed to all kinds of attempts to foster racial solidarity" (cited in Baker, "Research" 72).[52] This conviction may have grown from his own experiences growing up as a secular Jew in Germany. Since the late eighteenth century, German Jews had expressed a desire for, and had achieved, social advancement and integration by assimilating economically, and to a lesser extent socially and culturally, into the larger society. The diminishment of religious tradition and observance was one consequence of this process.[53] Yet the possibility for integration was not at all obvious for African Americans in the post-Reconstruction Era and early decades of the twentieth century. That period ushered in a multitude of instances of systemic racial violence and exclusion including the eruption of lynching incidents and race riots against African American communities, the institutionalization of Jim Crow segregation, and the wholesale disenfranchisement of Blacks from civic life, all of which made the goal of integration seem unlikely and the need for racial solidarity all the more necessary.

W. E. B. Du Bois, another, equally influential figure in the study of race and culture, keenly understood this. Like Boas, Du Bois was instrumental in the formation of a discipline in its modern form, namely sociology; and he made critical theoretical interventions in conceptualizations of race and culture at a pivotal point in the formation of the discipline. Unlike Boas, his influence is not always accepted as incontrovertible fact. Lee Baker, Faye V. Harrison, and Irene Diggs argue that although Boas's institutional base in the academy afforded him the opportunity to "redirect scientific approaches to race," other more marginalized scholars, like Du Bois, anticipated and even influenced Boas's scholarship.[54] Baker argues, for example, that Du Bois's early understanding of the color line contributed to the culture concept by distinguishing between "the cultural aspects of race and the social relations of race." In his 1897 paper "The Conservation of Races," presented at the first meeting of the Negro Academy, Du Bois argued that despite the existence of racial differences, "when we thus come to inquire into the essential difference of races we find it hard to come at once to any definite conclusion."[55] The reason Du Bois gave—that more differences exist within individual racial groups than between the different races—anticipates Boas's theory of diffu-sion.[56] Yet Du Bois's seminal role in modern American constructs of culture is often overlooked because he lacked the institutional power and authority that Boas possessed as a White scientist who was viewed as objective, and who held influential posts on editorial boards and in a prestigious depart-ment in the Academy.[57]

In the following chapter, I will discuss Du Bois's significance as a cul-tural and intellectual patriarch on New Negro artists and authors. His early career illustrates the many similarities between his struggle against scientific racism and Boas's own engagement with these issues. Yet his departure from academic discourse and engagement in social and political activism also points to the reasons why African Americans sought to cohere under a shared racial identity and illuminates the communal and cultural spaces in which they looked to find spiritual healing, political solidarity, and social justice.

Raising the Veil: Racial Divides and Ethnographic Crossings in The Souls of Black Folk

Objectivity, Authority, and Epistemologies of Difference

Like Franz Boas, W. E. B. Du Bois profoundly helped shape modern American thought on race and culture. As I have already mentioned, Du Bois's 1897 speech "The Conservation of the Races" was a landmark moment in the development of cultural pluralism. Biographer David Levering Lewis credits Du Bois with first articulating the principles of cultural pluralism in this speech to the American Negro Academy, long before the terminology to describe cultural pluralism even existed.[1] Lewis writes:

The writings of James and Dewey would point the way for the "cultural radicals," the pluralists of the near future, but the boldest signpost was first erected by Du Bois when he asked rhetorically of the seventeen attentive men in the Washington church: "[W]hat after all, am I? Am I an American or am I a Negro? Can I be both? Or is it my duty to cease to be a Negro as soon as possible and be an American? If I strive as a Negro, am I not perpetuating the very cleft that threatens and separates Black and White America? Is not my only possible practical aim the subduction of all that is Negro in me to the American? Does my Black blood place upon me any more obligation to assert my nationality than German, or Irish or Italian blood would?" (172)

In asking these questions, he began to unravel notions of citizenship and national identity, work that would contribute to a project of making America more inclusive and pluralistic. I will go on in this chapter to argue that Du Bois would prove to be a driving force in the New Negro movement, not only as a theorist of race and culture, but also as a literary figure. But in order for me to argue for his influence as a theoretician and social scientist, we must consider how the disciplines of anthropology and sociology paralleled each other at a time when both he and Boas embarked on their careers. In the latter part of the nineteenth century, sociology, like anthropology, broke with the less professional standards of writing upheld by earlier generations, by emphasizing empiricism and objectivity as proof of the disciplines' scientific legitimacy.[2] Each centered on the study of "primitive" societies—abroad in the case of anthropology and at home in the case of sociology—with ethnography functioning as a privileged mode of inquiry.[3]

Trained at Harvard primarily as a philosopher, historian, and political scientist, Du Bois acquired the skills and methodological approach necessary to conduct the empirical research that informed his earliest writings during his years at the University of Berlin (1892–94). Although he considered majoring in philosophy at Harvard, he eventually studied history because his professors warned him of the impracticality of the philosophy major, particularly for an individual committed to the work of racial uplift.[4] When he turned as a graduate student more decisively to the social sciences, buoyed, in part, by his studies at Harvard with the philosopher William James, Du Bois revealed a pragmatist's concern with the tangible application of ideas to the material world.[5] The years he spent studying at Humboldt University reinforced this approach. Carved above the university's entrance was the maxim, "until now philosophers have only explained the world, our task is to change it" (Lewis 142). Under the tutelage of Gustav Schmoller in Berlin, he learned to privilege inductive reasoning and analysis built on objectively accumulated historical and descriptive material. Schmoller "saw the goal of social science as the systematic, causal explanation of social phenomena, and he believed that social scientific facts, based on careful, inductive analysis, could be used as a guide to formulate social policy."[6] Until 1910, Du Bois's sociological works show ample evidence of Schmoller's influence, including his emphasis on empirical data collection, the use of facts as the basis for creating social policy, an underlying interest in social justice, and an emphasis on an historical approach, of which *The Philadelphia Negro* (1899) is a stellar example (Lewis 201).

After returning to the States in 1896 and a short stint teaching classics at Wilberforce University, Du Bois was offered a temporary position at the University of Pennsylvania to study the social condition and urban problems of Philadelphia's African American population. At that time, Philadelphia contained the largest community of African Americans in the North. Du Bois produced a 400-page monograph entitled *The Philadelphia Negro*, which analyzed the plight of the urban Black using survey and demographic data, much of which Du Bois collected during his stay in the city. Dan Green and Edwin Driver describe his sojourn in Philadelphia, during which he rented a room over a cafeteria in the "worst part" of the Seventh Ward, as an exercise in participant-observation, although the extent of his immersion in neighborhood life is debatable given his displeasure with the rougher element that populated the district. This fifteen-month appointment was followed by his employment at Atlanta University as a professor of economics and history, and as director of the Sociological Laboratory and the Atlanta University Conferences. Between 1897 and 1920, Du Bois took charge of this series of annual sociological conferences, which had been inaugurated in 1896 to study the effect of urban problems on African Americans. He also edited the annual volumes that issued from the conferences and taught a course on sociology. Yet by 1910 he moved away from pure sociology and toward other forms of address and redress, such as fiction, and his activism in the NAACP.[7]

Du Bois's early commitment to empiricism is uncontested, but the question of whether and if so, when his commitment wavered varies as critics consider the significance of his varied rhetorical strategies and methods in doing anti-racist work. Wilson Moses argues, for example, that Du Bois the scholar initially adopted the discourse of the social sciences because "as a youth Du Bois was romantically involved with the idea of social science, which he naïvely believed might yield a science of racial advancement."[8] To describe this commitment as romantic suggests that Du Bois's faith in empiricism as a weapon against social injustice was youthfully naïve, an interpretation that resonates with other critics who note that as Du Bois matured and became more aware of the roots of racial inequality, his approach to sociological research changed. Green and Driver note, "beginning in 1901 and continuing until his public split with [Booker T.] Washington in 1903, he was apparently moving through a transition period away from academic science and sociology toward action, agitation, and writing for popular magazines" (19). The lynching of Sam Hose, a Palmetto, Georgia farmer proved especially influential to Du Bois's diminished belief in the value of inductive reasoning as a tool for social engineering.[9] He became convinced, they assert, that scientific investigation was not sufficient to solve the problems of Black Americans because the problems were not, as he had initially and idealistically assumed, those of ignorance, but were instead based on the conscious determination of one group to suppress and persecute another.

In contrast, Robert Stepto argues that Du Bois adhered to a scientific language because of his desire for authentication. "He seeks nothing less than a new narrative mode and form in which empirical evidence, scientifically gathered in a literal and figurative field (for example, the Black Belt), performs the authenticating chores previously completed by white opinion."[10] And Houston Baker underscores Du Bois's lifelong commitment to scientific observation, stating that "while studying in Berlin under Gustav Schmoller (1892–94), Du Bois came to believe that the solution to the American racial problem was 'a matter of systematic investigation,' and throughout his life he was dedicated to critical objectivity—to what Mathew Arnold defined as 'disinterestedness.'"[11]

Du Bois's *view* of empiricism and inductive reasoning (which he never fully abandoned) is as important as his level of commitment to these methods. Even as a young scholar, his work shows that he reflected on the possibilities and limits of constructing a scientific discourse on race, even as he revealed an acute awareness of the cultural capital that science held. In 1903, when he published *The Souls of Black Folk*, the reader finds Du Bois wary of an unquestioning embrace of empiricism and even of the possibility of a Negro living a "life of the mind." Rather than advocating pure science early in his career, which he later retains or discards depending on the critic's point of view, we can see Du Bois inhabiting the middle ground, at the intersections of thought and action, reason and emotion, scholarship and activism.

Shamoon Zamir's argument that the empirical and emotional exist dialectically in Du Bois's body of work introduces an alternative to other critics' chronological or developmental narratives of Du Bois's thought on the uses of sociology. Reflecting on the importance of his writing the first chapters of *Souls* while in the midst of working on *The Philadelphia Negro*, Zamir identifies a "triumphant" conflict between scientific empiricism and political advocacy, or between "thought and feeling." He concludes, "if the different approaches represent conflicting understandings, then it is the very contradictions and struggles, not the straightforward triumph of one option over another, that must be accepted as the truth of Du Bois's thought" (55–56). Dialectical exchange can be seen as the operable mode not only among discrete periods of his career, or texts (*Souls* and *Philadelphia*), but also within the singular masterpiece, *The Souls of Black Folk*.[12] Thought and feeling, or science and activism, acquire meaning when we understand one in relation to the other. Du Bois makes evident his awareness of this fact in his layering and piecing together of different discursive traditions.

Race, Marginality, and the Formation of National Communities

The Souls of Black Folk is comprised of twelve essays and one short story, addressing a range of topics from the personal, to the sociological, historical, ethnographic, and political.[13] According to Gates and West, the breadth of topics and genres mirrors the scope of Du Bois's accomplishments. They call the book a monumental achievement that charts "the contours of the civilization [the Negro "nation-within-a-nation"]—the arts and sciences, the metaphysical and religious systems, the myths and music, the social and political institutions, the history both before and after Emancipation—that defined a truly African American culture at the outset of the new century."[14] The work's expansiveness was necessary for Du Bois to successfully portray Negro "civilization" from both internal and external points of view. Sociology gave him a framework through which he could produce an empirical and historical analysis of the state of Black America. Fiction allowed him to explore the post-emancipation dynamics between the emerging intellectual and professional classes and the masses of Black Southerners; and the "sorrow songs," as Du Bois called African American spirituals, voice the despair, longings, and hopes of Black people who had been historically silenced and subordinated because of the dual stigmas of color and poverty. In all these discursive moments, Du Bois presents himself as a representative subject who exhibits kinship and solidarity with the oppressed from a shared history of oppression, even as the adoption of the social scientist's identity in the service of racial uplift and activism produces a tension that threatens to unravel the affiliations he so fiercely maintains.

The Souls of Black Folk is not the first work in which Du Bois experiments with the rhetorical approach of simultaneously representing the Negro from "without" and "within," although he did not necessarily accomplish this through discursive hybridity, as he does in Souls. In "The Black North in 1901," he tackles the perception that Black communities in the North are homogenous by twinning his analysis of demographic statistics about social patterns such as domestic configurations and employment statistics with a brief psychological sketch of the "average New York negro" that attempts to describe the emotional and psychic resources on which Black people draw in response to racism. In the essay he observes, "they live and move in a community of their own kith and kin and shrink quickly and permanently from those rough edges where contact with the larger life of the city wounds and humiliates them" (reprinted in Green and Driver 151).[15] This description emphasizes that social contact across interracial lines is obstructed by a racism that can be palpable in its damaging effects. Du Bois states that racism is a force from which the Negro shrinks and retreats into the protective fold of a homogenous community in an act of self-defense. Yet this observation occurs in as essay in which substantial effort has been made to establish the high degree of social, economic, and moral differences among Blacks in New York's segregated neighborhoods. The incongruous representation of New York Blacks as both heterogeneous and insular suggests that both juxtaposition to and segregation from a dominant group can render a marginalized community cut off and isolated. Rather than positioning Blacks, the domestic U.S. version of the primitive others, as "out of time," Du Bois underscores the notion that segregation is directly caused by adverse social and historical forces.

Insights such as these were made possible by Du Bois's multiple allegiances to scholarly and racial communities. Inspired by the liminality of his own subject position, he introduces the symbol of the veil as a figure for the racial divide. The image can also be read as a symbol of the ethnographer as participant-observer. In the "Forethought" of *The Souls of Black Folk*, he conjures an image of a narrator unique in his ability to move and communicate across the color line: "Leaving, then, the world of the white man, I have stepped within the Veil, raising it that you may view faintly its deeper recesses, the meaning of its religion, the passion of its human sorrow, and the struggle of its greater souls" (359). This portrait illustrates an ideal relation between ethnographer and audience, characterized by the narrator's mastery of the nuances of transculturation and the reader's openness to greater understanding of the racial other, yet it is also a depiction rife with ambivalences. It hints at, for example, the narrator's liminality through the image of his stepping "within the Veil." To step within the Veil is to traverse anxiously between, and live partly in, both White and Black worlds, a circumstance that may lend its own insight but that also speaks of alienation. As Houston Baker argues:

The "veil" is Du Bois's metaphor for what might be thought of as the "edge" of the performative frame, the dissonant rim where safe, colored parochialism is temptingly and provisionally refigured as an anguished mulatto cosmopolitanism. The "veil" hangs in the performative moment like a scrim between dark, pastoral, problematic folk intimacy with black consciousness, and free-floating anxieties of a public mulatto modernism that subjects one to the white "gaze."[16]

That dissonant edge, the performative space inhabited by the cosmopolitan Black (or racially hybrid) modern is also a space of undefined possibility for the audience as much as it is for the narrator. The image of the reader viewing beyond the Veil "faintly" both promises and withholds the possibility of his identifying with the author's Southern Black subjects. This ambivalence over the narrator's ability to cross racial boundaries easily, or facilitate the passage of others, is rendered still more complexly in other parts of the book.

Du Bois queries the efficacy of scientific authority, for example, by rendering uncertain the possibility of the scientist (himself included) knowing his subjects fully. His description of the Georgia Black Belt, the "center of the Negro problem," commences with the narrator aboard a train rumbling through Georgia; its movement across the rural landscape allows the narrator to cover historical ground as well, from the slave trade, to the Cherokee nation's displacement by the U.S. government, and into the present moment of the plantation system's dissipation and disappearance. Du Bois's summons the reader—"If you wish to ride with me you must come into the 'Jim Crow Car' "—playing with the idea of simultaneous closeness and distance (440). While this invitation holds out the promise of a kind of intimacy that would grow commensurate with the reader's increased understanding of the Black Belt and proposes the closure of a social divide, it also accurately positions the narrator and Black folk in separate racial camps and social strata from Whites and indicts the nation for its failures to live up to its social contract with the Negro. Du Bois continues, "There will be no objection,—already four other white men, and a little white girl with her nurse, are in there. Usually the races are mixed in there; but the white coach is all white. . . . The discomfort lies chiefly in the hearts of those four black men yonder—and in mine" (440–41). The inability of the White passengers to share the Negroes' sense of constraint in movement and choice, limits their ability to truly empathize even as they share the same social space. Consequently, Du Bois's invitation to the reader to accompany him into the heart of the Black Belt, to delve deeply beneath the layers of history and social customs to arrive at a greater measure of understanding, is accompanied by a subtle reminder of the (white) reader's privileged social status that constrains his ability to identify with the experience of oppression that is *de rigueur* for the African American.

The (im)possibility of knowing the racial other deepens in Du Bois's representation of Albany, Georgia, a typical Southern town whose Negro inhabitants he describes as "black, sturdy, uncouth country folk, good-natured and simple, talkative to a degree, and yet far more silent and brooding than the crowds of the Rhine-pfalz, or Naples, or Cracow" (442).[17] The silence and brooding that Du Bois observes suggest a collective resistance to the clinical gaze of the observer, a wall of reserve erected to fend off the outsider who is the reader; and perhaps Du Bois the social scientist and light-skinned Yankee, despite his repeated claims of affiliation with Southern Black folk. The inscrutability of the masses, their refusal to be "read" as examples of a primitive type, rears up almost simultaneously with the narrator's assertions of his ability to represent them. And admittedly, it is this same narrator who observes about this landscape and the people who populate it: "How curious a land is this,—how full of untold story, of tragedy and laughter, and the rich legacy of human life; shadowed with a tragic past, and big with future promises" (447). Such statements make clear that the author's reservations arise from his sense that the reader will not or cannot adequately discern these individuals' humanity either through the poverty, disrepair, and despair that overrun their town, or through a totalizing scientific narrative, that would view them as an abstraction known as "the folk."

The narrative's shift from an ethnographic perspective to an elegiac one underscores this question by probing the ability of ethnography to adequately represent the Black Belt in all its complexity and prodding the reader to deeper levels of empathy. Du Bois thus moves from a survey of the dilapidated cabins, to a brief historical meditation, to a lyrical recounting of the Negroes' arrival in the American South:

Then came the black slaves. Day after day the clank of chained feet marching from Virginia and Carolina to Georgia was heard in these rich swamp lands. Day after day the songs of the callous, the wail of the motherless, and the muttered curses of the wretched echoed from the Flint to the Chickasawhatchee, until by 1860 there had risen in West Dougherty perhaps the richest slave kingdom the modern world ever knew. (448)

The portrait being drawn here, with its sentimental tenor, gothic images of enslavement, and hints at cultural richness yet to be discovered ("the richest slave kingdom the modern world ever knew"), differs strikingly from the earlier description of Black Belt inhabitants as "black, sturdy, uncouth country folk." The almost seamless narrative's transition from "clinical" observation to sentimental lyricism and grand mythmaking mirrors the perspectives of the narrator and reader, outsiders working to achieve a measure of closeness to the subjects under observation. As Hazel Carby argues, "In *The Souls of Black Folk*, Du Bois's initial premise was that black people and black cultural forms did not exist in opposition to the national ideals but, on the contrary, embodied those ideals. He thus attempted to rewrite the dominant cultural and political script by transferring the symbolic power of nationalism, of Americanness, into a black cultural field and onto the black male body."[18]

I want to suggest that the Southern Black folk, the narrator, and his readers are all active participants in a narrative whose intent is to make possible the formation of a more pluralistic national community. The narrator and his readers' passage through the Black Belt is the more obvious in that they are understood to be modern men of reason who *use* travel to understand and, hopefully, cross social and geographic boundaries. Yet even as the Black Belt inhabitants seem, in contrast, to occupy a typically static position—stuck in a backward society, rooted in tradition—Du Bois produces an alternative reading that underscores the Southern country folk's passage through time. He emphasizes, in other words, the importance of their temporal progress, their steady, collective march into the future not visible to the outsider unless he is willing to leave behind the comfort of racist ideologies and regimes to join Du Bois on the journey in the "Jim Crow car."

The challenges posed by African Americans' social marginalization provided much of the impetus behind Du Bois's sociological theories and methods. In "The Negroes of Dougherty County, Georgia," Du Bois described his methods for collecting data: "My first work [in studying small communities] was at Farmville, Virginia. What I did in that case was to go to a typical town and settle down there for a time. I made a census of the town personally, went to the house of each negro family in town, and tried to find out as much as I could about the general situation of things in that town" (reprinted in Green and Driver 154). Here he suggests settling within and blending into a community results in more acute observations; in *Souls* it allows for an empathetic linking of the individual and the group, the articulation of racial feeling, and the formation of a racial community. The privileging of communal relations in *Souls* marks a shift from *The Philadelphia Negro,* in which Du Bois writes in the voice of "classic social analysts [who] pretend to speak either from a position of omniscience or from no position at all," to his explicitly positioning himself within a particular social context.[19] Declaring in the Forethought, "need I add that I who speak here am bone of the bone and flesh of the flesh of them that live within the Veil?" Du Bois claims a racial and biological affiliation that minimizes the regional, educational, and class differences that distinguished him from the masses of Southern Black slave descendants (209). Where in *The Philadelphia Negro* he highlights intraracial difference, in this text, written almost contemporaneously, he underscores notions of attachment through kinship.

Stepto argues that "Du Bois's efforts at binding or combining create expressions of a special unity between 'we' and 'I,' 'our' and 'my,' 'theirs' and 'mine,' that is unquestionably central to the rhetorical and narrative strategies of *The Souls* and, quite likely, essential to Du Bois's personal sense of self."[20] This strategy also anticipates the Renaissance project of communal and cultural identity construction. By merging the "I" and the "We," the individual and the communal, he signals a shift toward the articulation of a common, modern identity emerging from the ashes of slavery. Du Bois turns to the South at a moment when Blacks were beginning to leave the region and its slaveholding legacy in increasingly larger numbers (the trickle he documents will, in a matter of decades, turn into a flood of urban migrants). He documents the development of an expressive culture that held traces of the old and new, the South and the North, the Black and the White. The ongoing importance of these ideas is signaled by the frequent turn by *New Negro* contributors to the folklore and culture of the African American slaves as a source of artistic inspiration, even as they announce a definitive break from the past.

The Literal and Figurative South

Members of the New Negro Renaissance legitimized the movement's progressiveness by underscoring the rural, slaveholding South's setting in the retrograde past; and looking back at the progress narrative intrinsic to the "Hampton Idea," we can see that this was not a formulation invented by the upwardly mobile African Americans of the 1920s. Du Bois's response to this impulse, however, was to suggest, through what I call the homecoming trope (in "Of the Coming of John"), that one must first revisit the past in order to move more assuredly into the future.[21] The reoccurrence of the Southern home as trope in the literature of the period gives weight to Sterling Brown's observation that Harlem was not the epicenter of the New Negro Renaissance. He insisted, "the New Negro movement had temporal roots in the past and spatial roots elsewhere in America."[22] Houston Baker provocatively suggests, "Modernism's emphasis falls on the locative—where one is located or placed—in determining how constricted the domain of freedom might be" (*Turning South* 69–70). Fiction as diverse as Jean Toomer's *Cane* (1923), Walter White's *Fire in the Flint* (1924), Nella Larsen's *Quicksand* (1928), Langston Hughes's *Ways of White Folk* (1933), and Zora Neale Hurston's *Their Eyes Were Watching God* (1937) repeat and revise Du Bois's story of education, migration from, return to, and uplift of Southern homes. These narratives of homecoming and cosmopolitan migration constitute a collective, fictive grappling with both the ethnographic imagination and its implications in the complex relations of the "talented tenth" to the "folk" he or she aspires to represent. Especially at this historical moment, the South represents, according to Baker, "a liminal zone, a middle passage of the imagination, a space of performance, a series of peculiar 'strips' of interactive behavior where *blackness* has played or performed toward the *scene* of modernity" (36). The South was a symbolic location with which New Negro intellectuals constructed and performed modern Black identities.

The social sciences' emphasis on fieldwork as a fundamental mode of inquiry established the notion of "the field" as isolated, set apart, and uncorrupted by outside communities.[23] Yet we should not attribute the place of the South in the Renaissance imagination solely to this fact. Because the Southern Black Belt is a central site of analysis for Du Bois he, as much as a figure like Boas, influenced Harlem Renaissance constructions of New Negro identity in relation to the Southern past. Alain Locke extends Du Bois's thesis when he argues in "The New Negro," for example, for the recognition of more progressive, assertive, and urban identified Negro, whose advancement was tied to a revaluation of the artistic and cultural roles Southern Blacks have played in the regional and national scenes. What was needed, in other words, for the advancement of the race, was a reassessment of the value of the culture from which it was born:

It must be increasingly recognized that the Negro has already made very substantial contributions, not only in his folk-art, music especially, which has always found appreciation, but in larger, though humbler and less acknowledged ways. For generations the Negro has been the peasant matrix of that section of American which most undervalued him, and here he has contributed not only materially in labor and in social patience, but spiritually as well. The South has unconsciously absorbed the gift of his folk-temperament. In less than half a generation it will be easier to recognize this, but the fact remains that a leaven of humor, sentiment, imagination and tropic nonchalance has gone into the making of the South from a humble, unacknowledged source. (15)

Locke's identification of the Southern "folk" as a point of orientation for the creation of an African American expressive culture corresponds with and is informed by a period in which Black writers absorbed the idea of the "field" as apart from the real and modern present because of their ethnographic training and/or interests.[24] In fact, Du Bois's representation of the Southern Black Belt anticipates the New Negro consumption of anthropological concepts when, in *The Souls of Black Folk*, he describes a Southern town as a product of the imagination of modern, urbanized Northerners:

Once upon a time we knew country life so well and city life so little that we illustrated city life as that of a closely crowded country district. Now the world has well nigh forgotten what the country is, and we must imagine a little city of black people scattered far and wide over three hundred lonesome square miles of land, without train or trolley, in the midst of cotton and corn, and wide patches of sand and gloomy soil. (442)

When writing from a distance, whether geographic or experiential, Du Bois suggests descriptions of the other inevitably leave something lacking because the writer endows them with characteristics of the familiar, or relies on easy stereotype. The city dweller, he implies, may aspire to represent "country life," but her or she may only be able to imagine a "little city" in which the relational geography assumes the characteristics of life in an urban setting, while at the same time imposing on the landscape stock features of associated with the rural: cotton, corn, and gloomy soil.

The irony is that while Du Bois certainly emphasizes the isolation of Southern towns because of historical circumstances (namely racial segregation), he also stressed its status as an ideal study site because the advent of emancipation allowed for the rapid social transformation of a once oppressed group of individuals. In "The Atlanta Conferences" (1904), for example, he wrote:

The careful exhaustive study of the isolated group then is the ideal of the sociologist of the 20th century—from that may come a real knowledge of natural law as locally manifest—a glimpse and revelation of rhythm beyond this little center at last careful, cautious generalization and formulation. For such work there lies before the sociologist of the Untied States a peculiar opportunity. We have here going on before our eyes the evolution of a vast group of men from simpler primitive conditions to higher more complex civilization. (reprinted in Green and Driver 54)

Du Bois's implicit suggestion is that we should not equate geographical isolation with temporal stasis; Southern Black society was caught up in a dynamic process of regeneration. Baker points out that the South became in the African American imagination a locus of sustained analysis, identified more than any other place with African American culture, not because of uncritical essentialism or nostalgia for a vernacular culture but because it was the home of the vast majority of Blacks after emancipation.[25] For Du Bois, the South was the birthplace of African American culture, but he also viewed it as a microcosm of a culture in the process of social advancement, progress writ large. And, just as importantly, he considered the Southern Negro condition to be intimately tied to the outcomes of their Northern kin. He wrote, for example, in "The Black North in 1901: New York," "The North . . . has much more than an academic interest in the Southern negro problem. Unless the race conflict there is so adjusted as to leave the negroes a contented, industrious people, they are going to migrate here and there. And into the large cities will pour in increasing numbers the competent and the incompetent, the industrious and the lazy, the law abiding and the criminal" (reprinted in Green and Driver 143). The suggestion here is that northward migration is not the only avenue to lead to socioeconomic progress, and the improvement of race relations was a—if not *the*—critical step toward collective Black advancement. In his early sociological works Du Bois not only emphasized North/South interconnectedness, he also differentiated among social and economic strata within urban Negro communities in order for Whites to better recognize the achievement of the "better classes."

This agenda is first apparent in *The Philadelphia Negro*. In his overview to this study, Du Bois writes:

It is often tacitly assumed that the Negroes of Philadelphia are one homogenous mass, and that the slums of the Fifth Ward, for instance, are one of the results of long contact with Philadelphia city life on the part of this mass. There is just enough truth and falsehood in such an assumption to make it dangerously misleading. The slums of Seventh and Lombard streets are largely results of the contact of the Negro with city life, but the Negro in question is a changing variable quantity and has felt city influences for periods varying in different persons from one day to seventy years. A generalization then that includes a North Carolina boy who has migrated to the city for work and has been here for a couple of months, in the same class with a descendant of several generations of Philadelphia Negroes, is apt to make serious mistakes. The first lad may deserve to be pitied if he falls into dissipation and crime, the second ought perhaps to be condemned severely. In other words our judgment of the thousands of Negroes of this city must be in all cases considerably modified by a knowledge of their previous history and antecedents. (reprinted in Green and Driver 127)

Du Bois's efforts to differentiate within the race implicitly challenged the ethnographic imperative to construct a narrative of a community, or "field" that was isolated, homogenous, and "authentic" because of the presumed lack of encounters with contaminating outsiders. Ironically, he reveals in this overtly sociological text his awareness that representing a community in a field site as representative of the whole race runs the risk of masking the reality of profound differences within it, a prospect that would have run counter to Du Bois's attempts to make visible different levels of accomplishment within Black communities. Although he stressed that the outside observer needed a sufficiently historical view of Philadelphia's Seventh Ward in order to recognize the different levels of achievement (or potential for achievement) within the urban enclave, he changes approaches in *The Souls of Black Folk* precisely because he has different rhetorical aims. In contrast to emphasizing a Northern Black urban neighborhood's heterogeneity, he seems to conclude that such a setting was less suited to the kind of collective cultural identity construction that he embarks upon in *The Souls of Black Folk*. There, he turns his prophetic vision southward to a region whose recognizable traits seemed to offer more to the cultural nationalist and ethnographer bent on drawing a unified portrait of a racial group with a cohesive cultural identity.

Du Bois anticipates New Negro constructions of identity construction when, in *The Souls of Black Folk*, he writes about the African-derived cultural origins of Southern Black American genius in his discussion of the sorrow songs. Black writers, including Du Bois, produced an equally compelling depiction of the South as a place of violence, dispossession, and displacement, a portrait perhaps epitomized by Richard Wright's post-Harlem Renaissance fiction. But because Locke and his peers—following in Du Bois's very large footsteps—were so bent on articulating the modern and progressive in African American culture and situating that culture within a expressive Black tradition, they initiated a sustained "reading" of the South as what French historian Pierre Nora has labeled a site of memory.[26] Nora suggests that acts of commemoration of a folk past are frequently deployed in the service of a particular kind of nationalism, which resonates with the New Negroes' incipient cultural nationalism. Farah Jasmine Griffin argues that the portrait of the South as home, site of ancestral wisdom and spirituality, finds its fullest articulation in post-Civil Rights era literatures of migration as a response to Northern experiences of violence and domination.[27] In each case—whether in the France described by Nora, the industrializing decades heralded by the New Negro, or the post-60s cultural dislocation captured in contemporary Black fiction—the construction of a cultural space of wholeness is pressed into service to represent an always desired, never achievable state of plenitude by a people contending with social fragmentation and ensuing crises of identity.[28] The paradox of the Harlem Renaissance era is that its writers, like Du Bois, initiated this trope while simultaneously contending with widely held assumptions that Southern Negro culture held not wisdom but indecipherability and little of true value. Sociology, like anthropology, could be a weapon in the anti-racist project, but it was not without its pitfalls in that both tended to deny individual agency and to generalize about a group based on the example of representative subjects.[29]

Creating a counter-narrative to this discourse of Negro primitivism required that Du Bois view himself as something other, or more, than a social scientist as he wrote about his own people, and that he recognize and validate the everyday knowledge and wisdom of common people. The ability to express what cannot always be articulated through language—the heights and depths of human experience—epitomized for Du Bois the best of African American expressivity rooted in the Southern slave experience and simultaneously illustrated the notion that culture and knowledge could develop in ways, and emerge from sources not recognized by hegemonic structures. Thus he devoted large sections of his book to rendering, indeed *articulating*, folk wisdom. Implicitly, Du Bois asks us to consider what happens when certain modes of knowledge production disallow certain kinds of knowledge. And also, he makes the reader see that these different modes of knowing need not exist in a racially or socially segregated vacuum. This fact makes *The Souls of Black Folk* an important *theoretical* intervention on the practices of doing fieldwork, writing ethnography, and producing culture.

The Sorrow Songs: Expressing the Incomprehensible

In order to construct an argument that is both culturally nationalist and humanistic, Du Bois emphasizes the *universal* significance of local forms of cultural expression. The Sea Islands, he writes for example, were "touched and moulded less by the world about them than any others outside the Black Belt" (537). Du Bois's emphasis on the Sea Islands' isolation follows what will eventually become standard ethnographic practice, localizing, and isolating the cultural field (at least rhetorically) from a contaminating exposure to modernity and difference. Yet despite the Sea Islanders' strangeness—that is, their alienation from the American majority—Du Bois implored, "their hearts were human and their singing stirred men with a mighty power" (537). His ensuing discussion makes clear that the spiritual and emotional pull of the music arises from its capacity to convey the most common and tragic of human experiences and emotions. The sorrow songs, we learn, are the expressions of exile, betrayal, despair, death, mourning, strife, fugitivity, and struggle (539–41). To Du Bois, their creation was made possible by intercultural contact and they promised social transformation.[30] Noting the nation's neglect of the slave songs before the Civil War, Du Bois identifies the war as a pivotal moment because "after the capture of Hilton Head, and perhaps for the first time the North met the Southern slave face to face and heart to heart with no third witness" (537). In the absence of the South's biased witness and interference, Du Bois implies, White Northerners would finally see Southern Blacks' humanity in its fullness.[31]

His decision to conclude *The Souls of Black Folk* with a passionate discussion of the sorrow songs underscores his conviction of their ability to convey information about and feelings for the African American. In other words, the sorrow songs' movement through history illustrates much about the Africans' movement through American history, at the same time that it also articulates their complex reactions to that passage in time and space, and through centuries of oppression. Du Bois represents the sorrow songs, following multiple models of travel, from the diasporic to the entrepreneurial. On the one hand, he identifies three steps in the development of Black music, from the "African," characterized by its "strange" and "primitive" chants; to the "Afro-American," to which Du Bois fails to ascribe any particular characteristics; to a "blending of Negro music with the music heard in the foster land" (541). He even suggests the possibility of identifying a fourth step in development, "where the songs of white America have been distinctively influenced by the slave songs or have incorporated whole phrases of Negro melody" (540). This trajectory focuses on a collective history of forced displacement, a cataclysmic break that is inscribed in spirituals which allow for the fullest expression of Black people's mourning and loss. Yet at the same time, Du Bois sounds a hopeful note by locating signs of transformation and renewal, evidence of which can be found in the hybrid notes sounded on both ends of the racial spectrum.

The Fisk Jubilee Singers signify for Du Bois the most accomplished and idealistic exemplars of this traveling musical form. Exiled wandering shapeshifts into a voyage of conquest as the Fisk Singers—"four half-clothed boys and five girl-women"—travel first across the country and then around Europe exposing nations to songs that "conquered till they sang across the land and across the sea, before Queen and Kaiser" (538). Du Bois's description suggests that the Fisk Singers' vocal soundings had the power to topple, if not actual empires, then certainly regimes of racist reasoning and uncivil action against people of African descent. Moreover, their travels bolstered newly freed Blacks' burgeoning entrepreneurial spirit by allowing the singers to raise and bring back "a hundred and fifty thousand dollars to found Fisk University" (538).

Racial uplift and the reformation of White racism were made possible by what began as the diasporic wanderings of enigmatic African song. From his great-great-grandmother's crooning in an unknown and half-remembered language—"Do bana coba, gene me, gene me"—to the "strange chants" of the most primitive, that is, least acculturated of the spirituals, Du Bois lays claim to a musical tradition that carries the awesome responsibility of conveying a people's history. It is not coincidental that Du Bois so often recounts musical expression emanating from women like his great-great-grandmother or the "girl-women" from Fisk, for femininity and emotion are typically linked in patriarchal discourse. Yet at the same time that Du Bois articulates the Black male subject's aspiring toward full masculinity through the mastery of language (here, the protagonist in "Of the Coming of John" will prove illustrative), he also problematizes the binary by calling into question the power and authority typically located in language (hence, reason). African American history's defining moment, the Middle Passage and ensuing enslavement, centers on an experience of cataclysmic rupture and loss that resists the author's attempts at mastery and translation because of language's failure to fully render the scope of human tragedy. Du Bois's turn to an artistic, emotive, nonlinguistic, and vernacular tradition at these moments suggests the limits of the ethnography and historiography practiced elsewhere in the volume. Musical soundings, in other words, must do the expressive work that language fails to achieve.[32]

The first indication that the music resists assimilation into a more transparent language lies in its uneasy juxtaposition with the poetic verses that introduce, along with untitled bars of music, each chapter. Du Bois offers no explanation for these pairings until the final essay, "The Sorrow Songs," in which he informs the reader of the slave-era spirituals each refrain is meant to represent.[33] At the time of the book's appearance, this pairing of African American music with European verse posed a radical intervention because, according to biographer David Levering Lewis, Du Bois intended "to advance the then-unprecedented notion of the creative parity and complementarity of white folk and black folk alike. Du Bois meant the cultural symbolism of these double epigraphs to be profoundly subversive of the cultural hierarchy of his time" (Lewis 278).

Sandra Adell's reading of this musical and textual juxtaposition echoes Lewis's in that she too sees it as an assertion of cultural parity. Moreover, Adell explicitly challenges Houston Baker's suggestion in *Singers of Daybreak* that the bars of music from the sorrow songs "displace" the poetic epigraphs. According to Adell, instead of displacement, Du Bois "merely foregrounds the very complex system of interrelationships that makes up his (con)textual field."[34] Parsing the particulars of this system of interdependence is difficult, however, when the reader is hampered, like the author himself, by a lack of musical training. Du Bois writes, "What are these songs, and what do they mean? I know little of music and can say nothing in technical phrase, but I know something of men, and knowing them, I know that these songs are the articulate message of the slave to the world" (538). How, then, to convey that message in prose when its meaning is embedded in the *sound* and not just in the words?

The question to consider then is not whether Du Bois privileges music over poetry or vice versa, for a reading of "The Sorrow Songs" immediately makes clear his belief in the profundity of both. What becomes apparent, however, is the inadequacy of language to narrate a medium that *performs* feelings that arise in response to inhumane conditions.[35] While one could argue that our understanding of the poetic verses is equally compromised because they too are removed from their context, the literate person can still read and interpret the fragments offered, an act which is virtually denied when we "read" musical notations that were meant to be sung or played. Thus, we are presented (at least until the final chapter) with only the "spirit" of the folk as represented by the untitled bars of music.[36] Lacking the immediacy of the kind of performances offered by the Fisk Jubilee Singers, the impact of the music can only be felt through the author's intervention.

Du Bois's mediating role, his impassioned explanation of the form and content of Black musical expression, opens up yet another site in which to consider the complicated role of the native ethnographer. For even as he attempted to impress upon his readership the complexity of Black feeling, he battled against the perception that African Americans while abundant in their reserves of feeling and emotion, lacked the critical capacity for logic and reason. Many of his readers would continue to equate literacy with a civilized status, even as they expressed appreciation for Du Bois's articulation of a more pluralistic constellation of cultures. For example, an anonymous review published in *The Nation* in 1903 asserts, "The bar of music from one 'Sorrow Song' or another which stands at the head of each chapter is a hint (unintended) that what follows is that strain writ large, that Mr. Du Bois's thought and expression are highly characteristic of his people, are cultivated varieties of those emotional and imaginative qualities which are the prevailing traits of the uncultivated negro mind. Hence one more argument for that higher education of the negro for which Mr. Du Bois so eloquently pleads."[37] The writer's application of an evolutionary trajectory to the narrative's use of a presumably more sophisticated emotional rhetoric to explain an emotive music betrays his misapprehension of Du Bois's point that the enigmatic sorrow songs were well equipped to articulate a complex—and universal—set of experiences and emotions; that the "primitive" music of a rough and rude folk was paradoxically sophisticated in its ability to express a range of emotions and human experiences, and that this artistic form was comparable to that produced by the most celebrated of European writers.

If we think of modernism as a movement fueled by the impulse to conceive of a once unimaginable future while standing on the brink of an era fraught with uncertainty, then it becomes clearer how Du Bois was able to discern complexity in cultural formations that his education and Northern inclinations could easily have led him to disdain. Writing and working at a point of social, historical, and disciplinary flux, Du Bois treated Negro culture, embodied by the sorrow songs, as not just a set of material artifacts, but as a humanist engagement with feeling and experience. He treats them, in other words, as living culture. Working from this assumption enabled him to advance theories of cultural pluralism and racial equality before a formal discourse had emerged fully to frame these terms and ideas.

The impressiveness of this achievement rests in the fact that Du Bois conceived of what Zamir describes as the "lyrical science" that characterizes *The Souls of Black Folk* just a few years after he had begun to employ the scientific empiricism in which he was trained as an undergraduate at Harvard in the service of conceptualizing and articulating a new scientific method for the study of racial groups.[38] The imaginative realm of fiction and the impressionistic realm of memoir which he enters in *Souls* offered Du Bois opportunities not available in other genres, opening up spaces for self-examination of his views, values, and positions on himself and the world. For example, the reflexivity that characterizes "Of the Coming of John," the sole work of fiction in a collection of mostly nonfiction, focuses the narrative on the racist conditions that compelled Du Bois to demand equal access to education for the most talented members of his race, and on the tensions between the upwardly mobile and working classes that threatened to create new social rifts within Black communities.[39] Indeed, Du Bois uses generic hybridity to articulate multiple, interlocking commentaries on race matters in a modernist mode of theorization. Multiple points of view signal his refusal to locate an authoritative voice and hegemonic gaze in a single subject or language. Du Bois's concern with the dislocation of knowledge and peoples in the modern world marks him as firmly situated in the twentieth century even though he had yet to relinquish the style and tone of a Victorianist.

"Of the Coming of John": Homecoming and Reflections on the Black Intellectual

In "Of the Coming of John," Du Bois reflects on the place of Black intellectuals in their communities, meditating as it were on the factors that hinder or facilitate their manipulation of the Veil. The story explores a number of themes running throughout the collection, including transcendent knowledge, double-consciousness, and leadership in Black communities. It is also a story of homecoming that considers the possibilities for return of the native son made prodigal by a transformational encounter with the world of Western thought and ideas. Zamir has identified as "the problematic of Du Bois's work" the relations of his European and Euro-American intellectual formations and the "concrete particulars of a life lived and understood historically"; in other words, the relation of theory to experience (2). In the narrative, Du Bois represents the Black intelligentsia, of which the native ethnographer is not only a part but also an emblem, as a problem for both his community and the larger society by dint of an educational experience that renders him profoundly outside his circle of intimates, as well as the more hostile world that surrounds them. Like the author, John too longs for the freedom made possible by living a cultured life of the mind: "A deep longing swelled in his heart to rise with that clear music out of the dirt and dust of that low life that held him prisoned and befouled. If he could only live up in the free air where birds sang and setting suns had no touch of blood!" (527). The concert hall, symbolic of the best of European art and culture, temporarily transports John from the reality that his racial identity determines and constricts the possibilities for his life. He resents the intellectual, cultural, and social narrowness assigned to him because of his race. But John's migration from rural to urban spaces and his transformation from illiterate to literate individual allows him to acquire the sensibility that fosters his appreciation of Western art and culture. That he is molded from a rough, boisterous, countrified child into a dignified, educated, and refined adult is meant to stand as proof of the inherent capability (as opposed to the assumed inferiority) of all Negroes.

Du Bois's eulogy of Alexander Crummel in chapter 12 can be read as a meditation on the subject of literacy and knowledge facilitating the Black subject's transcendence of racial barriers. According to Adell, Du Bois depicts Crummell as dwelling above the Veil because of his education. He exemplifies Du Bois's ideal of "book-learning" as the path "leading to heights high enough to overlook life" (Adell 24). For Du Bois the most advantageous and empowering position to aspire to is that of the observer/scientist whose goal is to "overlook life." But unlike Crummel, John falls victim to social obstacles that impede his attainment of transcendent knowledge because he fails to consider how experience informs the production of knowledge. According to Adell, John's "mode of thinking . . . is initially epistemological: why is a circle not square; why does this Greek word mean this and not that, and so on? What he learns is that there is no relation between this kind of knowledge— academic literacy—and freedom. The myth of the quest for literacy and freedom is nothing more than a myth for John Jones" (25). While there is no correlation between academic literacy and freedom for John, the narrative suggests that a strong connection can still be made among the acquisition of knowledge, the cultivation of a critical consciousness, and the pursuit of social justice. Ontology and epistemology could be mutually constitutive modes if John had been able to discern the relation between the two. Certainly, his story hints at the potential for this connection to exist, even as its trajectory heads inexorably toward the failure of that union being realized.

John's migration from home and exposure to Western art and culture initiate his awareness of racial difference and racism. With education, "he grew slowly to feel almost for the first time the Veil that lay between him and the white world; he first noticed now the oppression that had not seemed oppression before, differences that erstwhile seemed natural" (525). This passage implies that a formal education is necessary for individuals to have the capacity to recognize their own oppression. The conclusions critics draw from this assumption are revealing.

For example, Lewis suggests that double-consciousness, symbolized by John's awareness of the presence of the Veil, may be a formulation that has more relevance for acculturated Blacks who embraced "the values of the dominant class of the dominant society" (Lewis 282). Less privileged Blacks, Lewis writes, may have "had a simpler self-concept, one uninfluenced by Hegel and more fixed by a common identity based on color and raw oppression" (282). He makes explicit Du Bois's implied notion that an educated and acculturated mind is enlightened, and this state is a necessary prerequisite to recognizing that racial differences "that erstwhile seemed natural" are actually mechanisms for social control.

Accepting this presupposition, Ross Posnock argues that cosmopolitanism—the identification with things outside of one's particular local, or national, communities—is absolutely necessary for acquiring the means of political engagement. He writes that Du Bois conveys an idea of the political as civic participation by those whose qualifications are severed from family, tribe, class, and caste. This understanding of citizenship recalls a Hellenistic sense of the political. The *politicos* referred to those men permitted and willing to leave the private household for the *polis*, where men of various origins and social standing engaged in rational debate as they attempted practical problem solving for the community, an activity requiring intellectual improvisation in the face of uncertainty. In the polis one had to cope with *pragmata*, the contingencies of unsettled circumstances. According to one commentator, those outside political life, excluded from speaking the language of politics, were called *ethnos*, the root of ethnic. These provincial *idiots*, also known as *barbaros*, are embedded in nature, confined to a tight circle of blood relations, reliant on the habits and folkways of forefathers, and resigned to the monotony of time endlessly unfolding.[40]

Posnock underscores the fact that it is by leaving home for the "polis" that Black intellectuals acquire the qualifications and credentials to assume the position of race men and women who represent their peers within dominant cultural institutions. The irony is, of course, that it was precisely Blacks and women who were prevented by law and tradition from participating fully in the political life of the nation, which renders problematic the notion, embedded in this argument, that those confined to the "tight circle of blood relations" are incapable of full engagement in a democratic and modern society. Privileging the migrating or cosmopolitan subject as the knowing, thinking, more complex individual runs the risk of reinforcing the "historical effacement of blacks from public political life" by identifying reason and agency only in the experiences of the relatively few privileged elite.[41] When Du Bois writes in "The Atlanta Conferences" about the "evolution of a vast group of men" (reprinted in Green and Driver 54) in the South, he implicitly rejects his own view set out in *Souls* that progress is inextricably yoked to migration, and the privileged status that facilitates such movement. He is, in other words, a cosmopolitan subject who argues for the citizenship rights of those who are not. In fact, more than in any other pieces in the collection, John's story encourages the reader to speculate on the possibility that a "simpler self-consciousness," based on raw oppression can indeed lead to the desire for and movement toward larger societal participation and political intervention.

Du Bois's fiction, even more than his ethnography, reveals his unwillingness to accept the notion that "the folk" as primitive subalterns, cannot speak.[42] This unwillingness is illustrated by his depiction of the tension existing between literate and illiterate, cosmopolitan and tribal, representative and represented. The conflict comes to a head during the festivities organized to welcome John home and celebrate his ascension into the role of community leader. John's speech on the role "Negroes of this land would take in the striving of the new century" is met with a violent response:

Then at last a low suppressed snarl came from the Amen corner, and an old bent man arose, walked over the seats, and climbed straight up into the pulpit. . . . He seized the Bible with his rough, huge hands; twice he raised it inarticulate, and then fairly burst into words, with rude and awful eloquence. . . . John never knew clearly what the old man said; he only felt himself held up to scorn and scathing denunciation for trampling on the true religion, and he realized with amazement that all unknowingly he had put rough, rude hands on something this little world held sacred. He arose silently, and passed out into the night. (530)

The old man's denunciation signals the collective rebuff of John as leader. He and John end up mutually rejecting what each stands for. Although they stand for opposing values, Du Bois uses similar descriptions for them. Both are "rough" and "rude." Each is inscrutable to the other. The elder's words move the congregation, but they remain unarticulated in the story. This clash signals the break between the Altahama community's conviction that the exceptional individual endowed with a classical education can be their negotiable currency in a racist society and their realization that the individual's encounter with outside values can radically vex the association of the "I" with the "we."

While this exchange offers support for Posnock's reading of provincial, folk spaces as pre-modern and subject to exclusion from mainstream society, it simultaneously resists the suggestion that the answer to this dilemma resides in the infusion of select individuals into spaces designated as modern. The passage points to a failure of communication between John and the congregation due not only to the "folk's" lack of sophistication, but also to John's refusal to recognize their capacity for reason. While it is true that the narrative asserts that they cannot follow his argument for secularization and industrialization because "he spoke an unknown tongue," it also stresses their conscious refusal (as opposed to simple ignorance) of his logic because it flies in the face of the values central to their self-definition. They denounce him not simply because they cannot understand him but because his agnosticism has "[trampled] on the true religion," calling into question his right to represent their interests. The dynamics between John and the elder underscore the masses' grasping for an active voice in social and political discourse through the conscious cultivation of a *responsive* leader. This desire, half articulated by the old man's rough utterance, undercuts the notion that literacy and social mobility necessarily precede political consciousness.

"Of the Coming of John" functions as a cautionary tale for Black intellectuals, native ethnographers among them, warning them to tread carefully in their negotiation of the dynamics between individual and collective. The importance of these ties being carefully cultivated is made against a backdrop in which White society views the educated Black as a threat to its continued subordination of the race. A literate John has no place in a White supremacist society despite his mastery and admiration of its culture. Likewise, John fails to articulate a mutually satisfying place for himself in Altahama's Black community. For example, he is abruptly fired from his post as schoolmaster when Altahama's ruling class determines that he possesses an "almighty air and uppish ways"; even more threatening is the rumor that he has been instructing his impressionable students on "the French Revolution, equality, and such like" (532). At this juncture, John finds himself caught between an intolerant society and a needy and demanding community, neither of which know what to do with him. He stands at the hyphen between Black and American, paralyzed by his inability to function fully in either world, unable to communicate effectively with the multiple audiences with which he attempts to engage. John's only recourse is to strike out violently at the conditions that constrain him by bludgeoning a White man who is in the midst of assaulting his sister. Words and book-learning fail him because they offer no adequate model for alleviating his and his people's pain and suffering; yet violence leads him to an abyss. The narrative ends with his impending death by lynching as he hears Richard Wagner's *Lohengrin* sounding in his ears, the lyrics expressing his longing for spiritual, if not actual, material freedom.

This image speaks to the universality of music on the one hand, as did Du Bois's discussion of the sorrow songs; yet it also reinscribes John's entrenchment in Western civilization on the other; a possibility that is ironically and tragically refused by the White men coming to lynch him. This powerful image captures the acute irony of John's situation, lauding on the one hand art's universality; yet on the other hand implicitly condemning his classical education for not equipping him with the means to navigate the treacherous waters of the racist and uncivilized Southern society to which he returned.

Zamir argues that, for Du Bois, "the self is mediated by power and terror, but also by positive social location among others. At the heart of the book is an exploration of the dilemma of the black intellectual and artist caught between *communitas* and solitude, between the necessities of political activism and the requirements of the contemplative life. This is not a polarization between passivity and activity, as [William] James would assume, but a dialectics of two different kids of activity" (13). This insight underscores John's failure to achieve a positive social location among others, and locates that failure at the nexus of his inability to successfully merge political activism and intellectual activity. Yet, despite the double bind that he imagined trapping John, Du Bois unequivocally championed the role of education in Negro uplift. That conviction is voiced through John's earlier response to his sister's asking whether he is glad he studied despite the unhappiness it has brought him: " 'Yes,' came the answer, slowly but positively" (530).

Yet at the same time that Du Bois advocated increasing the access of talented young Blacks to a classical education, his portrayal of John demonstrates it was not always feasible or desirable to transcend social and political situations through the acquisition of dominant cultural literacy, particularly if that knowledge was attained at the expense of acquiring or retaining the kind of localized cultural literacy that would have enabled John to better navigate the politics of the Black church. Du Bois makes apparent in *The Souls of Black Folk* his belief in the necessity of the Black intellectual to accept the role of mediator between two worlds. And yet, his engagement with and examination of ethnographic methods of observation and narration illuminates the conflict, paradoxes, and challenges that result from the meeting of two, often conflicting, worlds. The next generation of culture writers— Johnson, Brown, Dunham, and Hurston—will experiment with different ways of addressing these conflicts, employing genres as wide ranging as autoethnography, fiction, poetry and dance, and strategies like irony and reflexivity, to comment critically on and expand the possibilities for Black intellectuals and the communities with which they affiliated themselves.

Striking Out into the Interior: Travel, Imperialism, and Ethnographic Perspectives in The Autobiography of an Ex-Colored Man

Franz Boas and W. E. B. Du Bois shifted the terms used to discuss race by foregrounding the cultural and historical conditions that determined racial formations. Inspired by their theoretical interventions, in *The Autobiography of an Ex-Colored Man* (1912), James Weldon Johnson uses a racially indeterminate character to illustrate what it might mean to conceive of racial identity as a social and historical construct. In this and other ways, we see in his *The Autobiography of an Ex-Colored Man* the extent to which the social sciences filtered through the New Negro literary imagination.[1] In addition to redefining race to be a historical and social construct, Johnson requires his narrator to travel to the South, implicitly treated as the site of his amateur fieldwork, to encounter African American culture in its "purest" form, and he uses fieldwork implicitly as a trope for the encounter between dominant and marginalized groups. He figures the protagonist's travels through the South as a kind of anthropological or sociological exercise, employing the ethnographic trope of uncovering and understanding difference through participant-observation, at the same time that the narrator also undergoes a personal journey of self-discovery. And finally, he makes a case, through the protagonist's involvement with African American ragtime, for understanding America to be a multiracial and pluralistic nation in which African American cultural contributions have played an important role. These are all examples of anthropology's influence on a literary figure, but this influence is not unqualified for Johnson asks the reader to consider the efficacy of the narrator's culture-work. We might consider *Autobiography* to be a revision of *The Souls of Black Folk* that points the spotlight on the intellectual and asks what the conditions are that facilitate his ability to discern and convey the inner lives of Black subjects.

Johnson is an important transitional figure between the pioneering work done by Boas and Du Bois and the younger generation of Renaissance scholars who would go on to revolutionize Americans' perception and understanding of African Americans. A poet, lyricist, novelist, educator, diplomat, and general secretary of the NAACP (1920–30), he was a multitalented individual who straddled both generations of culture-workers. Although he was not a sociologist, he did contribute his secretarial and/or research skills to the first two of the Atlanta Conferences of Negro Problems. This series of studies, produced by Atlanta University, would flourish under the future direction of W. E. B. Du Bois, but at the time of Johnson's participation, George Bradford, a White Boston businessman and University trustee supervised its production. Johnson's views on the importance of African Americans' cultural contributions to the nation were in accord with, and most likely were influenced by, the thinking of anthropologists and sociologists. For example, in 1917 when he gave a talk at the Intercollegiate Socialist Society in Long Island, it was still rather unconventional to focus on the Negro cultural contributions to America, as Johnson chose to do:

The common-denominator opinion in the United States about American Negroes is, I think, something like this: These people are here; they are here to be shaped and molded and made into something different and, of course, better; they are here to be helped; here to be given something; in a word, they are beggars under the nation's table waiting to be thrown the crumbs of civilization. However true this may be, it is also true that the Negro has helped to shape and mold and make America; that he has been a creator as well as a creature; that he has been a giver as well as a receiver.[3]

Even as Johnson's rhetoric echoed progressive social scientists who worked on redefining America as a pluralist nation, his limited participation in their academic milieu allowed him to assume a critical detachment from the disciplines of sociology and anthropology. Johnson's protagonist may be read as a sort of anthropologist/sociologist, and as a prototype of the New Negro intellectual. Ultimately the author shows the character's stance in relation to Black folk life and culture to have the potential to transform a society that is blind to its multicultural riches, but it is also problematic because his desire to use academic discourse to incorporate Black culture into the national body runs the risk of reinscribing African Americans' social marginalization and domination.

Masking the Narrative: Fiction as Autobiography as
Auto-Ethnography

Because the fictional *The Autobiography of an Ex-Colored Man* was marketed
as an autobiographical work when it was first published in 1912, and because
the novel's narrator assumes a sociological tone when discussing different
strata of Black society, it has often been read, and in fact encourages its audience to read it, as a kind of ethnography that promised to reveal the secrets
of Black culture to its White readership.[4] One might surmise that this is a
misreading because, from the outset, Johnson aspired to focus on the interplay between White and Black subjects and societies, more than to hone in
on the intimate lives of Black folk. The 1912 preface professes to show "in a
dispassionate, though sympathetic, manner conditions as they actually exist
between the whites and blacks to-day" (xxxiii). Because the narrator took the
phenomenon of racial passing as its subject matter, the narrative really promised to reveal the secrets of American society to itself, namely that the racial
binaries upon which segregation was based were untenable. When the post-
war era ushered in a period of heightened interest in Negro art and culture,
the novel was republished in 1927 with Johnson's authorship made explicit. It
became a classic of the Harlem Renaissance.

Johnson created a character that resembled him in striking ways. Both
author and protagonist share an interest in and talent for music; they each attended Atlanta University, during which time they had their first formative
encounters with the Southern Black peasantry; and more importantly, they
each grappled with the obstacles posed by their relative privilege to their political and activist ambitions. And yet the path of author and character diverge sharply because unlike the narrator, who cannot overcome his
ambivalence about his racial identity and therefore eventually abandons the
project of racial and cultural uplift, Johnson assumed and embraced the responsibility of racial uplift and, in fact, made it the source of his creative inspiration as both a writer and musician.

The novel-masquerading-as-autobiography was written almost a
decade after the publication of Du Bois's *The Souls of Black Folk* and takes up
Du Bois's mantle by exploring the life of a member of the "talented tenth"
who immerses himself in African American folk culture and hopes to emerge
a race leader. The publishers of the first edition of Johnson's novel allude to
Du Bois in their preface, stating, "In these pages it is as though a veil had been
drawn aside" (xxxiv). Yet the text is not so much a "true" account of Southern Black life as it is an account of a psychological journey taken by a man

who eventually rejects his Blackness and embraces a White racial identity. The entanglement of the narrator's personal conflict with his "objective" observances about Negro society adds a psychological dimension to Du Bois's earlier exploration of the dynamics and conditions that would render members of the Negro elite fit to assume the mantle of representing the marginalized communities from which they sprang and complicate portraits of "the Negro" that Black intellectuals sought to depict.

As I have already mentioned, Johnson simultaneously makes and withholds the promise to unveil a Negro subculture, first declaring that "whites know far less about blacks who are as enigmatic as a sphinx," then suggesting that the narrative may work to rectify this situation (xxxiii–xxxiv). Yet he also asserts, "it is curiously interesting and even vitally important to know what are the thoughts of ten millions of them concerning the people among whom they live," suggesting that the more vital project is to convey to Whites the perception that Blacks have of *them*. The intention of unveiling Black American life is unchanged, but the assumption that only one racial group possesses knowledge and self-awareness is overturned. Second, Johnson underscores the protagonist's views of Black culture as fictions, narrative constructions that are mediated by his severely compromised point of view. Finally, he reiterates that this narrative—really a *bildungsroman*—is a narrative of self-fashioning, a personal journal of self-discovery, as much as it is a window on the realities of the African American world. Ultimately, all these aspects show that the novel veils its true agenda, which is to compel White America to learn about its own conflicted society, what Langston Hughes (also "riffing" on Du Bois's *The Souls of Black Folk*) would call "the ways of white folk."

If Johnson intended for the text to function on some level as a sociological treatise, or as a type of auto-ethnography, his use of irony to undercut the narrator's reliability troubles the reader's search for truth and authenticity.[5] The debate over the narrator's reliability as a commentator on Black life, or on his own psychic and emotional states, and the lack of conclusiveness about which of the two we better comprehend by the end of the narrative, makes apparent the novel's emphasis on *how* knowledge is constructed by the narrator rather than *what* knowledge is acquired from him.[6] Just as the novel's passing as autobiography "sets up a narrative situation that makes possible the naming of the self, only to unname himself systematically . . ." its passing as ethnography establishes, then deconstructs, the possibility of naming and defining the other (Smith 45). Johnson's novel should be read as a narrative of self-fashioning, and as an exposé of how "ethnographic writings can properly be called fictions in the sense of 'something made or fashioned.'"[7] He compels the reader to consider that the protagonist's account of folk culture may reflect more on his own psychological needs and desires than on the culture he purports to describe.[8] At the same time, because the Ex-Colored Man strives to define his place in a world that insists that he choose between White and Black, he struggles to articulate a stable sense of self. In demonstrating the ways in which a text, or a self, is fashioned, Johnson illustrates the constructedness of identities, whether collective or individual.

The Ex-Colored Man's youthful confusion over his identity, coupled with class differences made visible when he enters different communities—and class *is* as much a category of analysis as race in this novel—apparently contributes to lifelong feelings of difference, detachment from, and even shame of Black folk, the poor and working-class masses who are participate in vernacular cultural traditions. One might argue that given the narrator's middle-class upbringing, his alienation from the masses of Black folk is unsurprising. Yet even when he strives to identify with an African American middle-class "gentleman" doctor his efforts seem contrived. On the ship returning to the States after he has traveled around Europe with a wealthy benefactor and made the decision to fully embrace the Negro race and culture, the narrator strikes up a conversation with a "gigantic, colored man" about racial discrimination. For the first time in the narrative, the narrator announces his racial affiliation as they discuss "different phases of the Negro question" (110). Nonetheless, the reader remains unconvinced that the narrator has fully internalized a collective identity perhaps because his repeated references to the man's size convey awe and astonishment rather than empathy. Fleming argues that because the doctor is a member of the talented tenth, he and the narrator share an affinity: "The narrator seems unaware that his high opinion of the doctor is determined by the many similarities between the man and himself. Like the protagonist, the doctor can discuss the 'Negro question' in objective, detached terms. Only when his personal freedom is threatened does the doctor become emotionally involved enough to resent racial prejudice" (Fleming 93). What seems apparent, nonetheless, is that the narrator must manufacture these feelings of empathy because, unlike the doctor, the narrator's careful cultivation of anonymity means he need never contend with the ill effects of racial discrimination because most people he encounters assume he is white unless he chooses to correct them.

The character's ambivalence toward his own Blackness leads him to use the language of ethnography to describe the African Americans he encounters. The academic tone and perspective acts as a substitute for the intimacy and affiliation he craves because it allows him to assume an authoritative stance on race issues. Whether describing a schoolhouse interaction, or the social networks of a Southern city, the protagonist uses specific occasions to explain or explore for the reader what it means to be black (see, for example, pages 14 and 54). Yet at the same time, the alienation he feels and struggles with generates that screen of objectivity. Under these circumstances, one questions the possibility of his keeping the self out of the social portrait that he paints. Ultimately, the narrator's ethnographic stance casts the shadow of imperialist domination over his actions, subverting his claim to ascend to a position of leadership in the race.

Racial Heritage and the Problem of Citizenship in *The Autobiography of an Ex-Colored Man*

Johnson, who was born in Jacksonville, Florida in 1871 to Bahaman parents who had immigrated to the States in 1868, assumed the public role of the race man that his character could only dream about. Johnson's entry into the world of racial advocacy came about after a childhood and youth characterized by educational advantages and comparative interracial harmony. At the time that his family immigrated, they moved into an integrated neighborhood in which Whites, Blacks, European and Caribbean immigrants, and native-born Americans lived peaceably side by side. Johnson joked in his autobiography about the unconventional nature of his racially harmonious upbringing. "So it appears that in the land of black mammies I had a white one," he notes archly about a White neighbor who nursed him as a newborn when his mother was too incapacitated to do so herself (*Along This Way* 9). In fact, "interracialism" as a fact of New World/American life is a theme that runs throughout Johnson's autobiography, which he initiates by recounting the fact that his grandfather, Stephen Dillet, was the offspring of a French army officer and an Afro-Haitian woman who would emigrate to the Bahamas with her children eleven years after the slave insurrection. Yet Johnson's genealogy is one not only of interracial hybridity but also of paternal and civic disinheritance when racial regimes are imposed and enforced. He writes, "when young Stephen landed in Nassau his entire clothing consisted of the long shirt in which he was clad; and his sole possession, one to which he had somehow clung, was a silver spoon. A silver spoon . . ." (*Along This Way* 3). Johnson repeats the phrase, emphasizing the irony of this scant inheritance, the ellipsis's pregnant silence mimicking the void left by the French officer, who left no other provisions for his children than a symbolic reminder of the wealth and status that his European background theoretically could have granted them.

This familial legacy echoes a similar moment in the novel in which the narrator remembers a frequent visitor to his childhood home in Georgia; a man we are meant to surmise is his White father, from whom he is estranged. While the narrator's memories of his mother are vivid, those of his father are much more elusive:

I remember that his shoes or boots were always shiny, and that he wore a gold chain and a great gold watch with which he was always willing to let me play. . . . I remember how I sat upon his knee and watched him laboriously drill a hole through a ten-dollar gold piece, and then tie the coin around my neck with a string. I have worn that gold piece around my neck the greater part of my life, and still possess it, but more than once I have wished that some other way had been found of attaching it to me besides putting a hole through it. (3)

By drilling a hole in the gold, the father renders it worthless monetarily. By failing to cultivate a relationship with his (colored) son, the paternal inheritance the coin might have connoted is rendered meaningless as well. Both Johnson's actual and fictive autobiographies represent the failure of paternal figures who also represent their nations' failure to nurture their African-descended (step)children. Valerie Smith views the coin as a marker not of denied familial wealth, but of the son/slave's value in a domestic arrangement stained by the economy of slavery: "The necklace functions as a yoke or restraint by means of which he [the father] continues to exert his control" (53). In either reading, what is conveyed is the repeated denial of full citizenship rights to the African American subject. This is a conundrum he repeatedly faces throughout his life. For example, Johnson recounts in his autobiography the experience of moving to Atlanta University with his Cuban friend, Ricardo. The two boys are about to be evicted from the first-class car despite the fact that they possess tickets when they begin to converse in Spanish; the conductor leaves them unmolested. "Fifteen years later, an incident similar to the experience with this conductor drove home to me the conclusion that in such situations any kind of a Negro will do; provided he is not one who is an American citizen" (*Along This Way* 65). Johnson underscores that something seemingly as innocuous as riding the rails proves his dispossession as a national subject. The desire for mobility, the freedom to travel, then, becomes a metaphor for the African American subject's desire for fundamental claims to liberty, happiness, and civic participation and national belonging.

Mapping the Racialized World

Having a mastery of foreign languages, and participating in travel—especially to Europe—proved enabling to Johnson, who had to learn as a young man that the crossing of racial boundaries was not as simple and uncontroversial as his upbringing in his Jacksonville neighborhood may have led him to believe. He found that the United States especially could be mapped along rigid racial demarcations and crossing these boundaries could be difficult at best, deadly under the worst circumstances. Johnson's first experiences with the most virulent and blatant racism took place in the deep South, in the "backwoods of Georgia," during a three-month summer vacation from Atlanta University, during which he worked as a schoolteacher. "It was this period," he wrote, "which marked also the beginning of my knowledge of my own people as a 'race' " (*Along This Way* 118). For Johnson, the South's methods of enforcing its racial regimes imposed on individuals an inferior and marginalized *status*, a state of being that occluded the significance of both personal and collective identities. To know his people as a race, Johnson clarified, meant that "now I began to perceive them clearly as a classified division, a defined section of American society. I had learned something about the Negro as a problem, but now I was where I could touch the crude bulk of the problem itself with my own hands, where the relations between Black and White in the gross were pressed in upon me. Here there were no gradations, no nuances, no tentative approaches; what Black and White meant stood out starkly" (*Along This Way* 118–19).

The exigencies of Southern racism were troubling, but nonetheless not debilitating. Johnson found himself identifying with the most dispossessed of this community despite the differences in class and education; and he found multiple sources of inspiration in the rich cultural traditions in which the Black community was rooted. He expresses, for example, an interest in the lower classes' use of dialect, even while feeling repulsed by their "unkempt appearance" and unrefined behavior, such as loud talking (*Along This Way* 40). He also points to the Uncle Remus stories, Jubilee songs, ragtime, and the cake-walk as incontrovertible proof of Negro originality and artistry, refutations of the charge of racial and cultural inferiority (*Along This Way* 63). After studying his charges and their parents with "a sympathetic objectivity, as though they were something apart," Johnson concluded, echoing Du Bois's reflections on being "bone of the bone and flesh of the flesh" of the folk behind the veil, "in an instant's reflection I could realize that they were me, and I was they; that a force stronger than blood made us one" (*Along This Way* 118–19). Like his creator, the narrator of *Ex-Colored Man* celebrates the creative genius of the Black masses, but he never conquers his feelings of ambivalence and embarrassment that inhibit his cultivation of feelings of racial affiliation. The question of whether he can transform "sympathetic objectivity" into filial loyalty remains a question throughout the novel.

In the novel, although the narrator of *Ex-Colored Man* must go south to claim his racial and cultural heritage, Johnson is distinctly uninterested in mythologizing the region:

The farther I got below Washington, the more disappointed I became in the appearance of the country. I peered through the car windows, looking in vain for the luxuriant semi-tropical scenery which I had pictured in my mind. I did not find the grass so green, nor the woods so beautiful, nor the flowers so plentiful, as they were in Connecticut. Instead, the red earth partly covered by tough, scrawny grass, the muddy, straggling roads, the cottages of unpainted pine boards, and the clay-daubed huts imparted a 'burnt up' impression. (37)

Just eleven years later, Jean Toomer would write lyrically of the piney forests, red earth, and radiant beauty of the Georgia landscape. For example: "Karintha, at twelve, was a wild flash that told the other folks just what it was to live. At sunset, when there was no wind, and the pine-smoke from over by the sawmill hugged the earth, and you couldnt [sic] see more than a few feet in front, her sudden darting past you was a bit of vivid color, like a black bird that flashes in light."[9] But where Toomer saw luminescent beauty in the Georgia countryside, Johnson's narrator, upon entering Atlanta, saw only "a big, dull, red town" (37). Yet he also acknowledges that the narrator's perceptions of his surroundings (and presumably its inhabitants) were directly affected by his own psychic and emotional states. The dullness he perceived "had much, I think, to do with the extreme depression of my spirits" (37). The narrator's observations, this statement reminds us, are always subjective, mediated by the emotional, psychological, and historical "baggage" that he carries with him on his journey.

This reminder shapes the reader's understanding of the narrator's reflections on Black Southern social mores and customs as much as it does his thoughts about Southern geography. The South (Atlanta and Jacksonville) reveals to him social distinctions, such as where "respectable" people find accommodations, with whom and how they socialize and how the different classes conduct themselves in public. Like the blatant racism of "backwoods" Georgia, these Southern cities foreground for the narrator social and racial hierarchies because there, more than anywhere, he struggles to figure out where he fits in.

In contrast, New York allows more freedom of self-definition. The descriptions of New York's "sporting life" when the narrator travels to the North are equally descriptive in the attention paid to manners of dress, style, speech, and behavior as he moves from pool hall to drawing room, but the tone is less clinical, the protagonist less prone to making generalizations and categorizing groups of people. There is something about the Southern experience of Blackness that inspires him to assume a clinical tone; perhaps it is the exaggerated perception of foreignness to the people he encounters there.

The narrator is certainly no intimate of gambling and drinking circles given his sheltered upbringing in Georgia and Connecticut, but New York City is full of striving strangers like himself. He views the city as a "great witch at the gate of the country . . . constantly enticing thousands from far within," whereas the South is full of intimate spaces, circles of kin, and community that he must penetrate and navigate (65). Even when he observes a situation that seems to invite sociological analysis—namely, a wealthy White woman who entertained (and paid for) the company of Black men—the narrator deigns to elaborate on the phenomenon that this illustrates. He refrains from generalizing about her behavior, remarking, "More that I learned would be better suited to a book on social phenomena than to a narrative of my life" (79). In contrast to the tone he strikes in his descriptions of his Southern travels, he firmly resituates this part of the narrative within the realm of the autobiographical despite the fact that the subject is so ripe for sociological analysis. The narrator's unwillingness to expand on the mores of certain classes of people can be attributed, as well, to his rapid, albeit temporary, descent into gambling addiction, which limits his interactions to a narrow circle of gamblers in a circumscribed midtown neighborhood of the city: "I regret that I cannot contrast my views of life among colored people of New York; but the truth is, during my entire stay in this city I did not become acquainted with a single respectable family" (83). These details suggest that family specifically, and communal affiliation more generally, demand a measure of conformity to collective values. By failing to make such connections and aligning himself with an underground subculture, however, the narrator perceives himself to be free from having to meet such expectations, a function of his not having a role to play in public (that is, polite) society.

New York City represents not only the freedom of self-invention, it also offers a cosmopolitanism that the narrator admires and toward which he aspires. In his autobiography, Johnson reminisced about a trip to New York taken with his grandmother in 1884 when he was twelve or thirteen years old. Johnson knew even at that young age that he was "born to be a New Yorker":

But being born for a New Yorker means being born, no matter where, with a love for cosmopolitanism; and one either is or is not. If, among other requirements for happiness, one needs neighbors; that is, feels that he must be on friendly terms with the people who live next door, and in addition know all about them; if one must be able to talk across from front porches and chat over back fences; if one is possessed by a zeal to regulate the conduct of people who are neither neighbors nor friends—he is not born for a New Yorker. (47–48)

A natural cosmopolite, like the narrator, we learn from both autobiography and novel, is open to meeting and learning from all manner of people. Yet while this openness facilitates the gathering of information, it prohibits his development of the kind of knowledge bred through intimacy. Cosmopolitanism was a desirable trait to Johnson, however, because he found that it freed people from racism since they did not fear the new and different.

The Ex-Colored Man's benefactor is such an individual. He is most likely modeled after Dr. T. O. Summers, a Florida surgeon and professor of surgery at Vanderbilt University for whom Johnson worked as a receptionist during a yearlong break in his schooling in Atlanta. Johnson describes Summers as a man of "great culture" who traveled widely, spoke multiple languages, and had garnered a literary reputation by writing poetry. Summers's cosmopolitan leanings meshed with Johnson's own. Thus, he notes, "Between the two of us, as individuals, 'race' never showed its head. He neither condescended nor patronized; in fact he treated me as an intellectual equal" (*Along This Way* 93–95). Summers so considered him a peer that they traveled together to New York and Washington by ship, shared a room, and socialized with their sailing companions and the ship's crew as equals (*Along This Way* 97–98). Johnson concludes after this sojourn, "I had made him my model of all that a man and a gentleman should be" (*Along This Way* 98). Like Summers, the Ex-Colored Man's patron is without overt prejudice, largely because of his urban sophistication.

Summers reintroduced the adult Johnson to the pleasures of New York and Washington, D.C.; the Ex-Colored Man's patron introduced his charge to the unfettered, apparently race-less territory of Europe. Again, Johnson's personal experiences shed light on his characters' perception of a particular landscape. When he accompanied his brother Rosamond and their collaborator Bob Cole on a three-month performance tour of Europe in 1905, Johnson noted the internal transformation that took place upon arrival. "From the day I set foot in France, I became aware of the working of a miracle within me. I became aware of a quick readjustment to life and to environment. I recaptured for the first time since childhood the sense of being just a human being" (*Along This Way* 209). His travels to Europe frees the protagonists from double-consciousness, from the psychic fragmentation wrought by racism, even though his Whiteness allows him an extraordinary ability to cross wide expanses of geographical space with relative ease. By declaring himself Black he is accepted in the best of Negro society that a city has to offer. By saying nothing, he is free to circulate among Whites as well.

Racial Ambiguity and the Traveling Subject

The narrator's assumption of an ethnographic stance (his movement through communities as a participant-observer) and his racial ambiguity enable his fluid passage between poor, Black communities and literate, cosmopolitan, interracial society; yet Johnson also depicts his attitude as a debilitation that prevents him from ever achieving a state of true belonging.[10] Johnson found the participant-observer to be an apt symbol for the talented tenth individuals who attempted to return to and reconstruct "home," and an incisive figure with which to explore and critique hegemonic attitudes (carried by these privileged persons) regarding Black subcultures. Joe Skerrett has argued that "through the duality of the tragic/ironic narrative, Johnson 'outers' and then exorcises the weakness he saw so clearly in (and shared with) D. [a childhood friend on whom the protagonist is based] the temptation to desire and to seek a less heroic, less painful identity than their blackness imposed on them" (558). The narrator's struggles to see his own fair skin and dark curls reflected in the faces of his African American classmates parodies the efforts of highly educated, socially refined, often light complected members of the talented tenth to find common interests with the Negro masses despite the increased social and economic differences that developed as the Black middle class grew in the post-bellum years. The narrator's ambivalence about being identified as Black manifests itself as a variety of disassociations from his African American classmates, anticipating his more adult hesitations with being identified with the ignominy of being Black in a

Jim Crow society. In his younger years, believing he is White, he uses the same racist language as his White classmates. He tells of chasing "niggers" from the schoolyard and fondly remembers "Shiny," a high-achieving Black schoolmate, apparently unaware of the nickname's racist connotations. Yet just a few sentences later he remembers White classmates taunting Blacks with the rhyme: "*Nigger, nigger, never die/Black face and shiny eye*" (10). The protagonist eventually discovers the truth about his identity when the school principal divides his class up by race, taking pains to place him with the other Black students. He reacts with shock, disbelief, and more importantly, with an ambivalence which intensifies as he grows older and gains more exposure to the masses of Black folk. Given the narrator's eventual recognition of the immorality of racism and his own imbrication in racial regimes as a "colored" man, his persistence in calling "Shiny" by that name even when they are adults seems suspect in that it perpetuates the process of othering that he participated in as a child, which he could then excuse as acts of youthful ignorance.

Throughout the Ex-Colored Man's life he remains ambivalent about his racial identity and his racial identification is ambiguous. Perhaps this is because he associates Blackness with the responsibility of racial representation. He makes this connection while watching "Shiny" deliver the valedictorian speech at their high school graduation: "I think that solitary little black figure standing there felt that for the particular time and place he bore the weight and responsibility of his race; that for him to fail meant general defeat; but he won, and nobly" (31). Although impressed with "Shiny's" oratorical power and proud of what his individual accomplishments represented for the race, the Ex-Colored Man remains throughout most of the text a solitary and self-absorbed figure—William Andrews argues that he "lived basically a self-centered life"—who would have chafed under the burden of communal responsibility.[11]

His initial unease at the thought of being Black is revealed when he returns home and asks his mother if he is "a nigger," and "looks at her critically for the first time," searching for "defects" such as brown skin and woolly hair (12). His mother's response is revealing: " 'No, my darling, you are not a nigger.' She went on: 'You are as good as anybody.' " And when he asks if he or she is White, she answers, "No, I am not white, but you—your father is one of the greatest men in the country—the best blood of the South is in you" (12). She suggests to him that to be Black is not to be inferior; yet she also, when confronted with the more direct question—"am I white?"—is unwilling to label her son Black. The specter of racial inferiority haunts their exchange despite her protestations to the contrary, which she deflects by focusing on class, hinting that his father's "blue blood" has the capacity to erase the taint of his newly discovered "black blood."[12] Implicit in the boy asking about his racial identity is his desire to situate himself in a particular culture and community, to figure out where he belongs.

Despite the narrator's troubled feelings about his racial identity, he is able to move from North to South to Europe and back, from middle-class Black society to poor and working-class communities with relative ease. His racial ambiguity appears to allow him to experience multiple sites of belonging. People accept him into their homes, often because a few well-chosen words allow them to see and accept him as one of them. But he never resolves the problem of belonging, and compensates for that lack by assuming the posture of a clinical, analytical observer.

The Ex-Colored Man's mother's displacement of racial anxiety onto class difference marks the protagonist's future interactions with African Americans. Even when he identifies openly as a Black man, living and working with other Black people, class, educational, and regional differences cause him to act like a detached observer of various communities. He moves through the world like a social scientist, categorizing Black people and their behaviors. When his journeys take him South, for example, he takes note of "the shambling, slouching gait and loud talk and laughter" of the lower classes (40) and organizes the Black community into three "classes"—the "desperate class" who "cherish a sullen hatred for all white men"; the "servant" class, who are "characterized as simple, kind-hearted and faithful"; and the "tradesmen . . . and educated coloured people," who are "as far removed from the whites" as members of the first class mentioned (55–59).[13] This sociological classification functions to distance him from other Black folk. This, however, is an insight he lacks as he unquestioningly equates distance with objectivity:

I had formulated a theory of what it was to be coloured; now I was getting the practice. The novelty of my position caused me to observe and consider things which, I think, entirely escaped the young men I associated with; or, at least, were so commonplace to them as not to attract their attention. And of many of the impressions which came to me then I have realized the full import only within the past few years, since I have had the broader knowledge of men and history, and a fuller comprehension of the tremendous struggle which is going on between the races in the South. (54)

These remarks anticipate the remarks of Zora Neale Hurston in *Mules and Men*, describing culture as a garment that can, indeed must, be viewed from afar in order to be properly appreciated. But at the same time, distance and a propensity for continual wandering function prophylactically, keeping the Ex-Colored Man from making a long-standing or meaningful commitment to others, and in particular to a community that he understands primarily through its social exclusion and degradation. As Eric Sundquist notes, "his overtly ethnological perspective derives from his own self-protecting disengagement from rural black culture."[14] The suggestion that psychological need provides the impetus for the narrator's social commentary subverts his claims to objectivity. Thus, Johnson's twinning of the narrator's bourgeois values and perspectives with ethnographic language serves as a subtle indictment not only of the protagonist's elitism, but also of the ethnographic imagination that informed the attitudes of race men and women toward working-class Black communities. The consequences are greater than one individual's vexed understanding of what it means to be Black.

The Perils of Traveling Cultures: Commodification and the Value of Black Folk

When the Ex-Colored Man sets out near the end of the novel to fully live his life as a Black man in order to contribute to the cultural life of the nation, he assumes that an anthropological method will give him the information (he does not really seek understanding) that he will need to accomplish his goals. When he attempts to transform ragtime into classical music, he is indeed operating as an amateur folklorist, traveling from Nashville to Atlanta to Macon: "All this while I was gathering material for work, jotting down in my note-book themes and melodies, and trying to catch the spirit of the Negro in his relatively primitive state" (126). Johnson alludes to the colonialist stance in an ironic moment that acknowledges the narrator and his audience's own unfamiliarity with African American life. He states, "When I reached Macon, I decided to leave my trunk and all my surplus belongings, to pack my bag, and *strike out into the interior*. This I did; and by train, by mule and ox-cart, I traveled through many counties. This was my first real experience among rural colored people, and all that I saw was interesting to me" (122, emphasis added).[15] It is not coincidental that when the narrator decides to fully embrace his Blackness, he goes to live among rural colored people in the South because his ethnographic inclinations lead him to the place where he would expect to find cultural artifacts in their presumably most authentic form.

The Ex-Colored Man's reasons for collecting folk music reveal the contradictions in his ethnographic methods. He argues against a strict division between high and low cultures: "Whatever new thing the *people* like is pooh-poohed; whatever is *popular* is spoken of as not worth the while. The fact is, nothing great or enduring, especially in music, has ever sprung full-fledged and unprecedented from the brain of any master" (73). Yet at the same time, his project hinges on the idea of refining, cultivating, and elevating materials he considered raw and primitive; in other words, the rhetoric of high and low reinserts itself into his thinking.[16] The narrator's ability to "gloat over the immense amount of material [he has] to work with, not only modern rag-time, but also the old slave songs—material which no one had yet touched" hinges on the assumption that only one trained in European classical music would count as a "someone" whose influence on the music could be recognized (104). The project is as much an exercise in upward class mobility through art, and *of* art, as it is a project that hybridizes Afro- and Anglo-American musical forms. [17]

Du Bois recognized the sorrow songs to be vital repositories of African American history, including processes of cultural and racial syncretism. In a similar way, the Ex-Colored Man framed his own project within a context of historical preservation. According to Eric Sundquist, he "participates in the work of historical recovery, the shaping and saving of memory, in which African Americans were especially engaged as slave culture threatened to fade from view by virtue of both the passing of the slave generations and the rising severities of Jim Crow. Johnson at once underscored the value of such historical recovery and subjected the acts of recollection and cultural recovery to merciless scrutiny" (4). The novel suggests that while cultural recovery is a necessary and important goal, the agenda and methods of those engaged in this project could be suspect and even sinister.

The protagonist's hesitant expression of caution regarding the behavior of the "millionaire friend" who becomes his benefactor illustrates the point (87). For example, while entertaining at a party hosted by the patron, the narrator remarks on the shocking displays of avant-gardism and unconventionality by the people gathered in the apartment. The women, for example, project sophistication by smoking and occasionally cursing. The narrator remarks with some unease that their host became more reserved as his guests became more animated; but he eventually learns that this behavior was common. "He seemed to take cynical delight in watching and studying others indulging in excess. His guests were evidently accustomed to his rather non-participating attitude, for it did not seem in any degree to dampen their spirits" (86). The description is nonjudgmental, but the characterization of the host's non-participatory stance as "cynical" makes suspect a figure who is also depicted as shadowy and opaque. It suggests also that the reader should regard the narrator with some wariness, for he has already proven himself to be equally detached from the circles in which he travels.

The narrative implicates the millionaire in the protagonist's collecting, for he acts as a benefactor, financially supporting the Ex-Colored Man in his venture. Johnson depicts the millionaire's interest in ragtime music as overbearing and overly proprietary. He employs the narrator as his personal musician under the condition that he play for no other engagements; the narrator occasionally finds himself on loan to the millionaire's friends and he is compelled to play for his benefactor for hours on end, sometimes to the point of exhaustion. "During such moments this man sitting there so mysteriously silent, almost hid in a cloud of heavy-scented smoke, filled me with a sort of unearthly terror. He seemed to be some grim, mute, but relentless tyrant, possessing over me a supernatural power which he used to drive me on mercilessly to exhaustion" (88). The narrator glosses over the ominous nature of their relationship when he hurriedly concludes, "But these feelings came very rarely; besides, he paid me so liberally I could forget much" (88). The musician and his listener are involved in an economic exchange that corrupts the New Negro ideal of cross-cultural awareness and appreciation. The brooding, tyrannical demands of the patron suggest that the musician offers his talent, his spirit—his soul—to the listener; and other than money, he receives nothing in return. The narrator's admiration for the older man's cosmopolitan openness to new experiences sours because "This man of the world, who grew weary of everything and was always searching for something new, appeared never to grow tired of my music; he seemed to take it as a drug" (95–96). Openness becomes insatiable desire for novelty. When the narrator decides that the best use of his talent will be in rendering African American folk music classical, he sounds alarmingly like his benefactor when he thinks, "I made up my mind to go back into the very heart of the South, to live among the people, and drink in my inspiration firsthand" (104). In both instances, they view folk cultural production as sustenance, available for consumption by the sophisticated, but spiritually empty cosmopolite.

We bear witness to the sophisticated urbanite's ability to render lived culture into a novelty item. We also observe his self-absorbed sense of entitlement, his sense that other cultures exist for the taking. Of course, the narrator fails to make this connection to his own attitudes, and he idealizes his plan to go "home," to realize, "my dreams, my ambition, and my decision" (105). In fact, he rejects the patron's views explicitly after he tries to discourage the protagonist from returning to the States and living as a Black man. His benefactor cynically informs him of the folly of his decision, "My boy, you are by blood, by appearance, by education, and by tastes a white man. Now, why do you want to throw your life away amidst the poverty and ignorance, in the hopeless struggle, of the black people of the United States? Music is a universal art; anybody's music belongs to everybody; you can't limit it to race or country" (105). Although the narrator finds his patron to be entirely free of racism after talking with him about "music and the race question," there is something troubling about the benefactor's position because he finds it so easy to take up Black culture, transform it into a commodity, and leave behind Black people and their needs and desires.[18]

The narrator fails to identify traces of his own elitism in the benefactor's statements, but he does reject the proposal because he associates these "old Southern songs" with his mother. "She would hold me close, softly crooning some old melody without words, all the while gently stroking her face against my head; . . . The memory of that picture has more than once kept me from straying too far from the place of purity and safety in which her arms held me" (5). Thus, he links his love of music to the idea of an emotional attachment to another person, an idea of interpersonal connection that he rarely cultivates after his mother's passing. This music also recalls a notion of affiliation with the racial community embodied by his mother.

Music connotes racial affiliation, but the protagonist also associates music with individualism because of the emphasis on the (accomplished) artist's personal interpretation of a piece of music: "I have never been a really good accompanist because my ideas of interpretation were always too strongly individual" (19). Music allows him to fully express all the dimensions of himself. It also allows him to indulge in emotion, to emphasize feeling over reason. Even as a child, he tells us, "I always tried to interpret a piece of music; I always tried to play with feeling. . . . I think this was due not entirely to natural artistic temperament, but largely to the fact that I did not begin to learn the piano by counting out exercises, but by trying to reproduce the quaint songs which my mother used to sing, with all their pathetic turns and cadences" (18). The feelings that he pours into his music, signs of his individuality, are paradoxically linked to his mother's old Southern songs, presumably the sorrow songs about which Du Bois wrote so eloquently. The narrator reconciles racial feeling, or consciousness, and individuality in the composition and performance of music, one of the few avenues that offer him this possibility when he often feels torn between these two competing impulses to identify with a group and to assert his individuality.

Social Critique, Self-Inquiry, and the Abject Negro

Ragtime, a hybrid musical form, symbolizes the potential for the harmonious merging of conflicting identities and values, but ultimately the protagonist fails to achieve this ideal because he finds the pervasive stigmatization of Blackness so demoralizing. The narrator's psychological trajectory plays a critical role in the development of the narrative. For example, he uses the same language of scientific analysis to examine his own reasons for self-revelation, remarking several times on his desire to "to analyse the motives which prompt me to do it" (1). A pivotal moment of insight occurs after the protagonist witnesses the lynching that initiates his decision to pass. The trauma forces him to recognize the impossibility of separating the culture from the people that create it. In other words, he finally acknowledges the fallacy in his as yet unspoken belief that he might embrace Black culture while remaining impervious to the physical and psychic violence perpetuated against Black people. Ironically, his analytical self-assessment reveals his decision to pass as White to be irrational and emotion-driven: "I understood that it was not discouragement or fear or search for a larger field of action and opportunity that was driving me out of the Negro race. I knew that it was shame, unbearable shame. Shame at being identified with a people that could with impunity be treated worse than animals. For certainly the law would restrain and punish the malicious burning alive of animals" (139). The narrator's feelings of shame, which more logically should be felt by the White perpetrators of this atrocity, suggests that he feels that the lynching victim is somehow complicit in the wrong acted upon him. As with Du Bois's portrayal of John, this depiction of a lynching underscores the denial of Black masculinity, power, and agency. In the novel, the protagonist chooses to pass after witnessing the utter negation of a Black man's humanity by a lynch mob.

In contrast, in his autobiography, Johnson reveals in an account of his closest encounter with a possible lynching that the slightest perception of shared humanity allowed him to retain his composure in the face of the mob's fury, and to save himself. After witnesses see him meeting an apparently White (but really African American) woman in a Jacksonville park, the couple are met by a furious group of men and dogs who have hunted them down: "Among the men rushing to reach me is a slender young man clad in a white uniform. He breaks through the men who have hold of me. We look at each other; and I feel that a quivering message from intelligence to intelligence has been interchanged. He claps his hand on my shoulder and says, 'You are my prisoner.' . . . As soon as the lieutenant put his hand on me and declared me his prisoner, the howling mob of men became soldiers under discipline" (*Along This Way* 167–68). No such momentary recognition of shared humanity (and shared class identity) passes between the novel's lynching victim and any of his assailants: "There he stood, a man only in form and stature, every sign of degeneracy stamped upon his countenance. His eyes were dull and vacant, indicating not a single ray of thought. Evidently the realization of his fearful fate had robbed him of whatever reasoning power he had ever possessed" (*Autobiography* 136). The narrator's shame at belonging to a race that could be so dehumanized has to do with the loss of human dignity that he witnessed. Being associated with African Americans, he concludes, is synonymous with "going about with a label of inferiority pasted across my forehead" (139). He feels also shame at being a citizen of a nation in which such atrocities could be committed. The lynch mob's refusal to recognize African Americans' humanity so troubles the narrator, that he turns away and rejects the possibility of having to see himself—or the White world's view of his people—in the wrecked and abject body of the corpse. The psychological and physical assaults to which Blacks are regularly subjected so unsettle the Ex-Colored Man that he gradually distances himself from other African Americans. That feeling of psychic assault, combined with a desire for class mobility, motivates the protagonist to pass as White after witnessing the lynching. Because class privilege is often equated with racial privilege, when the narrator chooses Whiteness, he also, and perhaps primarily, chooses upward class mobility.[19]

It is no coincidence, then, that the Ex-Colored Man becomes a businessman when he passes, relinquishing life as a musician and potential leader in an African American community. He gives up the cultural riches of Blackness in exchange for the social, political, and economic advantages of Whiteness, and struggles with the consequences of this trade-off for the rest of his life. Unsure if the "little money" he makes as a White man is significant to anyone but himself and his children, he laments that he may have sold his "birthright for a mess of pottage" (154). While the Ex-Colored Man toys with a hybrid cultural form when he tries to combine his classical European musical training with the rough exuberance of ragtime ultimately he feels compelled to choose between two racial identities, and unable to take full advantage of either. In this way he resembles the protagonist of Du Bois's "Of the Coming of John," who also feels divided between the White and Black worlds (although for different reasons). Whereas John dies because he cannot live fully in either world, the Ex-Colored Man settles for the meager advantages of Whiteness over the insecurity of Blackness, thereby suffering a spiritual death.

Kathleen Pfeiffer argues that critics who read this novel as being about self-hatred or disloyalty insist upon a "'racially correct' way of reading the text."[20] In contrast to such readings, she offers the notion that the Ex-Colored Man "resists categories" and argues that passing also indicates that he is "a person who values individualism" (403). She reads the passage in which the narrator decides to pass for White as not so much a rejection of his Blackness as a rejection of "the ontology of racial categories" (404). In this regard, I think it worthwhile to cite this passage: "I finally made up my mind that I would neither disclaim the black race nor claim the white race; but that I would change my name, raise a moustache, and let the world take me for what it would; that it was not necessary to go about with a label of inferiority pasted across my forehead" (139). While the Ex-Colored Man states that he will neither disavow one race nor claim the other, his unreliability makes it nearly impossible to accept this statement at face value. In fact, his attempts to bond with the Black doctor on the ship bound from Europe make clear his awareness of the necessity of making explicit his racial affiliation. On that occasion, when discussing racial matters the protagonist notes, "In referring to the race I used the personal pronoun 'we'; my companion made no comment about it, nor evinced any surprise, except to raise his eyebrows slightly the first time he caught the significance of the word" (110). The Ex-Colored Man indicates at the end of the narrative that he will passively accept whatever race the world chooses to foist upon him, but he knows that not to claim his Blackness can only mean that he will be taken for White.[21]

Rather than celebrating this decision as an act of individualism, the narrator expresses ambivalence about his choice to put his own safety and well-being over that of the race's. It comes at the expense of his belonging to *any* community outside of his immediate family, and he is acutely aware of the loss. Comparing himself negatively to Race Men like Booker T. Washington who choose to stand up for principles of equality and democracy and fight for "the cause of their race," he concludes, "Beside them I feel small and selfish. I am an ordinarily successful white man who has made a little money. They are men who are making history and a race" (154). The narrator's spiritual demise arises from his inability to locate himself within, or to feel closely affiliated to, a larger community outside of the nuclear (White) family. Where, as a youth, he expresses disappointment over his inability to claim his paternal line, as a mature adult he recognizes that claiming a cultural heritage, represented by the musical tradition passed on to him by his mother, may have offered him far richer rewards than the economic security represented by the gold coin given to him by his father. His sense of loss and regret suggests that his path toward upward class mobility results in ethical bankruptcy when it is rooted in a philosophy that conflates domination with representation, power with exclusion, and refuses communal identification or obligation to someone other than one's own self. If the novel begins by asserting its subject's indebtedness to W. E. B. Du Bois's thought and example, it ends with a deflated, morally bankrupt protagonist whose choices have led him directly away from the legacies of self-sacrifice, political engagement, and communal bonding set forth and embodied by Du Bois.[22] In the process, Johnson questions the usefulness of the ethnographic imagination to the collective good, suggesting that its efficacy lies in the attitudes the Black intellectual brings with him when he goes into the field to collect, preserve, and disseminate his culture.

Chapter 5

Living Culture in Sterling Brown's Southern Road

James Weldon Johnson's fiction implicitly challenged Race Men and Women to contend with class, gender, and regional differences within the race, despite the hegemonic tendency to view Black people monolithically.[1] Sterling Brown's body of poetry introduces a new set of questions of concern to Renaissance intellectuals because rather than exploring the dynamics between the bourgeois and proletariat classes, he puts the imaginative visions of ordinary Black people at the center of his poetry, and considers what *they* had to say about the state of the race. Brown's blues poetry puts him in the company of younger, more radical writers like Langston Hughes and Zora Hurston, who resisted their older, more conservative peers' desires to elevate African American culture to meet bourgeois standards of propriety and achievement, or to assume the passivity of poor and working-class African Americans. In this way, he departed from what Robin Kelley describes as a typical move in "race relations scholarship" to paint an "image of an active black elite and a passive working class."[2] He defined the "New Negro" as an individual oriented toward the idea of racial progress and advancement, rather than as an individual situated in a particular geographic location (Harlem) or social position (middle class), thus articulating a theory of vernacular culture that recognized the expressive and empowering potential of nonliterary forms of expression like the blues.

Brown's finely tuned ear for the subtleties and complexities of folk expressions had to be learned. This sensibility grew from his work as an amateur folklorist, which he commenced after graduating from Williams College with a B.A. in 1918 and Harvard University with an M.A. in 1923.[3] A succession of teaching assignments in the South, first at Virginia Seminary and College (1923–26), then Lincoln University in Missouri (1926–28), and finally Fisk University in Tennessee (1928–29), immersed Brown in the midst of the Black Belt where he spent time associating with people on their porches, in barber shops, and around jook joints. In those communal places, he honed his listening skills and learned from the people he encountered about their everyday experiences, desires, and concerns. After that period, in 1929 Brown commenced what would become a long and distinguished teaching career at Howard University at the same time he entered a successful period as a poet and critic. His early poetry was published in the twenties in *Opportunity* magazine and in anthologies like Countee Cullen's *Caroling Dusk* (1927) and James Weldon Johnson's *Book of American Negro Poetry* (1922).[4] *Southern Road*, his first collection of poetry, was published in 1932. Brown's work in ethnology continued when he assumed a post between 1936 and 1940 as the Editor of Negro Affairs to the Works Progress Administration's (WPA) Federal Writers' Project. He also contributed to Gunnar Myrdal's monumental sociological study of race in America, *An American Dilemma* (1944).[5]

Both the form and content of Brown's poetry revealed his encyclopedic knowledge of folklore. Poems might take the form of the blues or recreate the rhythms of a work song; and whether or not they were written in the vernacular, their themes and images reflected the perspectives of African American Southerners. The fact that so many of the poems in *Southern Road* explored the threat of individual and communal destruction from either social or natural forces suggests that he accepted the allegory of salvage articulated by modern anthropologists. In his poetry, the values and folkways of Southern rural Negroes were perpetually on the verge of disappearing, but the almost seamless continuity between the folk culture he observed and the poetry he wrote suggests that Brown's poetry, like an ethnographic narrative, aspired to preserve and transmit the source material. In addition to viewing Southern Black culture as a vanishing entity in need of preservation, Brown also saw and represented it as a culture of resistance whose significance would remain relevant even in the face of the rapid social changes American Negroes were experiencing. Thus, in *Southern Road*, he introduces the idea of mobility, embodied by the figure of the road, to underscore not only his awareness of the race's desire for social mobility, but also to mobilize a notion of African American culture as adaptable, supple, and multiply unfolding.

David Anderson argues for Brown's conceptualizing of culture as a process by pointing to his depiction of folklore as an instrument of adaptation and survival in the face of often cataclysmic change.[6] Brown uses the figure of the road to explore the influences of place, travel, history, and social relations in the production of African American culture. In his poetry, the South is not only the cradle of African American culture, and it is much more than a site of anthropological investigation. For Brown the South is best understood as a network of geographic and imaginative landscapes that mark the region as a place of complex cultural productions and negotiations. Brown showed the "Southern Road" to be inhabited by individuals who struggled not only for survival, but also for the freedom and agency to shape their own destinies, and expressed those desires in a range of cultural productions ranging from song to jokes to stories.

Collecting, Culture, and New Negro Poetry

Understanding the significance of Brown's use of the road as a metaphor for a Southern culture that is always in process of making and remaking itself demands that we examine the ways that scholars and intellectuals have traditionally theorized culture using more static frameworks. A glance back at anthropology's "museum age"—1880–1920—and the discipline's traditional practices of representation and exhibition offers some insight into the conventional ways that scholars represented culture. Again, Franz Boas played a pivotal role in the formation of these ideas and practices. During this period, Ira Jacknis argues, Boas made his first major theoretical statement in anthropology on the topic of museum classifications.[7] In opposition to the view of Otis T. Mason of the U.S. National Museum, Boas objected to dispersing artifacts from one tribal group around the museum and exhibiting them with specimens from other groups. Prior to his intervention in the field, Mason, the preeminent authority on anthropological collection and exhibition at the time, had arranged materials according to universal categories—fire-making, transportation, pottery, and so on—and in accordance with an evolutionary scheme (Jacknis 77).

In contrast to this model, Boas argued that ethnological materials could be "divided into families, genera and species," separated according to ethnic groups and therefore, he argued, more reflective of the historical circumstances that produced meaning for particular items. Jacknis argues that where Mason focused on the external form of each artifact, expressing interest in the utilitarian function of the item, Boas argued that anthropologists should direct their attention to an artifact's meaning. Boas wrote, for example: "The rattle, for instance, is not merely the outcome of the idea of making noise, and of the technical method applied to reach this end: it is, besides this, the outcome of the religious conceptions, as any noise may be applied to invoke or drive away spirits; or it may be the outcome of the pleasure children have in noise of any kind; and its form may be characteristic of the art of the people" (quoted in Jacknis 79). Boas argued that textual explanations were a vital component of the ethnological display, making clear the contextual and signifying import of the objects on display. Labels, pamphlets, and monographs were to provide the scientist's written interpretation of artifacts (Jacknis 103–4). Recognizing the difference between an object's physical presence and its ever changing meaning, Boas and his researchers used narrative to destabilize the notion of treating objects as material evidence from, and of, the past. Their intention was for ethnographic objects to signify something other than cultural essences unspoiled by the mutability of time, place, and historicity. In fact, they emphasized the opposite: that cultural objects or products were constantly being produced and reproduced by temporal, geographic, and historical forces.[8]

The Boasian approach to representing culture found an artistic and intellectual parallel in the poet's imagination. Brown's approach to his poetry suggests that culture acquired meaning only through a full accounting of the historical context that shaped it. And yet the ethnographic museum's reliance on artifacts to represent cultures proved too narrow a model for Brown's poetics, even as the Boasian notion of historical and cultural contextualization proved a durable influence. His poetry sought to represent Black subjects' agency and autonomy even as their experiences were molded by geographical displacement and the passage of time. Brown's insistence that literature should aspire to do something other, or even more, than sociology bears witness to his ambivalence about the ethnological model—as did Zora Neale Hurston's skepticism of the museum's ability to represent a complex African American subject or culture.

In an article published in 1950, "What White Publishers Won't Print," Hurston indicts the publishing industry and American reading public for their lack of interest in anything other than narrow and stereotypical representations of African Americans. This desire, she states, has its basis in "an intangible built on folk belief" called "THE AMERICAN MUSEUM OF UNNATURAL HISTORY."[9] In this essay, Hurston positions the ethnographic museum in direct contrast to literature in that the former offers nothing but a series of types, "lay figures mounted in the museum where all may take them in at a glance," while the latter at least retains the possibility of representing the internal landscape and complex emotions of the Negro (951). The distinction between exhibition and inspiration (in the sense of giving life to an object) informed not only Hurston's writing, but also Brown's. Just as Hurston would do in her novels and folklore collections, in *Southern Road*, Brown offers a model for representing a culture that resists the museum model's attempts to create order by containing and distilling dynamic cultures into easily consumable objects. New Negro writers like Brown used ethnography to acquire and argue for the relevance of African American vernacular culture, yet they distanced themselves from the discipline in order to represent Black subjects as multidimensional and, indeed, human. Brown's depiction of Southern African American as complex subjects succeeded in illuminating a racial group that contributed to and transformed the contours of the society to which it belonged.

The New American/Negro Poet

Brown's New Negro experience is atypical in that he did not reside in Harlem during the twenties, but his experiences as a young writer follow the imaginative and actual terrain of many New Negro writers. Brown's first job, teaching English at Virginia Seminary in Lynchburg, fostered his interest in writing because, he said in an interview, "I found something to write about. I found a world of great interest and it was a world of people and the poetry of the time—the poetry that I was reading—was a people's poetry" (Gabbin 33). Like Jean Toomer, James Weldon Johnson and W. E. B. Du Bois, and other New Negro intellectuals with teaching jobs that led them to Southern experiences that nurtured their artistic imaginations, Brown found himself as a writer and scholar when he discovered the stunning intricacies of Southern Black culture and history. At the same time that this professional commitment opened him up to a new way of seeing and of self-expression, he was also absorbing the populist ideas espoused by the New American Poets and the pluralist ideas of New Negro writers. Reading Claude McKay's *Harlem Shadows* (1922) supplied him with images of urban alienation and dissolution; Jean Toomer's *Cane* (1923) introduced him to the idea of a lush Southern landscape occupied by a people and culture in decline; and Langston Hughes's *The Weary Blues* (1926) revealed poetry written by a kindred spirit who shared his commitment to a vernacular culture that was innately artistic, but who focused his creative vision on Northern cities rather than the Southern countryside.

Brown's literary influences extended beyond the rich array of writers that converged in Harlem during the teens and twenties. The New American Poetry of Edwin Arlington Robinson, Robert Frost, Carl Sandburg, and Vachel Lindsay presented a model of creative writing that melded vernacular language and democratic values. Like them, he found poetic inspiration in American idioms and vernacular culture.[10] This school of poetry resonated

with Brown, who was in the process of developing a sensibility for the philosophical and poetic potential of Black folk life, lore, and language. He absorbed cultural and aesthetic influences on "folklore collecting trips" that
took him to jook joints, barbershops, and isolated farms. In 1941, for example, as he traveled around the Black Belt while funded by a Rosenwald Fellowship to write a book he planned to call *A Negro Looks at the South*, he set
out to collect a "sampling" of Negro speech and perspectives. He would
record interviews on the spot or record conversations in his notebooks.
In a 1973 address at his alma mater, Williams College, Brown equated his
Southern travels with the education he received at institutions of higher
learning:

> These men taught me to think. At Harvard, I went into careful study of American po-
> etry. I learned from Edwin Arlington Robinson's *Tilbury Town*, where he took up the
> undistinguished, the failures, and showed the extraordinary in ordinary lives. I
> learned Robert Frost. I learned from my own; the man I was brought up on was Dun-
> bar. I learned from Claude McKay. I participated in what I called the New Negro Re-
> naissance. I wrote poetry. I went South. I taught at Virginia Seminary, where I learned
> a great deal that I could not learn at Williams. I learned the strength of my people. I
> learned the fortitude. I learned the humor. I learned the tragedy. I learned from a
> wandering guitar player about John Henry, about Stagolee, about "The Ballad of the
> Bollweevil." I learned folktales. I learned folkstuff. I was like a sponge. I had a good
> eye. I had a good ear. I had a good mind trained by people like Dutton [George Dut-
> ton, a professor of English at Williams].[11]

While so much of Brown's experiences are typical of members of the Black
elite who worked as Southern teachers engaged in the project of racial uplift,
there is one crucial difference in his approach and that is his presentation of
himself (at least in retrospect) as a *student* of "folkstuff." He includes people
like Calvin "Big Boy" Davis, the "wandering guitar player" he mentions
above, among the men who taught him to think, on par with his professors
at Williams and the great writers of the Harlem Renaissance. Davis and other
Southern Blacks became both his mentors and the source of the materials
that he refashioned for his poetry. Brown's Boasian leanings led him to reject
"the narrow interpretation of culture meaning 'cultivation' or 'sophistication'" and embrace a more pluralistic understanding of culture.[12] One might
argue that he is even more of a Boasian than either Johnson and Du Bois in
that he did not describe his work as elevating or "cultivating" folk materials
into the stuff of true art, or "high" culture. Like other younger, more radical,
members of the New Negro avant-garde, Brown created literature that
blurred the boundaries between what was understood to be high modernist

art and primitive folk art, and in the process, made the meaning of artistry more democratic.

The poetry collected in *Southern Road* (1932) challenges James Weldon Johnson's dictum in the preface to the first edition of *The Book of American Negro Poetry* (1922) that conventional uses of Black dialect in American literature lacked subtlety, limiting the range of uses of the vernacular to either pathos or humor.[13] Brown viewed much of Johnson's argument as valid because he launched it from "a literary point of view, rather than from that of 'respectability.'"[14] Yet he also emphasized that the problem with earlier dialect poetry was not in the language itself but in the writers' narrow vision of Black humanity, a view that echoed Johnson's own sense of the limited literary uses to which the vernacular had been put in the past. In contrast to Johnson, who saw the abandonment of vernacular language as an appropriate response of the modern writer to this precedent of stereotypical fiction, Brown demonstrated that dialect could still be a supple mode of expression. Johnson notes in his introduction to *Southern Road* that Brown "began writing just after the Negro poets had generally discarded conventionalized dialect, with its minstrel traditions of Negro life (traditions that had but slight relation, often no relation at all, to *actual* Negro life) with its artificial and false sentiment, its exaggerated geniality and optimism."[15] Johnson identifies the authenticity in Brown's poetry, its "genuine characteristic flavor," in his evocation of "*real* life," in other words, the contextualizing details that ground his poetry in lived experience. In this, Johnson articulates a Boasian notion of making representations of culture as approximate as possible to lived experience by describing the environs and histories that give cultural artifacts and locally specific language their meaning.

Brown (like Hughes and Hurston) demonstrated the aesthetic potential of Black speech when it is centered in careful study of the folk themselves. His move from an interest in local color to an interest in the context, feelings, and experiences from which the lore and music emerge would prove to be critical in the development of Brown's poetics. He viewed local color as an important stepping stone toward the development of a meaningful literature by and about African Americans that would depart from the long history of stereotypical portraits in American literature. But he was also clear about the limitations of local color fiction: "Local color stresses the quaint, the odd, the picturesque, the different. It is an attempt to convey the peculiar quality of a locality. Good realistic practice would insist upon the localizing of speech, garb, and customs; great art upon the revelation of the universal embedded in these local characteristics."[16] Brown rejects the narrowness of regionalism when he suggests that it emphasizes the local in order to generate notions of quaintness and exotic otherness. Yet, as I have already suggested, Brown did not conclude that local subjects or cultures needed to transcend or quit their particular locations in order for them to acquire greater significance. He understood the "local" subject to possess the inherent ability to communicate universal values that speak to an outsider. His poetics suggest that the outsider/reader, like the poet, needs to cultivate his or her perceptiveness in order to discern that capacity for universal significance.

Brown deplored the kind of poetry that reified racial and class hierarchies by maintaining a sociological distance from the poetic subject. Thus, he viewed Lindsay's 1914 poem, "Congo," as flawed because, although it captured the rhythms and cadences of jazz and ragtime, it failed to enter the inner world of its subjects.[17] The poem's subtitle, "A Study of the Negro Race," signaled its sociological ambitions. Brown's criticism of the poem had more to do with his expectations of the appropriate poetic approach than with any deep dislike of the social sciences, for any artist who tried his hand at "race portraiture" dabbled in pseudo-science and propaganda and thus was doomed to failure ("Our Literary Audience" 141–42). In fact, while teaching at Howard in the 1930s he found much to admire in his colleagues in the social sciences such as Ralph Bunche (political science), E. Franklin Frazier (sociology), and Abram L. Harris (economics). In *The Negro Caravan*, he credits these scholars with adding "enormously to the new realism about Negro life of which America is becoming aware and must become even more aware. . . . They are social analysts rather than solvers of a race problem."[18] One can conclude from these statements that Brown believed that social sciences and literature should be held accountable to different standards of reality: the social analysts would attend to an analysis of the material and social aspects of reality, while the literary artists would concern themselves with human truths that they could get at through portraits of individual lives and circumstances. In yet another venue he again denounced the attempts of artists, such as Roark Bradford, author of *Ol' Man Adam an' his Chillun*, to "advance themselves as sociologists and ethnologists. Mr. Bradford's easy pigeonholing of an entire race into three small compartments is a familiar phenomenon in American literature, where the Indian, the Mexican, the Irishman, and the Jew have been similarly treated. Authors are too anxious to have it said, 'Here is *the* Negro,' rather than here are a few Negroes whom I have seen" ("Negro Character" 150). The many character portraits that Brown composes in *Southern Road* such as "Maumee Ruth," "Georgie Grimes," "Johnny Thomas," "Sam Smiley," and "Sister Lou," illustrate his commitment to the notion that artists should strive to depict "the countless human beings called Negros," as opposed to a fruitless search for the representative Negro type ("Negro Character" 150).

In contrast to those whose professional ambitions as anthropologists were oriented toward a more scientific methodology, Brown considered himself an amateur folklorist.[19] Influenced by folklorist Benjamin Botkin, the folklore editor at the Federal Writers' Project with whom he worked during his tenure as Editor of Negro Affairs, Brown believed that folklore was something more than collecting, verifying, indexing, and annotating sources; it was people talking, doing, and describing themselves, and it should aspire to being "broadly human," "deeply interpretive," and indigenous as opposed to merely provincial ("Negro Character" 174). Where a professional folklorist might be inclined to map folklore patterns over specific geographical areas or across multiple generations, Brown chose a less methodical, but more intimate, approach of visiting, listening, and writing down what he remembered of the conversations he held in the communities to which he traveled. Gabbin writes, "In his role as casual observer, Brown avoided the natural barriers of distrust and deception put up by some folk informants, who were intimidated by the collector with pen and pad or recording machine. He listened to the people when they were least self-conscious and recorded in his mind the subtle inflections, pauses, nuances, and gestures that annotated their speech and songs" (87). He might more accurately be described as an observant-participant than a participant-observer in these encounters. Hurston's reflections on her experiences of collecting in *Mules and Men* suggest that other factors such as dress, comportment, and speech patterns can signify class differences within a community; and that these class signifiers can stand in for the collector's alienating pen and pad. But this is a point that Brown does not dwell on; instead he associates his amateur status and his reluctance to stand apart from his informants with his ability to acquire and represent a realistic (meaning recognizably human) folk idiom.

The ethnographic imagination runs throughout Brown's conceptualization of Southern Negro culture. For example, in a 1950 essay entitled "Negro Folk Expression," he remarks on the geographical and social isolation that compelled Black people to create their own forms of self-expression and self-understanding. Brown argued that geographic and social isolation due to segregation, coupled with a lack of educational and economic opportunity, led to a kind of creative ferment that resulted in the musicality, irony, and innovativeness that he aspired to in his poetry.[20] The folklorist's achievement, he later declared, was the ability to force the recognition of material that had previously been "set in isolation" as an "integral part of the American experience."[21] And while he recognized the vitality of folk culture, he also argued in this essay that it was increasingly incommensurate with contemporary African American experiences, and argued that literature would provide "the fullest expression" of a passing phase of Negro life (202).

The poems in *Southern Road* that focus on death and dying suggest that Brown understood it to represent a transition from one stage in life to another; thus, for him to declare that Southern slave society was passing away under the force of modernity was not synonymous with his declaring it to be obsolete or irrelevant. In fact, Brown reveals a clear commitment to the representation of folklore and folk culture as dynamic and adaptable. In this, Johnson again provides some insight into what is distinctive about Brown's poetry. He writes, "he has made more than mere transcriptions of folk poetry, and he has done more than bring to it mere artistry; he has deepened its meanings and multiplied its implications" (xiv–xv). Seeing Brown's poetry imbue folklore with a multiplicity of meaning makes his artistic and cultural contributions part of the pluralist and uplift projects; but it also makes his achievements larger and more profound than the goals set by each of these movements. The principle of cultural pluralism invites dominant society to recognize the existence and inherent value of Negro folk culture; for this, the folklorist's transcription should suffice as a contribution to the cause. The New Negro philosophy might encourage artists to view these materials as inspirational fodder for their creative endeavors; a poet might bring to the folklore formal techniques and poetic devices, such as meter, rhyme, and lyrical language. But Johnson suggests that Brown reaches the heights of artistry not by virtue of what he brings to the poetry, but by revealing folklore's capacity to hold a multiplicity of meaning, inspiring the reader's empathy for the poems' personas, and introducing his audience to a rich interpretive field where previously it had viewed little of great importance.

Ironically, Brown's commitment to "literariness" is what allowed him to make visible the subaltern strivings of the Negro, to see and depict Black communities as something other than a social problem in need of scientific analysis. Yet, his concern with the discursive and the literary had political implications. His poetry anticipated what Robin Kelley describes as a fairly recent development in Southern labor and urban historiography, namely the exposure of the "hidden social and cultural world of black working people" in order to determine its political meanings. Scholars like Kelley and George Lipsitz are now theorizing as oppositional the "social spaces" created by Black people because these spaces "constituted a partial refuge from the humiliations and indignities of racism, class pretensions, and waged work. African American communities often created an alternative culture emphasizing collectivist values, mutuality, and fellowship."[22] Sterling Brown's exploration of themes such as migration and pleasure, and his use of the blues as a mode of resistance and occasion for communal fellowship anticipate and illuminate these contemporary trends in scholarship.

A Poetics of Migration: Dreams of Freedom, Sites of Resistance

In *Southern Road*, the poems are collected and divided into four sections that together constitute a narrative of communal endurance, resistance, and transformation. Beginning in the unpredictable landscape of the historical South, Brown's poems then move through the causes and catalysts for migration, to a reflection on the culture carried by Southern migrants as they leave home. The poems loosely follow a cartography that progresses from South to North; they shift from male to female perspectives; and settings range from cotton field to chain gang, to the railroad car, to dance hall, and city street. The migration experience, and the desire for change that it represents, functions as the critical link that joins past and present, country and city, South and North.[23] Brown depicts Negro culture, regardless of location, as constituting a site of resistance and communal affiliation that enables Black people to negotiate the trials, tribulations, and challenges that they confront. His poetry, based as it was on African American work songs, blues, folktales, and legendary tricksters and bad men like Casey Jones, Stagolee, Big Boy, and Slim Greer, gave voice to Black people's opposition to and strategies for surviving the daily indignities and regular injustices of the Jim Crow South. Racial segregation and racial violence, floods and other natural disasters that put farmers' livelihood in peril, poverty and other social inequities all wreaked havoc on Black communities.[24] Yet at the same time, the existence of communal and kinship ties, an optimism rooted in religious faith, and the refusal to passively accept everyday assaults on their dignity all attest to Southern Blacks' strength and determination.

Section one of *Southern Road*, "Road So Rocky," sets the tone by historicizing the South and also establishing Southern men as laborers and traveling men, sojourners in permanent exile who find temporary resting places, but who continually seek the next stopping point or destination. These two images, of the Southern cradle and Southern migrant, reside together in productive tension, composing a picture of the region as always in process of creating and recreating Negro identity. The second section, "Onrestless River," focuses on the reasons for the migrants' exodus, with the flooding rivers functioning as a metaphor for the random violence, both human and natural, that inflict suffering on the Southern Negro. In the third section, "Tin Roof Blues," Brown focuses on experiences of migration, with poems that depict both cityscapes and traveling blues. The fourth and final section, "Vestiges," is unique in that it is the only section written solely in standard English and apparently voices the reflections of New Negro sons and daughters whose literary language simultaneously signifies their evolution from the historical roots Johnson has just limned, while retaining traces of the values, knowledge, and memories of their Southern ancestors.

In *Southern Road*'s inaugural poem, "Odyssey of Big Boy," Brown articulates the Negro claim to national belonging while also painting a portrait of a restless subject who remakes his identity in each new location. The poem chronicles the epic travels of a man whose journey parallels that of the mythic Odysseus in his desire to find his way home. While matching the Homeric protagonist in his heroism, Big Boy differs in that his final destination is unnamed, unclaimed, and perhaps unattainable. Big Boy ironically enacts the historical disenfranchisement of African Americans at the same time that he memorializes the mark he has made on the nation through the contributions of his physical labor, and implicitly through his cultural innovations: "Done shocked de corn in Marylan', / In Georgia done cut cane, / Done planted rice in South Caline, / But won't do dat again, / Do dat no mo' again" (5). The poem's pattern—three longer lines, typically followed by two concluding lines that are shorter, with the last line repeating the language of the penultimate—"But won't do dat again / Do dat no mo' again"—mirrors Big Boy's own migrations, which are characterized by movement followed by rest. The resting places signified by the repetition are inevitably transitory, as the rhythm picks up again and Big Boy continues on to another destination. The reader follows him through a variety of jobs through the agricultural South, the industrial North, the coal mines of West Virginia, and the ports of Baltimore. That Brown chose to write a Southern poem that recounts the persona's travels around the nation suggests that the birthplace of New Negro culture is also an originary location for America. "Odyssey of Big Boy" is a ballad that testifies to the scope of Negro contributions to the building of the nation in a musical mode that Mark Sanders reads as an "extra-literary mode of self-articulation." This exercise in self-articulation, Sanders argues, is at the crux of Brown's conceptualization of a New Negro modernist aesthetic, "thereby acknowledging and celebrating the multiple ways in which

New Negroes formulated and expressed their modernity and claim to full participation."[25]

Brown combines his vision of national pluralism with a critique of the racial exclusions that historically have contributed to the subordination and marginalization of Negroes. In "Ruminations of Luke Johnson," the persona uses his observation of a young girl's daily walk home from work carrying a basket of leftovers from her employer's table to reflect on slavery's hidden and enduring legacy. This poem focuses implicitly on what in the successive poems, "Sam Smiley," "Frankie and Johnny," and "Johnny Tomas," will be explicit reflections on Southern experiences of rape, lynching, and coerced labor. But in "Ruminations," the social critique is milder and acts of resistance are covert. Puzzling over the sight of Mandy Jane "trompin' to huh wuk / Wid a great big basket," Luke Johnson reflects on the difference between mornings when she walks unburdened and evenings when she returns with her basket full of the remainders from her employer's dinner. The narrator's overt concern with economic exploitation hints also at the possibility of sexual exploitation when he observes that, "She picks all de darkest / Places in de lane, / Where de hungry hounds sniff / An' foller huh about" (25). The image of a Mandy Jane, vulnerable to unseen predators, unfolds into an overt indictment of White privilege wrenched from Black bodies when the narrator declares that the lady she works for lives on the money made from "niggers pickin' cotton," and "ebbery dollar dat she squander / Nearly bust a nigger's back" (26). He notes ironically that Mandy Jane is able to wrest a bit of pleasure from this exploitative relationship by at least ensuring that she carries home enough to feed herself and her family. Whether or not she has obtained permission to bring home the food, Mandy Jane's visage suggests and the narrator openly insists that she is entitled to the basket's contents:[26] "So I'm glad dat in de evenin's / Mandy Jane seems extra happy, / An' de lady at de big house / Got no kick at all, I say; —/ Cause what huh 'dear grandfawthaw' / Took from Mandy Jane's grandpappy—/ Ain' no basket in de worl' / What kin tote all dat away" (26).

Mandy Jane's daily traversing of the road between work and home is mundane and uneventful, yet it is also ripe with association of racial inequality, enslavement, and other forms of coercion and her slow and deliberate movement away from that history and toward an idea of justice. Despite the obvious differences with Big Boy's epic, explicitly masculine journey across the nation, Mandy Jane's travels are like his in that they are expressions of each subject's desire for freedom and self-determination.[27] By associating both individuals with the road, the poet reflects on the experiences of exile and belonging that are the divided legacy of African Americans. The dual themes of estrangement and kinship are encoded, Vera Kutzinski argues, in Brown's image of the road, which signifies both the Negro need to escape from the South and an affiliation with it as an ancestral home. "The characteristic referential ambiguity of 'Southern Road' derives from the fact that it leads both away from the South to a symbolic North, and thus becomes an emblem of [alienating] adversity, as well as back toward the South, in which case it is transformed into an 'image of kin.' "[28] Luke Johnson's concern for the well-being of Mandy Jane gestures toward the kinship ties he feels as she walks by him each evening; yet the image of her in motion underscores her refusal to accept her servitude unconditionally. It hints at her desire for personal and social change.

The sexual and economic violence recalled in "Ruminations of Luke Johnson," gives rise to feelings of despair and defiance that find their fullest expression in the blues. Brown's "Tin Roof Blues" in section three speaks to the disenfranchisement that resulted in Black migrants being torn from, or abandoning, their Southern homes: "I'm goin' where de Southern crosses top de C. & O. / I'm goin' where de Southern crosses top de C. & O. / I'm goin' down de country cause I cain't stay here no mo'" (105). If the blues provided a forum for the expression of social alienation, it also proved redemptive by reminding Black subjects not only of the histories they attempted to evade but also of the strategies they used to challenge racial and class injustices: "I'm got de tin roof blues, got dese sidewalks on my mind, / de tin roof blues, dese lonesome sidewalks on my mind, / I'm goin' where de shingles covers people mo' my kind" (105). The tin roof of the railroad car provides little comfort and scant shelter, but nonetheless it ushers the migrant into a new and more positive place where he will find kinship with "people mo' my kind," who share his desire for autonomy and agency. When the persona refers to "sidewalks on my mind," or taking his "foot up in [his] hand," he equates getting up and leaving with the exercise of free will. He may not have the power over his employment situation or race relations, but he has ownership over his own body and the right of self-determination. "Tin Roof Blues" is typical of cultural productions that provide opportunities for African Americans to remind themselves of their humanity, and to celebrate real heroes like Jack Johnson and mythic ones like Big Boy and Slim Greer, who insist on fighting back, walking away from, or laughing in the face of the mundane, arbitrary, and hateful insults heaped on them by a hostile society.[29]

Another poem, "Ma Rainey," illuminates the communal dynamics that create an opportunity for expressions of cultural resistance. This poem recollects a performance by the "Mother of the Blues," Gertrude Rainey, of "Backwater Blues," a song that memorializes a Mississippi River flood that decimated communities along its banks.[30] Brown portrays the experience of listening to Rainey recall the traumatic events as a communal ritual in which a fragmented people gather and re-collect themselves through the performance of the blues. The first stanza identifies the diverse locations from which Rainey's audience originates—Cape Girardeau, Poplar Bluff, Black-bottom cornrows, and labor camps, among other locations—conveying a sense of distance and fragmentation momentarily overcome (62). The individuals who come flocking from these parts to "hear / Ma do her stuff" take part in a pilgrimage to pay homage to the legendary singer because they expect the experience to be transformative (62). An informant, identified as "a fellow," tells the poem's narrator, "She jes' gits hold of us some kindeaway," suggesting a kind of spirit possession in which the audience loses hold of its self and is taken over by the spirit of communalism embodied by Rainey (63). The audience raises a unified voice to call Rainey to the stage: "O ma Rainey, / Sing yo song; / Now you's back / Whah you belong, / Git way inside us, / Keep us strong" (63). The repetition of a bell-like sound in "song," "belong," and "strong" underscores the notion that Rainey ascends not just a stage but an alter; she is called to minister to her "flock." Brown recognizes and gestures toward the connection between the sacred and profane in another poem, "New Steps," which celebrates the construction of "new steps a-climbin' to de little Church do'—" (91). In the poem the narrator takes notice of the church and the poolroom's location within eyeshot of each other, separated only by "de muddy road . . . de sinful road" (92). Recognizing that both church and jook joint draw from the same population (in this case, the pool den "snatchin' from de church pews all de men"), he joins the sacred and profane in "Ma Rainey" by endowing the raunchy, outspoken singer with a transcendent grace.

The blues Rainey sings chronicles a natural disaster with imagery that symbolizes the myriad of social hazards that Black Southerners face: "*It rained fo' days an' de skies was dark as night, / trouble taken place in de lowlands at night*" (64). Farah Griffin, discussing the significance of "Backwater Blues" and other blues songs that recalled the flood writes, "while the song specifically focuses on the Mississippi River flood, it reveals much more about the conditions under which poor Blacks lived in the South and it articulates their relationship to American society in general."[31] The performance has an immediate and profound effect on the audience. Brown writes, "An' den de folks, dey natchally bowed dey heads an cried,/ Bowed

dey heavy heads, shet dey moufs up tight an' cried" (64). This deep and grat-
ified silence conveys the audience's sense of how aptly the song reminds
them of what and how much they have endured. The blues is about exile
and alienation; but the poem itself is about communion. After the respectful silence, we learn "An' Ma lef' de stage, an' followed some de folks outside"
(64). In other words, she becomes one of and one with her audience. While
the singer depicts an individual experience of the trauma and dislocation,
her audience hears and receives it as a communal story, so it is fitting that at
the end of the performance, the individual folds into and merges with the
collective body.[32]

Female Roots and Male Branches: Gender and Migration

"Ma Rainey" is unique in *Southern Road* in that it imagines a woman giving
voice to African Americans' feelings of exile and displacement and forging
community in the intimate spaces that foster self-expression despite the migrant's distance from home. A woman, in other words, uncharacteristically
speaks for and to the migrant's condition. In "It Jus Be's Dat Way Sometimes:
The Sexual Politics of Women's Blues," Hazel Carby explored women's blues
lyrics for the attitudes revealed by Black women at the prospect of migration.
Carby argues that for most women, the iconic symbol of the blues narrative,
the train, signified not freedom, but abandonment and loneliness.[33] Brown's
poetry typically confirms this dichotomy by inscribing the figure of the single male traveler as the symbol of restless autonomy, and positioning women
as immobile, fixed in place, constant, and unchanging. In "Riverbank Blues,"
for example, male travelers are associated with perpetual, even compulsory,
mobility: "Man better move some, better not git rooted, / Muddy water fool
you, ef you stay" (100). Big Boy's masculinity is affirmed in "Odyssey of Big
Boy" by his cataloguing not only of places to which he has traveled but also
of his female paramours in those various locations: "Had a stovepipe blond
in Macon, / Yaller gal in Marylan', / In Richmond had a choklit brown, /
Called me huh monkey man—/ Huh big fool monkey man" (6). In Brown's
oeuvre, women remain, for the most part, fixed in spaces that symbolize do-
mesticity and home, even when the "home" is a temporary one as it is in
these cases. The male persona in "Long Gone" expresses compassion for the
woman he will leave behind while asserting a strong and irrepressible male
instinct to roam: "You is done all you could do / To make me stay; / 'Tain't no
fault of yours I'se leavin'—/ I'se jes dataway" (9). "I'se jes dataway" articulates

an unyielding masculine prerogative that contrasts starkly with the resignation suggested by Carby's "It jus be's dat way sometimes."

In contrast to his depiction of male travelers, Brown's portrait of "Bessie" offers a pessimistic view of the migrant woman that sharply contrasts with his heroic male travelers. Bessie's move "to the cities to get her share of fun" sets off her decline. The natural beauty Brown idealizes in Southern women, witnessed in Bessie's "bird voice, and laughter like the sun," dissipates as she withers into a woman "gaunt of flesh and painted, / Despair deep bitten in her soft brown eyes" (41). The move to the city, almost always for women, less frequently for men, precipitates a moral and physical decline as migrants lose touch with their ancestral values and communal ties nurtured in the South and embodied by maternal figures like "Maumee Ruth."

It becomes evident when Brown moves from the romantic liaisons described in "Odyssey of Big Boy" and "Long Gone" to the maternal hearth depicted in "Maumee Ruth" that separation and loss are common experiences that link the themes of travel and death in his poetry. In "Maumee Ruth," the narrator announces, "Might as well bury her / And bury her deep," rooting the ancestral Black woman firmly in the Southern soil (10). The poem laments the abandoned, lonely mothers who grieve the loss of their wayward children, while recognizing that they have no one to mourn their own passing (10). The departure of her son and daughter to the city foreshadow a more permanent separation of family members through death, and most egregiously, forgetting. The narrator associates the urban environment with isolation, dissolution, and estrangement when he counts the "boy that she suckled," now "hiding in city holes, / sniffing the 'snow,'" and Maumee's "baby gal," now living in Harlem "sodden with gin" (10–11). Like Jean Toomer, who also links women and landscape in *Cane*, Brown's depiction of the Southern Black mother suggests that with the commencement of a new and more modern era, Southern folkways were in danger of passing out of existence.

The idea of death links Brown's elegy of Maumee Ruth to "Virginia Portrait," a poem that covers very similar terrain with a critical difference. "Virginia Portrait" recollects a Southern culture and traditional way of life that is in decline, presumably with the onset of industrialization and migration trends. The poem begins with the declaration "Winter is settling on the place," a metaphoric reference to the death that descends on a "wizened woman" who embodies the South: "But she has strength and steadfast hardihood. / Deep-rooted is she, even as the oaks, / Hardy as perennials about her door. / The circle of the seasons brings no fear / '*Folks all gits used to what dey sees so often*'" (27–28). Both women and region are characterized by their endurance, dignity, faith in providence, and wisdom. In contrast to Maumee Ruth's tragic isolation, however, this woman relies on the companionship found through friendship and marriage, in addition to her religious conviction, to provide her with strength. We discover, "She has been happy, and her heart is grateful. / Now she looks out, and forecasts unperturbed / Her following slowly over the lonesome hill, / Her '*layin' down her burdens, bye and bye*'" (28). The italicized verse from well-known spirituals is presumably spoken or sung in the woman's voice, with the italics setting it apart from the narrator's observations. The difference in typography highlights both the fact that the woman speaks, as well as what she expresses. In contrast, Sanders argues that Maumee Ruth's silence underscores her lack of agency.[34] This comparison of poetic representations of women reveals that Southern women's exercise of their creative powers through participation in song can be evidence of their agency. The snatches of spirituals suggest that culture functions as a vehicle for their beliefs and values, and provides occasion for communal interaction, both of which makes them, like perennials, capable of regeneration.

This illustration of communal and individual fortitude should not be confused with an idealization of rural Southerners, for Brown recognized the dangers in romanticizing Southern Black beauty (and beauties). The skepticism he expresses in regards to the artistic project was fed in part by his aversion to pastoral poetry. Gabbin argues that Brown favored regionalism and realism in place of the pastoral view that he associated with Paul Laurence Dunbar.[35] He meditates on the limitations of the poet who fails to render the complexities of a vibrant woman—"She who was easy for any chance lover"—even as he attempts to honor her beauty in "Effie" (106). The artist inevitably fails, as "She who was clay for any clumsy sculptor / Becomes inflexible; fixed of form at length" (106). Clay, the sculptor's medium, calls forth images of the dust to which Essie will return upon her death, suggesting that the artist, like death itself, runs the risk of leeching away her vitality rather than adequately capturing it. The poem questions the logic of any imagination, whether ethnographic or artistic, indulging in the desire to render as an aesthetic object and to preserve for posterity vernacular culture and the people who produce it. What the artist described in the poem fails, or refuses, to recognize is Effie's changeability, her unpredictability, for these qualities run against the desire to depict her as timeless, transcend Beauty. The problem the puzzling Effie poses to the poet who would memorialize her is how to render these complexities and do them justice. The poem ends on an ambiguous note. The final guise of aloofness leaves out her many other aspects, making a difficult subject all the more "inflexible" to the clumsy sculptor; and yet the narrator concludes that this aloofness "is the Paradise crowning her days" (106).

"Young lambs gotta find de way": The Language of Modernity

In *Southern Road*, Brown thematizes the poet's representation of the past and its inhabitants. Brown introduces the collection with an epigraph from a spiritual—*O de ole sheep dey knows de road, / Young lambs gotta find de way*—that announces the collection's intention to face in two directions simultaneously. Looking forward into the future at the same time that they face backward toward the past, the poems in this collection consider the relation between the two and its relevance to Black people entering into modernity. As I have already mentioned, Brown's most optimistic poems equate death with passage and change, rather than with oblivion. Although many of the poems associate burial of the dead with rootedness and fixity, they also suggest that burial lacks the dynamic, life-giving force associated with remembering. Forgetfulness, nostalgia (false memory), and romanticization are all linked in poems that depict the New Negro of running the risk of overlooking the values that proved empowering to so many generations that came before. "Children's Children" depicts just such a predicament "When they hear / These songs, born of the travail of their sires, / Diamonds of song, deep buried beneath the weight / Of dark and heavy years; / They laugh" (107).

Rather than wisdom or insight, these children hear nonsense or ridiculousness because "they have forgotten, they have never known / Long days beneath the torrid Dixie sun" (107). Ignoring their own history in favor of assimilation and materialism symbolized by their "paled faces, copper lips," these children turn defiantly toward a future that promises little of lasting value. Too often the South's New Negro offspring fall for the seductive charms of the city as in "Mecca." In this poem, Maggie a migrant form Spartanburg, meets Tom who has migrated from Martinique. Both dress themselves in finery (a derby, pearl gray spats, a sealskin coat) whose aristocratic sheen speaks to their ambitions for social mobility. Yet Brown hints that they may not have arrived in a meaningful sense in the final stanza: "O Milk and honey of the promised land! / When Sunday rolls round again, / Lady Margaret, lord! . . . She tips for fair, / And Lord Thomas . . . twirls his cane" (109).

Where exactly, the poet implicitly asks, is the promised land located? Is the North the ultimate destination, or have Maggie and Tom fallen short because their flight northward is for material comfort rather than freedom and self-determination. The question remains unanswered, and yet the ellipses indicate a gap or silence to these unspoken ruminations, making one wonder what will occur "when Sunday rolls round again," and if Maggie and Tom will be adequately equipped to answer the query themselves. Northern cities beckon, offering new possibilities for employment and more egalitarian social relationships, but migrants frequently discovered upon arrival the promise was often hallow, masking spiritual malaise, social isolation, and dislocation.[36] In "Chillen Get Shoes," for example, the narrator reassures Lilly, "Don't you cry; / You'll get your silver slippers / Bye and bye." But his model of urban sophistication is "Good-time Moll," a prostitute whose image—"plump legs clad / In openwork hose"—is anything but reassuring.

Brown's poems of urban life tend to emphasize the unsettling and disillusioning nature of the experience, epitomized by the polyvocality and discontinuities of the third section's "Cabaret." In "Cabaret," the narrator describes a scene in which "Hebrew and Anglo-Saxon" consumers of jazz culture carelessly wield power over the Negro performers in a cabaret. The poem's first stanza narrates the scene from the point of view of an omniscient, third-person narrator while the second expresses the sentiments of the rich and powerful: "*Now, now, / To it, Roger; that's a nice doggie, / Show your tricks to the gentlemen*" (115). This thought may be submerged in the subconscious of an audience member, or perhaps it expresses the feelings of a performer who recognizes and resents the class and racial hierarchies implicit in this scene of cultural co-optation. Regardless of the source, Brown brings to the reader's attention the presence of oppositional communities and conflicting identities within this shared space. The narrator informs us that the jazz musicians respond with music that "wails," "belches," "clashes," and "twitches." This description of sonic dissonance conveys their lack of ease, even as they submit to the command to "show your tricks." It recalls a description Brown once gave of jitterbug dances he witnessed in Atlanta. After describing the "weird" and "wild" gyrations of the dancers, Brown wrote, "I thought how often I had resented the charges against my people that they were merely happy, carefree dancers. This dancing had been skillful, certainly. But it wasn't free of care, the way I saw it; it was defiant of care instead. It was a potent drug, a reefer smoke, a painkiller shot in the arm."[37] Brown intercuts the jazz inflected moments with lyrics that suggest that this cabaret scene and its production of cultural commodification and co-optation are as threatening as the flooding rivers and acts of racist violence that produced the sounds of the original blues.

Ironically, the lyrics are actually from a Tin Pan Alley song, "Muddy Water (A Mississippi Moan)," that bastardizes blues conventions and reproduces a nostalgic idea of rural Southern life that minimizes the severity of its conditions. One stanza declares, for example, "Southland has got grand garden spots / Whether you believe it or not / I hear those trees a-whispering, 'Come on back to me.'" According to Angela Davis, "A patchwork of discordant imagery, reflecting the South of White aristocrats with their 'grand garden spots' and the home of working class Black people 'reelin' and rockin' to them low down blues,' 'Muddy Water' appears to have been thrown together without any sensitivity to real social relations—racial and class—of the South" (87–89). Davis asks with acuity how Black people listening to the song's description of whispering trees could not be reminded of the crimes of lynching that made trees into "instruments of terror" (88). Brown frames the most nostalgic lines from the song, which refer to muddy water as being sweet and express nostalgia for "sweet home" with more enigmatic lines that enable the references to water to retain the connotation of suffocation it possesses in earlier poems. Thus, the stanza that describes the belching, twitching jazz musicians is followed by another that declares, "Muddy water / Round my feet / Muddy water" (115). In part two, "Onrestless River," the muddy waters signify threats barely submerged under the surface of daily experiences; here the juxtaposition suggests that this is a fact of Northern urban life as well. And while the chorus of "Creole Beauties from New Orleans" generates feelings of nostalgia in the audience that thinks "Muddy water, river sweet" at the sight of the costumed women, the narrator has already exposed their performance as illusory, for the chorus girls originate from places as different as Atlanta, Louisville, Washington, and Yonkers. The threat signified by muddy waters, of course, is posed not by lynch mobs, chain gangs, sharecropping, or the floods that threaten the farmer's subsistence; instead it derives from the casual racism that reduces African Americans to stereotypes and mindless entertainment and that simplifies their history to meaningless platitudes.

The poem refuses the reader a simple identification with the audience by reminding us in yet another disembodied, unidentified voice, "(*In Arkansas, / Poor half-naked fools, tagged with identification numbers, / Worn out upon the levees, / Are carted back to the serfdom / They had never left before / And may never leave again*)" (116). "Cabaret" makes explicit what "Mecca" only implies: there is no real future in Northern cities when their inhabitants are isolated and alienated from their histories. Blues performances served other purposes, not necessarily in the best interest of Black people, when they took place in public spaces where capitalism and individualism held greater sway than the communal ethic that characterized the more intimate spaces of performance in the South. And yet the final wail of the song lyrics—"My heart cries out for / M U D D Y W A T E R"—manages to capture and convey the loss and dislocation that characterizes the migrant experience despite the actual song's corruption of their memories (118). The line's expressive power resides in its ability to so aptly express the torment of desiring the very thing that will ultimately lead to one's destruction, like the siren song of money, or of nostalgic memories of the past. The poem ends with a final sounding that echoes the lyric's expression of ambivalence and defeat—"Dee da dee D A A A A H" (118). John Callahan describes this as an untranslatable sound that "cast[s] doubt on whatever expectations linger of modernism's ability to affirm convincing new beginnings either for self or for community without the low, painful fires of critical intelligence and historical consciousness."[38] This moment of wordless expression conveys a lack of closure, appropriate to the end of this migration narrative, which gestures toward a desire for agency and self-determination that Southern migrants sought but had no guarantee of finding.

"Cabaret" suggests that the future of the New Negro spills over with a multiplicity of possibilities, desired and foreclosed, that no single language or idiom can contain and communicate. Strikingly, Brown follows the wordless sounding of the end of "Cabaret" with a turn back to the South and the sureness of not only verbal expression, but of Standard English, Romantic poetry that seems at odds with the vernacular sounds, rhythms, and language of the first three sections of the book. Anderson argues that the final section of ten poems, "Vestiges," is an "evolutionary dead end because they ignore social problems for the sake of literariness" (1024). But this assessment is not entirely accurate because it overlooks the fact that Brown picks up and extends many of the themes explored in the first sections of the book in these Standard English poems (and quite a few poems in the first sections are written in Standard English even though the content is indigenous, or vernacular). In this final section, as in the previous ones, Brown looks backward and forward, southward and northward simultaneously. While the use of Standard English and the self-conscious literariness of the poems signal their origin in the New Negro imagination, other aspects of the section indicate that the poet continues to be rooted in and concerned with the South's influence on his imagination.

Brown introduces "Vestiges" with a picture by E. Simms Campbell of a traveler returning home. A man and woman, perhaps his mother and father, greet this traveler, whose turns his back to the reader. This image of domestic tranquility is composed with all of its elements (the landscape, architecture of the domicile, and human bodies) in their proper and "natural" places. The artist roots the trees in the earth; places the hills in the backdrop; arranges the house in the center of the frame and the road in the foreground. This image of tranquility departs from the three earlier images that introduce the other sections, which all are composed with modernist angles, linear breaks, and sharp juxtapositions of images of people, nature, and material objects that are rendered abstract by the rupture of their forms. This visual fragmentation mirrors the instability of Negro life. Only in the return journey—taken in memory and imagination—can the poet assume tranquility. This is something Brown acknowledges in his poem, "Return," in which he writes, "I have gone back in boyish wonderment / To things that I had foolishly put by" before concluding, "I have found peacefulness somewhere at last, / Have found a quiet needed for so long" (129).

As I have indicated earlier, Brown regarded nostalgia with wariness, and thus the poems in "Vestiges" refuse to indulge in the act of remembering as an exercise in aesthetics or abstraction, and focus instead on the uses to which memory can be put in the race's advancement toward the future. This suggests that we might regard the final visual composition not as an image of idealized harmony but of the uniformity and reparation that can be achieved through the cultivation of what Callahan calls a historical consciousness. In "Salutamus," Brown again returns to the theme of death, but simultaneously salutes the next generation who will take up the mantle of its predecessors. When the narrator asks, "What was our crime / gloomy path that we must go," he echoes the sentiment of many of the poems in "Road So Rocky" that ruminate on the lasting legacy of slavery and racism (123). When he concludes on a note of optimism that relief will come from the youth "who will plant and find a fairer crop than ours," and declares, "We must plunge onward," he recalls the forward momentum and future orientation of "Strong Men," the final poem in section one (123).

"Strong Men," like so many of the poems in this collection, brings together different voices and points of view. Of all the poems in *Southern Road*, it seems most influenced by Du Bois, who in *The Souls of Black Folk* merges historical, philosophical, sociological, and creative narratives. The historical voice in "Strong Men" recounts Negro history: "*They dragged you from homeland, / They chained you in coffles*" (51). It also recalls and brings to the foreground a folk perspective that expresses itself through song: "*Keep a inchin' along / Lak a po' inch worm*" and "*Bye and bye / I'm gonna lay down dis heaby load*" and so on (51). These two voices merge into a declaration whose collective force is suggested by the shift in typography from italics to normal. In other poems, differences in typography signify the depiction of different subjects or consciousnesses; in this poem it signifies the difference between historical and future oriented points of view. "The strong men . . . coming on / The strong men gittin' stronger. / Strong men . . . / Stronger . . ." (53). This declaration, like "Salutamus's," "We must plunge onward," functions as a collective call to action. It signals to the reader that the idea of return through memory only retains its significance if it recognizes the political and social meanings of the past and vernacular traditions.

Although Brown was totally committed to the creation of aesthetically pleasing and philosophically meaningful literature about African Americans, what is at stake in his concern with culture and memory is more than discursive; it is political and material. Brown understood that culture was not about the placement of artifacts in an arrangement that made a pleasing picture or told an interesting "story"; rather, he depicted folk and popular culture as "contested terrain, something to be struggled over by producers and consumers," making him an early and important contributor to cultural studies, decades before the field was defined and institutionalized.[39] Moreover, Brown's use of the trope of the Southern Road breaks apart the idea of the "Harlem" Renaissance as bounded in time and space. *Southern Road* highlights his commitment to and virtuosity in communicating fully with two locations (South and North) and two orientations (past and future) so central to articulations of the "new" in the New Negro movement.

Chapter 6

Woman Dancing Culture: Katherine Dunham's Dance/Anthropology

Like Sterling Brown, Katherine Dunham's youth and association with environs other than New York make her an unlikely subject to include in a study of a movement typically associated with Harlem in the twenties and thirties. While she was a young student at the University of Chicago between 1927 and 1936, however, Dunham's intellectual formation was influenced by key figures associated with the movement, like Charles Johnson, and her artistic and social agenda mirrored those of New Negro artists and intellectuals including Hurston, Brown, Johnson, and Du Bois, all of which merits her inclusion in considerations of this period.[1] If we think of the Renaissance as a discursive formation rather than as a geographically and temporarily delimited period, then Dunham's investment in reclaiming African Diasporic folk traditions, her belief in the socially and politically redemptive power of African American artistic and cultural achievement, and her use of anthropology to radically re-envision discourses on race and culture make her a critical member of the New Negro movement.

Dunham was born in 1909 into a middle-class household in Glen Ellyn, Illinois, near Chicago. She is best known as a dancer and choreographer who appeared on Broadway, on concert stages, and in Hollywood films, especially during the 1930s and 1940s but also for many years after that. The place of her choreography in the canon of American modern dance was cemented by her creation of an eponymous modern dance technique that combines Afro-Caribbean, modern, and ballet styles and by her creation of the first African American dance troupe to appear on the concert stage and in films. Finally, she is recognized for her pioneering work in the field of dance anthropology. Dunham went on to write an important ethnography of Haiti that focused on dance traditions called "Dances of Haiti" (1947). Her work in dance circles closely followed the model of other Harlem Renaissance intellectuals in that she saw herself as an artist who translated African American and African Diasporic folk materials in an effort to transform mainstream perceptions of the people who produced these dances and to expand conceptions of American cultural and national identities to include the contributions of Black people.

Dunham possessed the New Negro conviction that artistic excellence could change opinions and lead to a more egalitarian society for Blacks, and she sought to reclaim and recuperate African Diasporic folk traditions. On the concert stage, she explored the transmission and invention of African American identity through performance. Even when her choreography focused on representing traditional settings or dances, her emphasis was on re-envisioning African Americans' future possibilities. Dunham's stage work and film choreography participate in a symbolic New Negro progression into modernity. Moreover, her writing, specifically her memoir, shares with her choreography a concern with diasporic continuities and discontinuities. Dunham is, in other words, a significant theorist of culture and identity, who should be associated with the New Negro movement and whose legacy we must fully reckon with.

Despite her importance as an artist, writer, and anthropologist, Dunham's influence was not fully recognized until recently outside of modern dance circles. Her influence as a scholar is still not adequately appreciated and accounted for in histories of the formation of modern anthropology. Nor has literary criticism of African American modernism fully accounted for her importance, despite the fact that her presence offers an ideal opportunity to consider more broadly the cultural achievements of the Renaissance beyond the literary successes of its members. We can attribute Dunham's marginalization in both histories of the Harlem Renaissance and of American anthropology to the male-oriented focus of early and influential histories of modern anthropology and the Harlem Renaissance.[2] Reading these texts underscores several commonalities across the wide spectrum of intellectuals and culture-workers on whom they focus. The primary actors in both of these movements (Boas and Du Bois would be the models against which others were measured) shared a passion for and investment in intellectual work; they took advantage of and indeed where shaped by opportunities to travel internationally, which contributed in large part to the self-identification of the New Negro as cosmopolitan subjects; and they possessed, to varying degrees, institutional power that enabled their efforts to define and shape academic, cultural, and political developments. New Negro women, while they shared the same intellectual and political commitments, were often overlooked because the perception was that they lacked institutional power in the academy, or in activist or political organizations, and they did not travel widely. If they did travel, like Dunham and her contemporary

Zora Neale Hurston, they went to places other than the European metropole, thus those journeys were discounted as irrelevant.

Cheryl Wall comments in her study of women in the Harlem Renaissance on the perception that these women were sometimes homebound, and often perceived as being more physically restricted and less intellectually expansive than their male peers. Nonetheless, she argues, "despite restrictions against it, [women of the Harlem Renaissance] traveled widely in fact and in imagination."[3] A number of factors contributed to the perception of women's absence from Renaissance activities, including the fact that many of the women writers and artists did not live in New York for substantial periods of time, with the exception of Jessie Fauset, Nella Larsen, and Zora Neale Hurston; married women's career goals often took second place to their spouse's aspirations; and gendered and racial stereotypes about Black women's sexual availability and the corresponding insistence on propriety placed limits on women's freedom of mobility. Wall argues, "The Harlem Renaissance was not a male phenomenon," asserting that such an assumption is possible only if one insists on a narrow definition of the movement as centered exclusively in Harlem and within a narrow period between 1919 and 1929 (9). By widening the temporal and spatial lens through which the period is viewed, Black women intellectuals can emerge from out of the shadows.

Dunham's artistic and intellectual legacy is important to consider because, like the male culture-workers I focus on in the first half of this book, she forged connections between the social sciences and the creative arts. Her interest in anthropology as an undergraduate inspired the direction of her dance, and her approach to studying dance broadened the practice of writing ethnographic narratives. However, Dunham's early dance and theatrical experiences did not intersect with her academic pursuits, although they were enabled by her presence in Chicago to study at the university. While an undergraduate at the University of Chicago, she studied ballet with Ludmila Speranzeva, who studied with the Chauve Souris Dance School and passed on to Dunham a technique that stressed mime and acting. She also joined an arts group called the Cube Theatre, founded by her older brother Albert and some of his friends. Despite her youth and inexperience, Dunham founded three ballet schools during this early period. These schools failed because they were underfunded, and because Dunham struggled to find young students whose parents were open to the idea that other forms of dance besides ballet might be useful for their daughters to learn. Throughout, Dunham continued to take ballet lessons from Speranzeva, as well as Mark Turbyfill, and others.

It was during this period that she attended a lecture given by Robert Redfield, a professor in Chicago's Anthropology Department, in which he discussed African survivals in African American culture. The talk, and more specifically his discussion of the African roots in popular Negro dances such as the Lindy Hop and the Cake Walk, fascinated Dunham and piqued her interest in the field of anthropology.[4] While Dunham found her anthropology courses to be engaging and exciting, she noticed their omission of dance as an "important social act" (Haskins 48). This prompted her to pursue a Rosenwald Fund grant to study dance practices of cultures outside of America. She believed that in other societies dance continued to fill a more central role in the formation of communal bonds, in contrast to the more formal dance forms that American society recognized and performed.[5] In 1935, the Rosenwald Fund granted Dunham a fellowship to study dance in the Caribbean. Included in the grant was enough tuition for her to study under Melville Herskovits for a semester. Herskovits was then chair of the Department of African Studies at Northwestern University. From him, Dunham learned fundamental ethnographic methods, including the necessity of approaching a culture as a whole rather than exploring the parts that interested her. He taught her good recordkeeping practices, including the use of cameras and tape recorders, so her research would gain credibility in the eyes of professional researchers. Lastly, he taught her to use patience and to minimize the obtrusiveness of her presence in order to increase the likelihood of being treated as an insider by those she hoped to make her informants (Haskins 50–51).

After studying with Herskovits, Dunham proceeded to conduct fieldwork in Haiti, Martinique, and Jamaica in 1935 and 1936, but he was not the only individual who played an important role in her formative years as a student of anthropology. Dunham's work with Herskovits introduced her to a Boasian approach to the study of culture, which differed from the methods of most scholars working in what has come to be known as the Chicago School of Sociology.[6] Herskovits used Boas's diffusion theories to study the cultural continuities between Africa and its Diaspora. His most controversial, and influential, claim was that African Americans' speech, religion, family formations, music, and food retained African influences. Where most scholars in Chicago argued that processes of assimilation through education and urbanization would gradually transform Black culture, Herskovits emphasized the resilience of African cultural patterns.[7] Dunham believed in the inevitable loss of village values as rural societies became more urban, industrialized, and modern, but she learned from Herskovits to attend to African Americans' cultural strengths, an aspect that many of the Chicago as-

similationists overlooked because they tended to emphasize and argue for societal causes (racial oppression, for example) for Black people's social and
psychic pathologies (Jackson, *Gunnar Myrdal* 219). In that way, her approach
resembled that of scholars who held more nuanced views of Black culture
like Du Bois, Hurston, and Charles S. Johnson (who also trained in sociology
at the University of Chicago), and differed from novelist Richard Wright,
who like her, was also influenced by the Chicago School.[8]

Dunham embraced the New Negro/Boasian anthropological focus on heritage, but the Chicago School's evolutionary theories of culture also influenced
her. Robert Park, the Chicago School's leading scholar, argued that race relations
made a dynamic progression through four stages: competition, conflict, accommodation, and assimilation. Park argued that African Americans would eventually assimilate into American culture, but he also asserted that minority groups
could equally influence and transform the majority group as well (Jackson,
Gunnar Myrdal 95). While not as directly influential as Boas, Park helped re-
frame racialist and racist ideologies by shifting the emphasis from biological to
cultural explanations for racial difference. Also like Boas, he strove to establish
his discipline's legitimization by emphasizing empirical research and scientific
objectivity, and by refraining from attempts at social engineering. Dunham's
conventionally written ethnography conforms to all of these disciplinary expectations, but just as significantly she chose to depart from and implicitly challenge these standards in later works that deliberate more reflexively on
ethnographic constructions of other, non-Western cultures.

As a college student, however, Dunham worked directly and most
closely with Robert Redfield, a professor of social anthropology at the University of Chicago, who fueled her interest in the study of Caribbean dance
and culture. Because of a lecture given by Redfield at the University of
Chicago, Dunham grew interested in the African heritage of African American dance, yet his evolving interest in cultural and social acculturation also
made a lasting impression on her. Where Redfield referred to acculturation,
Park may have preferred the term assimilation, but in either case the Chicago
School's emphasis on the inevitability of cultural syncretism made its impression on Dunham. And finally, A. R. Radcliffe-Brown, who replaced Edward Sapir as chair of the department of anthropology at Chicago when
Sapir left to pursue a research project on the East Coast, contributed a British
perspective on social anthropology to Dunham's toolkit. Radcliffe-Brown
contended that the functions of social forms should be studied ahistorically,
in contrast to the Boasian approach, which emphasized historicity and other
contextualizing details. Radcliffe-Brown represented a school of researchers

who sought to generalize about universally held cultural truths by seeking commonalities across social behaviors of diverse cultures. From him, Dunham learned to ask about function, to look for the purpose and uses to which dance was put, and to seek out cross-cultural similarities, as she observed their performance in the Caribbean societies she visited.

The Ethnographic Gaze and the "Unplaceable" Diasporic Subject

In her choreography, Dunham strove to represent Afro-Caribbean dance in its "proper" contexts, something shared with her writings about culture, like "Dances of Haiti," *Island Possessed*, and *Journey to Accompong*. Her written work adds a layer of critical engagement to this project, however, by illuminating her role as translator and mediator between cultures. Dunham's writings belong to a tradition of feminist ethnography that makes explicit issues of positionality and is more ambivalent, and therefore implicitly critical, about claiming the ethnographer's scientific authority. Faye V. and Ira E. Harrison argue that these characteristics, combined with their blurring of generic boundaries like "social science and art, folklore and fiction, ethnography and autobiography, and social analysis and journalism," undermined the credentials they strove to attain in the academic establishment.[9] It is therefore all the more ironic that their ethnography anticipates and so closely resembles the "new" ethnography that emerged in the eighties in response to anthropology's crisis of representation.

Clifford asserts in *Writing Culture: The Poetics and Politics of Ethnography* that a new approach to ethnography would reject any claims to being unmediated, realistic reflections and records of culture and would acknowledge the tradition's legacy as a body of writing with all the attendant complexities of any attempt at representation.[10] In her introduction to the collection *Women Writing Culture*, Ruth Behar offers a summary of this period of crisis and its aims and then indicts it for the absence of women anthropologists. She argues that women who traversed the borders between anthropology and literature did so " 'illegally' as aliens who produced works that tended to be viewed in the profession as 'confessional' and 'popular. . . .' Even the personal voice, undermined when used by women, was given the seal of approval in men's ethnographic accounts, reclassified in more academically favorable terms as 'reflexive' and 'experimental.' "[11] In focusing on Dunham's contributions to the field of ethnography, I examine the ways she makes explicit the politics and power that accompany representations of the other and how her writing enacts a kind of deconstruction of the ethnographer's positionality, an endeavor which has clearly become a central concern for contemporary writings on and about culture.[12]

Approximately ten years after reconstructing Caribbean culture and dance for the American stage, Dunham wrote up and published her field-work as the ethnographic narrative, "Dances of Haiti," in 1947. Its publication contributed to a movement by Black intellectuals of the New Negro and Negritude movements to place Haiti and its revolutionary tradition within an emergent history of the African Diaspora. C. L. R. James's play *Toussaint L'Ouverture* opened in London in 1936; he published *The Black Jacobins* in 1938; Jacob Lawrence painted a series of paintings on Toussaint L'Ouverture between 1937 and 1938; and Langston Hughes wrote *Troubled Island* for the Federal Theatre. The recuperation of Haiti's revolutionary history appealed largely, although certainly not exclusively, to Black male intellectuals who embarked upon the construction of an alternative diasporic history by priv-ileging the island as a site of struggle and resistance. Black intellectuals con-structed this heroic and masculinocentric narrative of Haitian history to counter another, powerful narrative of Black savagery that made use of racial and gendered stereotypes: namely, the Black (implicitly male) savage and the idealized White and female victim. Joan Dayan recalls that in 1801, Pauline Bonaparte-Leclerc, the sister of Napoleon Bonaparte, accompanied her hus-band Victor-Emmanuel Leclerc as he set off on his mission to suppress the slave revolt on the island of Saint-Domingue. While her husband fought what would eventually be a losing battle to put down the revolt, Pauline lux-uriated in "lace, linen, silk, and sex" at the retreat her husband built for her on Isle de la Torture, Habitation Leclerc. Dayan uses this memory to medi-tate on "a strategic feminization of the tropics: the white lady necessary to the invention of the black threat."[13] The brutalization of Black people at Habita-tion Leclerc by these colonial masters was long submerged by the memory of Pauline's indulgences and luxurious surroundings. "Opulence and charm on one side, demonism and ferocity on the other. Haiti is one of those places all too easily represented by extremes" (282).

Dunham constructs yet another image of the island that mobilizes a rad-ically different symbol of the place and the women who define it. Rather than invoking male heroes or images of White female vulnerability, Dunham nar-rates Haiti as a feminized space in which African culture is carried and passed on largely through the ministrations of the women who shepherd Vodou ini-tiates through the rituals. For example, she describes her lave-tete, or initia-tion, ceremony in the following way: "I had seen gods only when already in possession of their 'horses,' not in that in-between limbo stage, which in the uncertain lamplight gave me the feeling that the god would emerge from between the priestess' wide-open legs and trickle into the ritually matted head of Alliance."[14] These images of women figuratively giving birth—to truth and the gods—invoke the proverbial motherland. This gesture toward African origins is consistent with her belief that Haitians and Vodou are closer to their African origins than other African Diasporic peoples.[15] According to Dunham, Haitian practitioners of Vodou shared the belief, or perhaps inculcated her with the notion, that she could get closer to these mythic origins through her initiation into Vodou. She writes in "Dances of Haiti":

When the stigma of being an American had worn off, there was great and protective interest in the recognition of my 'Guinea' blood tie, and great concern for my ancestors who had not received the proper ritual attention because that group of their brothers in the Caribbean and had forgotten these practices. In some instances . . . it seemed that the welfare of the entire negro race might be improved if these unfortunates to the north could be acquainted again with the rituals of ancestor worship and the *Vaudun*.[16]

This image reverses the stereotypical notion of a feminized island, open to foreign intervention, signified by the mambo's open legs. It offers instead a counter-narrative in which the island has something to offer to, and therefore some power over, the "unfortunates to the north" instead. Nonetheless, the memoir is more concerned than the ethnography with the reincorporation of the diasporic subject into the collective "African" body.

"Dances of Haiti" offers a brief history of the island, a description of Vodou ritual, and then an extensive discussion of the forms that Haitian sacred and secular dances take, as well as their functions. This discussion elucidates the ritual purposes for dance (to summon the *lwa*, or spirits, for instance), as well as psychological functions (for purposes of auto-intoxication, among others). She emphasized the centrality of dance to communal life and cultural identity, a foundational assumption in the field of dance anthropology. In "Dances of Haiti," the emphasis is always on the cultural aspect, the part—in this case the dance—that conveys something essentially true about the values, beliefs, and/or identity of the communal whole. To meet this goal, Dunham minimizes those experiences that troubled her attempts at narrative control, and positions the Caribbean as a site suitably isolated to allow for proper scientific study. For example, she depicts Haiti in "Dances of Haiti" as an appropriately primitive site of culture untouched by encounters with the outside world or by the corrupting engine of industrialization: "Excepting for differences of name and perhaps slight alterations in ritual significance, the dances of peasant Haiti today might well be those of slave Haiti in the 17th century" (5).

In contrast, in *Island Possessed*, Dunham's examines the limits and possibilities of African Diasporic connection in conjunction with exploring the culture shock she experienced as an outsider traveling to an unfamiliar society. Roy Wagner defines culture shock in such a way as to underscore not only the disorientation of encountering the other, but more importantly to highlight the invention of culture that such encounters enable: "In [culture shock] the local 'culture' first manifests itself to the anthropologist through his own inadequacy; against the backdrop of his new surroundings it is he who has become visible."[17] Dunham's work makes visible experiences of encounter and inadequate adaptation, and identifies communal and social differences as unique cultural phenomena. Wagner argues that the anthropologist is trained to manage feelings of disorientation and alienation by labeling differences cultural: "We might actually say that an anthropologist 'invents' the culture he believes himself to be studying, that the relation is more 'real' for being his particular acts and experiences than the things it 'relates'" (4).

Fieldwork required that Dunham inhabit liminal zones between cultures. Her discussions of that liminality suggest that the paradoxical experience of the participant-observer resides in the fact that her exceptional status as a privileged American in an impoverished, "third world" nation facilitated her attempts to gain access to communal settings and interactions typically closed to outsiders. In other words, being an outsider (the category the detached observer finds most enabling) cleared a space for her to assume the status of an insider (a necessary condition for her to fully participate in and gain knowledge of cultural mores). Describing herself as a lone young woman "easy to place in the clean cut American dichotomy of color, harder to place in the complexity of Caribbean color classifications," she finally names herself "an unplaceable, which I prefer to think of as 'noir'—not exactly the color black, but the quality of belonging with or being at ease with black people when in the hills or plains or anywhere and scrambling through daily life with them" (4). Not fitting local definitions of middle-class, Black womanhood allowed her to take part in activities usually restricted to Whites, men, or peasants—all classes of people to which she did not belong. We might go so far as to label her "unplaceable" within the field of anthropology because her ethnography disrupts and challenges its orthodoxies.

Although she is clearly pleased with the fluidity of social categories afforded her when she is away from home, she does problematize at an early stage of the narrative that access and mobility by associating conquest and invasion with her ethnographic venture. She introduces the text with the declaration, "It was with letters from Melville Herskovits, head of the Department of Anthropology at Northwestern University, that I invaded the Caribbean—Haiti, Jamaica, Martinique, Trinidad, passing lightly over the other islands, then Haiti again for the final stand for the real study" (3). While the association is made in the spirit of heroic adventure and conquest, its declaration just a year after the departure of the last American marines from Haitian soil (the U.S. occupied Haiti from 1915–34) would be highly provocative, especially when the memory of the occupation still stung. In contrast, "Dances of Haiti" begins: "In a consideration of the dances of the island of Haiti, accounts of early voyagers contain quantities of useful descriptive material from which it may be concluded that both the form and the function of these dances have remained relatively constant during the two centuries since the earliest records" (5). Although this introduction also begins with the historical fact of colonial expeditions onto the island and interaction with Haiti's population, in the memoir, Dunham makes the anthropologist's presence as a social and historical subject more visible and tangible, more immediate. Later in the memoir, Dunham will inscribe herself as unplaceable, located in a liminal zone between insides and outsides; yet her investment in exploring social and historical dynamics and events—as well as her own implication in these milieus—undercuts notions of cultural or diasporic identity grounded in essentialized origins. In lieu of understanding unplaceablity as synonymous with either exceptionalism or easy affinity, it is useful to imagine it as a description of the diasporic subject that encompasses the ambivalence, affiliation, disaffection, and ever present efforts at translation that attend the workings of race in social formations.

Dunham's description of the three-day initiation ceremony into a Vodou sect illustrates the paradoxes of the unplaceable subject. During the ritual, she is made to fast and maintain an uncomfortable position for long periods of time. The monotony of the long days is broken by the first possession (by Gede) of one in their midst. She writes that the *lwa's* (god's) obscene postures might have been amusing or exciting under other conditions:

But I was hungry and thirsty and thought only of how I would be able to swallow the sacrificial food to be brought around later in the morning and how I would avoid tasting whatever would be passed out again before the ordeal was over. Then to pass time I tried to figure out just how I happened to be here in the plains of the Cul-de-Sac not far from the capital of the island of Haiti at four in the morning wearing a nightgown wet by someone else's urine, chilled, disconsolate, feeling none of the promised ecstasy, and no signs of it, alien to gods, people and land. (65)

This is but one passage in which Dunham attempts to describe the sensation of existing on what she calls "the fringe border of belief and nonbelief" (105). Her open acknowledgement of the difficulties—at this point one might even call it impossibility—of assuming any measure of affinity with "the ancestors" or their keepers in Haitian Vodou casts a critical gaze on the complexities of interactions in the field, which were typically rendered invisible in order to underscore the ethnographer's authority; and illustrates the complexities of diasporic affiliation that Dunham's Afrocentric orientation might want to obscure.

What accounts for her willingness to write these moments of ambivalence into the narrative? I would argue that the participant-observation method posed a unique risk to the Black female ethnographer, who can never fully acquire the disembodied omniscience of the White male "scientist." Ruth Behar writes, "When a woman sits down to write, all eyes are on her. The woman who is turning others into the object of her gaze is herself already an object of the gaze" (2). Behar's language recalls the Du Boisian notion of double-consciousness, yet she discusses the predicament of women writers of culture without specifying the relevance of race. Black women, whose experiences of being at minimum doubly marginalized, experience the duality described by Behar (and Du Bois) especially keenly. What Dunham's narrative reveals, however, is that the risk of looking at an other, while recognizing that one is also subject to others' gazes, is a risk-taking act that can allow for other possibilities of recognizing and interacting with difference. Dunham's duality, which she describes elsewhere as "unplaceability," has generative consequences because it disrupts traditional hierarchies in the field (the Caribbean) and within her field of study (anthropology). The embodied ethnographer has a heightened awareness of the ways that the hegemonic gaze operates, and Dunham's turn to the memoir in 1967 makes possible her exploration of the politics of that gaze.

Her descriptions of her participation in Vodou rituals turn repeatedly, sometimes implicitly, sometimes explicitly, to the subject of looks and counter looks. Another example will suffice: Her initiation to the second stage of worship involves an offering to Dambala, her patron *lwa*, of his favorite food: a raw egg placed on top of a mound of flour. Dunham's anxiety rises to a pitch as she grapples with the fact that the sight and taste of raw eggs has always repulsed her, she has never experienced possession before, and views that fact as an indication of her inadequate belief. The eyes of the temple priest on her and feeling judged, Dunham decides to feign possession. I quote the relevant passage at length because I think it is revealing:

I froze for a moment, then went into action, inching and undulating in rhythm toward my sacrificial plate. I reached into it and tilting my head away from the houngan to cover my face, crushed the egg with my chin, praying to some Christian or at least non-vaudun god to come to my rescue, to work some miracle so that the dish would disappear or I would be able to overcome my repugnance, which was augmented by the fact that the egg was not fresh. The miracle did not happen. Julien watched me. . . . There was no way out. I heard the singing come to an end and felt fresh air on my face as the sheet was snatched back. A kata drummer had appeared and the staccato beat introduced a shoulder dance. I stood up, my face smeared with flour and egg, Dambala's offering untouched. Julien lifted my plate and took it to the houngfor, and when he returned the hounci and La place were in a frenzied 'zepaules, but I stood where he had left me, feeling sick and helpless as tears streamed through the flour and egg. Someone handed me a kerchief, I wiped my face and started to dance. I danced more than I have ever in my life, before or after. I danced out all my anger at unknown things and at myself for trying to know them, frustration at the rotten egg and weariness with strange mores. I found myself alone with one, with another, or just by myself while others clapped and sang and it dawned on me that it was with affection and encouragement. I hadn't dared look at Julien, but at last I did. He was puzzled, speculative, but benign. He nodded to me, and seemed to be telling me that everything was well, that the gods were happy, that things were now in my hands, even the decision as to how long we should dance. (234–35)

I find this passage illuminating for several reasons. First, it points to spirit possession as the edge over which this Westernized women cannot or will not cross. Dunham deliberately focuses on the complexities of participant observation, casting an unrelenting eye on her inability to understand and accept "strange mores" in the same narrative that seeks to explain those customs to the curious. The anxiety that pervades her initial description of this moment is shot through with her discomfort, her worry, about the threat of invasion, by the egg, the spirit, and the condemning gaze of the priest, Julien. In contrast, the end of the passage is a wonderful example of dance's function as cathartic expression. The idea of "dancing out" her disaffection, the ability to turn inward while engrossed in the movement, suggests that dance can be a space where the invasive gaze of others need not intrude. And ironically, this moment emerges in a written text in which the author feels compelled to contend with the perceptions and perspectives of the other. Dunham destabilizes the colonizing gaze of ethnography by recalling that the "native," Julien the temple priest, is not merely subject to the colonial gaze; he can not only look back at her, he also sits in judgment. *Island Possessed*'s achievement lies in its depiction of the failure of the anthropological gaze to manage the other by categorizing differences. Dunham's experiences testify to the multiple ways that communities and individuals insist on self-definition and resist imperialist powers' efforts to collect, contain, and delimit the meaning of their behaviors and their identities.

Dunham was interested in the thinness of the line between possession and performance. Her ethnographic writing and dance performances position her on the brink between possession (which demands the loss of self in the interest of group cohesion) and theatrical performance (which allowed for the retention of the notion of an autonomous artist-as-creator). In contrast, we might consider Charles Williams's staging of African dance during the early 1930s at Hampton Institute.[18] Williams, the athletic director at Hampton Institute, attended the performances of dancers from Nigeria, French Equatorial Africa, Algeria, the Belgian Congo, the French Congo, and "Kamaroon" at the 1933 Chicago Exposition, Century of Progress, a celebration of the world's scientific achievements with geographic exhibits on subjects ranging from the Walled City of China, to the Streets of Paris, and "Darkest Africa" (Perpener 85) These performers, including the Nigerian dancer, Abdul Assen, who would later appear as the witch doctor in Asadata Dafora's *Kyunkor*—the first staged performance of West African dance for mainstream American audiences—and the Royal Ashanti Ceremonial dancers and Drummers of Ghana, acted and danced in a model African village. Inspired by these performances, Williams returned to the Hampton Creative Dance Group, which he had organized, and choreographed many concerts in which he depicted an "idealized African community" (Perpener 97). Perpener argues that Williams's romanticized African ideal did not allow him to tolerate the kind of dance that might result in "disorderly outbreaks of spiritual possession" (97). It is exactly such outbreaks that fascinated Dunham, however, because they initiated the dissolution of personal boundaries that opened up spaces for collective bonds and values to take shape.

The passage about Dunham's "failure" to experience spirit possession offers another opportunity for connection and redemption. It suggests that dance offers a more acceptable avenue toward diasporic affinity for Dunham, one that allows both the singularity of experience and the collective solidarity that she craves, one that allows her to dance "alone with one, with another, or just by myself" (*Island*, 234) Here Dunham's description of one of the psychological functions of sacred dance in "Dances of Haiti" offers some insight for she argues that dance in sacred settings can function not only to "induce hypnosis," but also to allow the individual to experience "complete unity with the mystère, unity to such an extent that the body of the possessed becomes a temporary bode of the god" and to experience cult solidarity (49–50). According to Dunham, the Haitians she encountered instilled in her the notion that she could get closer to her African cultural origins through her initiation into Vodou. She came to the island with the idea that its "roots were still firmly planted in Africa, the motherland."[19] And in "Dances of Haiti," she writes:

When the stigma of being an American had worn off, there was great and protective interest in the recognition of my 'Guinea' blood tie, and great concern for my ancestors who had not received the proper ritual attention because that group of their brothers in the Caribbean had forgotten these practices. In some instances . . . it seemed that the welfare of the entire negro race might be improved if these unfortunates to the north could be acquainted again with the rituals of ancestor worship and the *Vaudun.* (9)

Despite this sense of redemption through cultural origins, Dunham resists simple essentialisms by reflecting on the outsider's feelings of cultural estrangement and problems decoding social and cultural mores. By positing culture as an interpretive field, she complicates primitivist constructions that assume a deep, pre-rational understanding that bypasses the need for acts of translation and interpretation.

At the same time, Dunham believed that dance had the potential to transcend linguistic, national, and political barriers, and she argued that "the arts, visual and performing, are, because of their freedom from language barriers among the most effective agents of contact, communication and persuasion."[20] Dunham's success as a performer led to her troupe being informally designated ambassadors of the African Diaspora. An anecdote recounted by Dunham's biographer Ruth Beckford serves to illustrate this point. In 1939, while the company was performing *Cabin in the Sky* at the Biltmore Theater in Los Angeles, Warner Brothers filmed it in a color short, *Carnival of Rhythm.* During the shooting, they noticed a conference among several rather distinguished-looking men, and later found out that someone had gone to the Brazilian Embassy and asked, "Are you going to let these colored people represent Brazil?" As a result, several embassy officials decided to watch the filming. The diplomats themselves were of mixed racial background and thus representative of one of Brazil's major races. After the viewing, they said that they were "charmed and pleased to see this presentation of the art of their country" (47).

The troupe's authority to represent Brazil was predicated on the accuracy of their choreography. And ironically, meeting expectations of cultural authenticity enabled these African American dancers to improvise and imagine an African Diasporic identity through dance. Beckford recounts how in 1965, upon traveling to Senegal, Dunham met with President Leopold Senghor, who told her that her company's appearance in Europe "had caused a cultural revolution that paralleled their political and economic revolution. Different people's chiefs-of-state in sub-Sahara Africa had been encouraged and inspired by her formula and format, adding course material from their own countries." Beckford concludes of the African students in Europe who comprised part of Dunham's audience, "They felt she belonged to them" (61). Dunham's company and its performances are repeatedly associated with the performance of a pan-African and/or Diasporic identity. Yet as Ramsay Burt reminds us, Dunham's motive for traveling to places in the Caribbean that retained traces of African cultural origins was to "re-establish a positive sense of American Negro identity" by demonstrating the cultural achievements in Black people's African heritage.[21]

One could argue that Dunham's facility with dance enabled her to achieve communal solidarity, but her experiences also taught her that any measure of belonging does not come automatically because of shared phenotype or pigmentation. In fact, Dunham can only conceive of some fantastical creature "still damp with sacrificial blood from his own temples and scared with tribal markings and jangling gris-gris from neck to ankle, as is the custom in Africa, [that] could so impart his 'belongingness'" (59). If such an individual could ever exist (and it is clear from Dunham's satiric tone that she does not believe that to be possible), then he would still, she states, have to submit to the protocol of the local vaudun, of which the Haitians are very proud. While Dunham strives to conceive of a diasporic consciousness that acknowledges belongingness as much as it recognizes its own fragmentation and exile, she nonetheless suggests that a diasporic consciousness is constructed not only through the recuperation of lost memory, but also through the acquisition of knowledge and a willingness to submit one's self to the will and ways of others. This formulation suggests a give and take, a surrender of one's autonomy, that flies in the face of Western ethnographic and artisitc paradigms.

Dance, Identity, and the Black Female Body

Dunham's approach to dance revealed a range of complexity and meaning in Black bodies and physical movement that was not always recognized in conventional portrayals of Black dancers. During the Harlem Renaissance, writers and artists habitually portrayed the dancer's body as a site of and medium for the African American's atavistic connection to her African roots. Claude McKay's "The Harlem Dancer" (1917) depicts a Black woman who suffers the indignities of being sexually objectified by a careless audience composed of "applauding youths [who] laughed with young prostitutes" as they watch her "half-clothed body sway."[22] The dancer remains aloof from this scene of debauchery, and the poet salvages her dignity with tropical imagery ("To me she seemed a proudly-swaying palm") that suggests that she possesses an idealized, natural, and Africanist beauty that her audience does not recognize. Dance historian John Perpener remarks that poets like McKay and Langston Hughes depict the dancer, always female, as "basking in sensuality and free from the shackles of modern society" (17). In cases such as these, stereotypical notions of Black women's sexuality converged with notions of modern industrial society's depleted spirit to result in representations of the Black dancing female body as vital and sensual.

It is important to note that when we refer to Black dance in the twenties, thirties, and forties, whether looking at literary examples or at those from stage and screen, the most popular images were of Black vernacular dances and dancers because dance crazes, such as the fox-trot and cake walk, swept the nation and Black dancers performed with regularity and much acclaim in cabarets and on vaudeville.[23] Katherine Dunham holds a prominent place in histories of this period and in histories of modern dance because her choreography combined modernist notions of primitivity with explicit challenges to the widely held assumptions that Blacks had an innate and natural aptitude for dance and not much else; certainly nothing that required advanced intellectual or artistic abilities. In contrast to these essentialist ideas, Dunham suggested that Black dance, both religious and secular, was sophisticated and had to be learned through rigorous practice and sustained exposure to cultural mores; that these dance traditions could have a legitimate place on the American concert stage; and that dance could provide a lexicon with which to articulate a modern Black subjectivity.

Not only did Renaissance writers link Black dance to Africa and femininity to signify "natural" eroticism and sensuality, some also recognized that dance was a social phenomenon, so they used it to imagine the formation of communal identities. For example, in Nella Larsen's *Quicksand*, the protagonist Helga Crane finds herself in a storefront church in Harlem at a moment of emotional crisis.[24] Larsen describes a world of lower-class Black religiosity that is fearsome in its relinquishment of reason and control: "So she stayed, listening to the fervent exhortation to God to save her and to the zealous shoutings and groanings of the congregation. Particularly she was interested in the writhings and weepings of the feminine portion, which seemed to predominate. Little by little the performance took on an almost Bacchic vehemence. Behind her, before her, beside her, frenzied women gesticulated,

screamed, wept, and tottered to the praying of the preacher, which had gradually become a cadenced chant" (113). In this passage the body and its movement are pivotal to Helga's transformation from nonbeliever to (temporary)
believer. While Larsen does not identify with any particular denomination or
forms of worship, one can surmise from the setting and description that this
is a Black church by the congregation's physical and vocal expressiveness.
Dunham has noted that some North American religious forms of expression
resemble West Indian religious rituals, like Vodou, in which dance plays a
central role. Of the storefront churches in North American cities, Dunham
had this to say: "The rhythmic percussion-type hand-clapping and foot-
stamping, the jumping and leaping, the 'conversion' or confession in unknown tongues which is a form of possession or ecstasy . . . , the frequent
self-hypnosis by motor-activity of the shoulders—all these African forms
were present. . . . In general form, even in function, the motor activity connected with the religious expression of 'store-front' churches in this country
is strikingly similar to that of the Haitian peasant."[25] Helga's religious conversion, temporary though it may be, occurs in response to the other women's
physical movements, which lead to her own feelings of spirit possession and
her attendant loss of reason, apparently leading her to go against all the cosmopolitan, avant-garde values she had previously held. This spiritual transformation is instrumental in motivating the defiantly, yet ambivalently,
individualistic Helga's last-ditch attempt to become fully a part of a Black
community. Thus, her religious conversion is the catalyst for her marriage to
a minister, their move to Alabama, and the births of the five children, which
will eventually lead to her physical and spiritual depletion. One could argue
that the church women's ritualistic, improvisational dance possesses Helga
with the desire for community because they act out physically a social cohesion and sensual expressivity that Helga is keenly aware of lacking in her own
life. But Larsen's skepticism about the loss of autonomy that such a conversion demands, again signified by dance that emphasizes somatic expression
over the rational workings of the mind, endows this pivotal moment with an
ominous undertone.

Like Larsen, Zora Neale Hurston identified in dance the potential for
creating communal bonds through dance. But her depiction of collective
identity formed near the end of *Their Eyes Were Watching God* is far less pessimistic and wary of a loss of self than Larsen's. In the novel, Hurston describes how Bahamians and Black Americans working in the Everglades
overcome their initial trepidation over each other's foreignness by dancing
together. The chapter that introduces Mrs. Turner and the divisive power of

her color-struck beliefs actually begins with an image of danced affiliation. Janie, Hurston tells us, "began to look around and see people and things she hadn't noticed during the season. For instance during the summer when she heard the subtle but compelling rhythms of the Bahaman drummers, she'd walk over and watch the dances. She did not laugh the 'Saws' to scorn as she had hear the people doing in the season."[26] Janie's openness to another community's rhythms signals her openness to difference and anticipates her eventual rejection of Mrs. Turner's attempts to cordon her off from the darker and poorer members of the Everglades community. Both Hurston and Larsen explore dynamics in communities that are stratified by class and ethnic divisions, and they create characters who wrestle with feelings of alienation from and struggle to identify with the communities they enter. Passages that evoke these negotiations using images of dance make brief, but memorable appearance in each text because the Harlem Renaissance artists were concerned not only with the form but also the function of dance in African American communities.

Form, Function, and the Meaning of Tradition: Authenticity on the Concert Stage

Dunham took up and explored through dance similar questions of identity and community formation. The Dunham technique, a dance idiom that combines Caribbean and African dance forms with ballet and modern dance, performs the vibrancy of syncretic cultural fusion at the same time that it was used to create a portrait of an authentic Afro-Caribbean culture and subjectivity. Many of Dunham's most well-known stage pieces, such as *L'Ag'Ya* (1938) and *Rites de Passage* (1943), incorporate the knowledge she gained of Caribbean dance after conducting anthropological fieldwork, and are propelled by narrative and thematic threads that provide context and meaning for the dance. Because her choreography sought to reclaim, recreate, and universalize African and Caribbean traditions that had long been considered lost to African Americans, we can view Dunham's performances as attempts to enunciate an African Diasporic identity in which the body functions as the medium for the transmission of tradition. Dunham's stage and film work can be read as performances of culture that not only transmit, but also reinvent collective identities.[27]

Dunham stressed authenticity in her performances of culture, emphasizing the importance of knowing both dance forms and their function.[28] At the same time, the staging of her choreography could just as easily refuse to conform to the demands of realism, particularly in the dancer's costumes. While in some pieces the troupe would appear in typical "island" garb (*Carnival of Rhythm*, for example), in others (like *Rites de Passage*) they might be dressed in costumes that brought together the aesthetics of classical antiquity, the spare lines of modern dress, and the natural fibers of traditional African clothing. The flexibility of Dunham's imagination in staging these works did not detract from her desire to represent Afro-Caribbean dance authentically, for she considered the most realistic representation of the dance to convey the social and psychological meaning of movement, even as those movements were moved from their original cultural contexts, and were assumed to possess a universal significance. This particular understanding of authenticity, knowing and communicating why "primitive" people danced, Dunham believed would distinguish her work from the mainstream representations of primitive and exotic others. She wrote, "It never seemed important to portray as such the behavior of other peoples, as exotics. But the cultural and psychological framework, the 'why' became increasingly important. It became a matter of course to attack a stage or production situation in the same way in which I would approach a new primitive community or work to analyze a dance category."[29]

Dunham's production of *L'Ag'Ya* illustrates how she put authenticity to use. *L'Ag'Ya*, named after a Martiniquan fighting dance, was commissioned by the Federal Theatre Project and premiered on January 27, 1938. It opens in a typical village. The audience witnesses the courting of a beautiful girl, Lalouse, in the marketplace; the second scene, set in the jungle, introduces a villainous rival, Julot, who uses witchcraft to seduce the girl; and the third scene features the *Ag'Ya*, during which the hero, Alcide, and villain battle for the object of their mutual desire. This dance is based on footage Dunham filmed while conducting fieldwork in Martinique. The ethnographic film captures a ritual fighting dance called the *Ag'Ya*. In it men dance with a loose limbed, bent-kneed, rhythmic bounce; at some unspoken, mutually agreed upon moment, they strike out in a series of jabs, roundhouse kicks, and swipes of the hands and feet. The film shows drummers and audiences typically composed of men, but occasionally including women and children. The footage that precedes the demonstration of the Ag'Ya emphasizes geographic landmarks like the sea and the mountains and social settings like the local market. The images that follow are of couples, and occasionally individuals, performing social dances like the beguine. In her staged interpretation of this footage, Dunham translated and interpolated the movement into a romance narrative that has elements of courtship, romantic rivalry, conflict (during which the Ag'Ya is danced), and denouement.

Dunham's investment in translating Caribbean dance clearly called for some obvious level of mediation. There is obviously a difference that can be discerned between a peasant woman walking along a country path, goods balanced gracefully on her head as she marches to the marketplace, and the rolling, majestic, signature "Dunham walk," which she modeled after such women and which all dancers trained in the Dunham technique are taught to do. The walk, like the dances themselves, sought to capture something essential either in the character of the movements or in the significance they held at the same time that it sought to render the everyday into the aesthetically pleasing. Dunham then translated that perceived essence into a coherent narrative whole. VèVè Clark argues that Dunham's performances should be read as sites that "perform the memory of difference"—between modern dance/ballet and Old World/New World, for example—and that "envision modernism" (194–97).[30] Recognizing the performative aspect of the dances Dunham witnessed in Martinique, as well as of the dances she choreographed upon her return, Clark argues that critics' expectation that she would represent regional dances in a documentary form is "irrelevant, because it fails to understand that Caribbean dance has been stylized and transformed throughout its history" (191). This approach compels us to recognize that ritual dance performance does more than transmit; it invents the memory, and thus the identity of African Americans. That act of translation required that Dunham seek both cultural continuities and discontinuities in the Caribbean.

Thus, in a 1939 *Esquire* article about the Ag'Ya, written under the pseudonym, Kaye Dunn, Dunham stated, "I continue to think of the sons of Nigeria."[31] Yet, she also acknowledges that the reasons for dancing may change over time: "The Earth Mother is appeased. Her sons have forgotten the significance of this dance, but the blood of their ancestors is strong. They have not forgotten the dance" (49). The overt reasons for performing the ritual may change with historical and geographical shifts—they may even be *forgotten*—but Dunham's attunement to the psychological functions of dance led her to discern that it could fulfill certain, essential functions regardless of changes in time, space, or venue. The anthropological training she received taught her to perceive the universal emotional experiences, patterns of expression, and historical perspective to "discern the developing motifs and consistent trends" in many kinds of dance, whether performative or ritualistic (56).

If Dunham sought to "recreate the dances as authentically as possible" for the stage, this project was inevitably complicated by the change in setting.

The performance may recreate the village, in other words, but it is not the village; and that discrepancy inevitably changes the function that Dunham argued was wedded to dance form in African and Caribbean cultures. Thomas minimizes the significance of Dunham's transformation of ritual competition into a cathartic act that resolves her dance plot's dramatic conflict by arguing that she captures the "ethos" of the original ritual.[32] The suggestion is that an essential meaning can be culled from the source material that is then translatable to other settings if the dance fills a similar function in its new environs. To illustrate the point, Dunham has argued, "What would be the connection between the carnival dance, whose function is sexual stimulus and release, and almost any similar situation in a Broadway musical—for example, the temptation scene on the River Nile in *Cabin in the Sky*? It would be the similarity in function, and through this similarity in function the transference of certain elements of form would be legitimate" ("Thesis Turned Broadway" 57). What *I* am arguing is that the process of translation also creates new possibilities of signification that are only visible when we relinquish the hold on the language of authenticity.

This is a possibility that Dunham flirted with, but which she often turned away from in favor of the more reassuring picture of unchanging tradition that she painted, for example, in the *Esquire* article. In that piece, for example, she privileged dance that took place in intimate settings, untainted by the prying curiosity of an audience of outsiders and uncorrupted by money as a motive for movement. For Dunham, the Ag'ya in its purest form arose naturally, in a fishing village, as part of a continuum of the community's dance "vocabulary." It might, for example, follow a morning of commerce conducted among fisherman, marketwomen, and housewives, after one such character has danced the *beguine*, a creole dance. Dunham's ethnographic training conditioned her to perceive traditional cultures and their primarily oral and bodily retentions, what Pierre Nora described as "environments of memory," as on the verge of disappearance. Thus her recreation of this scene for the stage can be understood as a site of memory, a "moment of history torn away from the movement of history."[33] Dunham implies that modernity imposes on Martinique's traditional culture a different and compromising set of conditions against which the dance is performed, as part of an economic exchange or captured by the voyeuristic gaze of the tourist: "No lurid spectacle under flickering kerosene torches, while callow-faced men place a piece for the breaking of a companion's skull. No exhibition for the tourist to come and see and feel a little ill and go away and write about the savage beat of the tom-tom, the bloody attacks of the two naked combatants, and the mad, primitive frenzy of the onlookers" (46–47). This understanding of the authentic as insular clearly played a role in her choreographed piece, which borrowed from the memory recounted for Esquire's readers: The marketplace setting and communal dynamics are all recreated for the stage performance. But as Roach reminds us, "collective memory works selectively" (2). In this case the notion of insularity obscures the fact that cultures inevitable perform themselves in opposition to others; they "[perform] what and who they thought they were not" (5).

Dunham remarked in a 1938 interview with Frederick Orme, "the value of transplanting the dance as such is mostly educational. My West Indian examples, so far have been authentic, but my ultimate achievement must be to modify this, that it may be applicable to whichever theme I choose."[34] Dunham considered her greatest achievement to be proving the translatability of primitive movement and tradition, so that one could educate the audience to become cognizant of the functional, ritual, ceremonial, or recreation values of movement. This would presumably place primitive or folk movement on par with classical and modern dance in their expressive capabilities. This is an understanding not always shared by Dunham's viewers. For example, New York Times dance critic John Martin praised a performance by the Dunham Company not for its psychological or emotional expressivity, but for its presentation of what he saw as the release of pure, natural physicality: "There is nothing pretentious about [the Negro dance]; it is not designed to delve into philosophy or psychology but to externalize the impulses of a high-spirited, rhythmic and gracious race. That Miss Dunham's dances accomplish this end so beautifully can mean only that she has actually isolated the element of a folk art upon which more consciously creative and sophisticated form can be built as time goes on."[35] Although both reviewer and performer considered folk materials to be the building blocks of high art, they diverged in that Dunham considered those materials to contain the purest expression of philosophical thought or psychological yearning, suitable and sophisticated materials for the artistic expression of human, not just Black, experience.

It is possible to read competing narratives of African American identity through dance. Thomas, for example, notes that White filmmakers traditionally filmed Black dance "to provoke laughter." Audiences frequently filtered performances by Blacks through stereotyping lenses. Thus, despite the complexity and sophistication of Dunham's choreography, her performances were often interpolated by viewers into exoticizing discourses, as evidenced by one reviewer who described her Haitian ceremonial dances as being illustrative of "the very essence of mysterious primitive humanity."[36]

Other critics frequently misread the dancers' pelvic movements as titillating and sensationalistic, like John Martin of the *New York Times*, who winkingly warned readers, "better not take grandma!" at the end of his largely positive review (65).

Nonetheless, the concert stage did offer opportunities to create alternatives to the entertainment industry's formulaic performances of Black dance and identity. For example, Edna Guy, Allison Burroughs, and Lenore Cox organized the Negro Dance Evening in March 1937, introducing Black dancers to the White concert stage and, according to Julia Foulkes, announcing a "call to independence" by revealing the Africanist roots of (African) American dancing. The concert progressed from the dances of Africa to slave dancing, spirituals, social dances such as the lindy hop, and concluded with modern dance pieces. Foulkes argues that "the variety of dance styles, and particularly the inclusion of more abstract modern dance, went beyond stereotypes of the natural dancing ability of African Americans—most commonly associated with tap and social dancing—although the dancers and choreographers of the evening did not deny these traditions either."[37] The concert stage, then, was viewed as a performance space that allowed for an oppositional construction of African American identity, in contrast to the images of Blackness transmitted on film and in vaudeville. Dunham and her troupe appeared in this concert, and their performances—like that of all the featured performers—functioned as living memory. They resisted the forms of forgetting characteristic of modernity, and revealed themselves to be improvisational and creative in the sense of imagining new possibilities for African-derived subjectivities. Yet these efforts, like all attempts to present Black dance as serious art was met with mixed reviews, at times praised for its artistic innovation, at other times viewed cryptically as evidence of the inadequacy of Blacks who were accused of acting as "cultural interlopers."[38]

From Stage to Screen: New Negro Identity and the Hollywood Musical

If Dunham's stage performances were generally celebrated for their innovation and respectful presentation of folk traditions, the reception of her film choreography is more fraught. Foulkes recounts how, as Dunham performed in Hollywood musicals in the early 1940s, her reputation was diminished in some circles. She writes, "the worry masked a concern that Dunham had fallen sway to white ideals of entertainment, copying their idea of dance for African Americans—with its emphasis on sexual provocation—and losing the racial originality she had possessed earlier" (76). In *Carnival of Rhythm* for example, the female dancers wear swirling skirts and brightly colored head wraps; and the men show off their virility by baring their chests. This sketch of Brazilian life centers on a man and woman's flirtation with and seduction of each other. The short ends with the suggestion that their romance will be consummated. Sexual desire, sensuality, and freedom are all associated with the dancers' dark bodies and rhythmic, Africanist movements. The film exoticizes and romanticizes their "primitive" sexuality, yet there is something disconcerting about Dunham's almost aggressively wide and frozen smile in the opening shot of the film. Rather than drawing the viewer in, it undercuts the voiceover narration's celebration of Third World sexuality as a dance of seduction that might include the viewer.

Thomas asserts that if her film choreography fell short of her stage work, the fault lay in her lack of authorial and directorial control: "When Dunham was invited to Hollywood in 1941, she came as choreographer, performer, and camera person. Her discrete experiences with the Hollywood studios were less than satisfying: she was particularly displeased with the stilted and unimaginative camera shots of her Company in most of the films. Nor was she unaware that the dances in most of the feature length films were additive, not an integral part of the story" (115). Hollywood convention undercut Dunham's efforts to bind form and function in her choreography, often reducing it to its most base and simplistic uses where rhythmic isolations were linked to sexual impulses. At first glance, it might seem that dance in the 1943 film *Stormy Weather* is even less concerned with conveying authentic contextual meaning than it was in *Carnival of Rhythm*, serving merely as ornament. The plot barely holds together except to give the characters a reason to dance or otherwise perform. Essentially a musical revue, the film holds more in common with a dance concert than with a typical film since plot is second in importance to movement, and the movement tells the story.

The film is loosely based on the life of Bill Robinson. Robinson portrays the protagonist, Bill Williamson, who recounts his memories of starting out in the business and eventual success. This narrative is coupled with a romantic plot that could be summarized as such: Bill and Selina Rogers (the latter played by Lena Horne) get together, break up, and get back together again. Yet despite the thin narrative construction, a second narrative, what I would call a danced narrative, can be discerned about New Negro progression into modernity. The couple's travels from implicitly Southern spaces to wider urban and cosmopolitan circles parallel, in other words, that of the New Negro described by Alain Locke.[39] Yet the narrative differs from that presented in *L'Ag'Ya* and the Negro Dance Evening in that it is neither linear nor cohesive. Instead, it is characterized by fragmentation, disruption, and ellipsis. A pseudo-Africanistic number, for example, presents characters beating drums, garbed in tribal costumes, and making use of the isolations typical of this dance tradition. While it happens relatively early in the story, it is presented as a cabaret act, taking place in the present, and it speaks more to Bill and Selina's burgeoning romance than it does to any historical narrative of urbanity and progress. In fact, by equating the characters' almost subliminal romantic desires with sexuality, and appealing to a mainstream audience's association of Black sexuality with primitivity, there is an obvious, and non-ironic, use of stereotype in this story. It mirrors, then, Dunham's description of spectacle and commodification as corrupting influences on the functions to which dance can be put and minimizes the subject of African origins of African American dance.

Dunham's sole appearance in the film is equally elliptical, but it also provides a striking assertion of Black Modernity. She performs during the famous "Stormy Weather" scene in which Lena Horne sings the solo looking out of a window into a stormy night. The camera then cuts away from a close-up of Selina to a shot outside of the window against which she stands, and onto the rain-drenched streets where we see a handful of prostitutes and their customers lingering under a street lamp. Film lore has it that the film's director, Andrew Stone, wanted Dunham's choreography to retain the focus on the prostitutes, but she refused. As opposed to the *Ag'Ya*, this is not the performance of memory but the performance of abstraction. We are suddenly in a dream world in which the dancers, dressed in costumes that refuse historical specificity, move in the fluid, multidimensional ways characteristic of early twentieth-century modern dance. To argue that this sequence is modern in its abstraction is not to advocate a notion of primitivism as the polar opposite of modernity. For, as Burt argues, the sequence moves from balletic choreography to the Africanist isolations characteristic of the Dunham technique. Yet we see none of the Caribbean dress, or vernacular movements and rhythms typical of Dunham's most celebrated pieces. The sequence disrupts the plot by refusing historical specificity; it is a performance that forces the viewers' attention to the aesthetic dimensions of the dance. In so doing we see a rejection of stereotypical representations of Black characters (the Jezebel, in this case) and the construction of a modern Black subject that refuses narrow categorization. In this way, it may have something in common with the tap performance in the film's penultimate number, which features the virtuosic Nicholas Brothers dancing to the Cab Calloway

Orchestra's "Jumpin' Jive." Arthur Knight reads this performance as a leap into modernity: "Their athletic, acrobatic dance takes the energies of all the performances that have preceded them, encapsulates and embodies those energies, and attempts—quite literally—to take performance *vertical*, not just to carry *on* but to carry *out*, to carry *over*, to carry *beyond*" (156).

Nonetheless, the film's structure denies the possibility of considering the future without pausing to look backward to the past. Robinson narrates his story to a group of children gathered in his home. Both Robinson's present-day success and wealth, and his more homely beginnings are represented by the house, whose pristine grandeur signifies professional success and material wealth at the same time that its simple architecture, porch, and prominently placed rocking chair signify the warmth of home and vernacular traditions such as storytelling associated with the star's humble origins. At one point, the group of children and Robinson practice some steps on the front porch, signifying the passing on of vernacular culture from an elder to the youth. The more earthbound hoofing of Robinson provides a counterpoint to the gravity-defying Nicholas brothers. Knight asserts that "any vestige of the rural or low, and certainly any explicit trace of blackface minstrelsy, is banished and replaced by the urbane" (118). But Bill *is* the central character, and it is important to note that past and future are tightly bound together in the story's structure of reminiscence. In other words, Robinson goes home at the moment that marks his successful ascent in show business, and he passes his knowledge, and his memories, onto the children some of whom will presumably follow in his footsteps. Knight argues that the virtue of *Stormy Weather*'s merging of a biopic and backstage musical is that it "allows history and memory into the form and thus makes carrying on— in the sense of continuing, persisting—a subject" (155). The interaction between old and young serve as reminders that, especially against the backdrop of enslavement and ensuing displacement, New World African memory and culture have been transmitted through the body.

Dance proves itself to be, on stage and in film, living memory, both resistant to the forms of forgetting characteristic of modernity, and revealing itself to be improvisational and imaginative. *L'Ag'Ya* and *Stormy Weather* seem so different: one employs narrative fragmentation and dances a story of urbanity; the other is more linear in its narration and is rooted in tradition. Yet, both are engaged in similar projects of imagining an oppositional, radically new Black subjectivity that both transmits and recreates history in terms of art that remembers.

Chapter 7
Narrative Dissonance: Conflict and Contradiction in Hurston's Caribbean Ethnography

Zora Neale Hurston's southern roots and anthropological traing make her a key figure in this study. She and Katherine Dunham knew of each other and had even met when Hurston attended a party thrown by Dunham in Chicago, but personal differences and regional separation kept them largely apart. Nonetheless, their careers overlap in ways that are remarkable and noteworthy. Like Dunham, Hurston worked with Melville Herskovits, Franz Boas's student and colleague. She assisted both men in the two summers preceding her graduation from Barnard by measuring the heads of African Americans in Harlem in order to disprove the assumption that Blacks lacked the cranial capacity and intelligence of people of European descent.[1] Hurston's contributions to Boas's project of providing a scientific basis for disproving notions of racial inferiority included not only the study of Harlemites' physiognomy, but also the collections of Negro folklore she would go on to produce. Boas used these materials as evidence for his argument that "historical events rather than race appear to have been more potent in leading races to civilization than their faculty, and it follows [that] the achievements of races do not warrant us to assume that one race is more highly gifted than others" (225).[2] The anthropological theories that he articulated etched a permanent imprint on Hurston whose own writing revealed their academic affinities. For example, in her autobiography *Dust Tracks on a Road*, she wrote: "It seemed to me that the human beings I met reacted pretty much the same to the same stimuli. Different idioms, yes. Circumstances and conditions having the power to influence, yes. Inherent difference, no."[3]

Boas and Herskovits's influence on Hurston extended beyond the concept of cultural relativism to include the importance of African survivals in New World Black cultures. Prompted by this research focus, Hurston applied for and received a fellowship from the Guggenheim Foundation "to make an exhaustive study of Obeah (magic) practices . . . to add to and compare with what I have already collected in the United States."[4] By April 1936, she was in Jamaica collecting folklore and writing. Her research agenda took her along many of the same routes followed by Dunham just a year earlier.[5] Like Dunham, Hurston aimed to represent African American and Afro-Caribbean cultures in a populist format, thus she did not limit herself to writing academic texts for scholarly venues. In addition to staging concerts, such as *The Great Day*, that showcased the songs and lore she collected during her folklore collecting trips in Florida, she also tended to include in her ethnographies, *Mules and Men* and *Tell My Horse*, contextualizing details about social dynamics among her informants, and between herself and her informants that were designed to capture the interest of the nonacademic reader. In a letter dated August 20, 1934, in which she asked Franz Boas to write the introduction to *Mules and Men*, Hurston wrote, "So I hope that the unscientific matter that must be there for the sake of the average reader will not keep you from writing the introduction. It so happens that the conversations and incidents are true. But of course I never would have set them down for scientists to read. I know that the learned societies are interested in the story in many ways that would never interest the average mind. He needs no stimulations. But the man in the street is different" (Kaplan 308). The "unscientific matter" added to the richness of *Mules and Men*, which represents Hurston at her best as a folklorist. The narrative is full of details of Floridian Black life. It also paints a precise picture of the negotiations Hurston had to perform in order to ingratiate herself into the life of the communities she studied, and provides a complex analysis of the social dynamics within each of those communities.

On the other hand, *Tell My Horse*, the ethnography she wrote upon her return from the Caribbean, provides a more conflicted representation of Hurston as ethnographer, and a more problematic depiction of the societies under scrutiny. Joyce Aschenbrenner argues that Dunham was more successful at integrating herself into the peasant and elite social circles of Haitian society, resulting in a narrative that is more nuanced, subtle, and respectful than Hurston's. In contrast, Hurston seemed unable or unwilling to get close to any individuals other than the urban elite and American expatriates that she relied on as her informants. Despite the obvious flaws of this narrative, I will argue in this chapter that these contradictions are the most interesting and critically engaging aspects of the work.

Hurston is occasionally, but certainly not always, intentional in producing or exposing the moments of conflict and contradiction in her fieldwork. Regardless of her narrative control, reading *Tell My Horse* compels the reader to question the idea of the ethnography as an objective and unmediated narrative, and implicates the genre as an instrument of imperialist containment. Kevin Meehan argues that Hurston's greatest contribution to anthropological writing and theory is her exposure of "the implicatedness of ethnographic projects (including her own) in imperialist political economy and [her movement] to decolonize ethnography by manipulating it away from a tendency to represent native populations as exotic and dependent Others."[6] To make this case, with which I tend to agree, is not to suggest that Hurston was hostile to the ethnographic project. Her biographer, Robert Hemenway, recalls the extent of Hurston's appreciation of Boas, who she called "king of kings" and "the greatest anthropologist alive" (63). He also argues that Boas's science "provided a taxonomy for her childhood memories" (63). Yet Meehan is correct in asserting "even progressive and radical ethnographers must contend with the way in which anthropological labor helps manage the transition from direct colonial rule to indirect neocolonial domination . . . by packaging indigenous cultures" (259). Meehan concludes that Hurston's response to this dilemma was a disengagement from "ethnography's codification/commodification program" (260), but drawing this conclusion appears to me to read a consistent point of view into the narrative that is difficult to support. It seems more precise to focus on the text's uneven or conflicted perspective, what I call its narrative dissonance. Hurston makes full use of her ethnographic authority, while signaling in occasional and oblique ways her skepticism toward the ethnographic project. Because she was doubly marginalized as an African American and a woman, her efforts to perform the ethnographer's role became a delicate and fraught operation. The ethnographer's assumed omniscience, invisible and simultaneously all seeing, ran directly in opposition to the double-consciousness she certainly experienced as a woman of color. The narrative effect of these conflicting ways of seeing and being seen is a disorienting fragmentation of the narrative. Does *Tell My Horse* depict another culture in all of its complexity, or is it a racist and ethnocentric text that lacks any merit? Depending on the point of the view of the reader, the conclusion drawn can easily be either of these.

I want to suggest that both of these interpretations have merit precisely because *Tell My Horse* shows Hurston speaking in multiple registers to different, at times conflicting, audiences. The narrative's unwieldy juxtaposition of different modes of narration and different points of view has the effect of narrative dissonance.[7] The result has been a long critical reception that is often scathing or dismissive, and occasionally appreciative of the narrative's strengths. The textual quality that I am calling dissonance, Hurston might have identified as asymmetry, a "definite feature," she claims of Negro art. In

"Characteristics of Negro Expression," she uses musical metaphors to elucidate the concept of asymmetry, describing it as "the abrupt and unexpected changes. The frequent change of key and time [that] are evidences of this quality in music" (835).[8] The narrative equivalent of these abrupt and unexpected changes would be Hurston's movement from ethnocentric travel narrative, to naïve political commentary to respectful and complex rendering of Vodou ritual. Critics have typically had a number of responses to the text's dissonance: aversion (Hazel Carby's critique of Hurston's ethnographic imperialism, for instance), selective "listening" (Ishmael Reed's praise of and almost exclusive focus on the narrative's contributions to scholarship on Vodou and New World Black cultures being one example) and the imposition of "sonic" uniformity (for instance, Rachel Stein and Kevin Meehan's tracing of Hurston's feminist politics as a unifying theme throughout the text's disparate parts).

But Hurston offers another model of reading (or listening) in her analysis of asymmetry as a characteristic of African American expressive culture, namely searching for the paradoxical presence of rhythm in asymmetry. She writes, "The presence of rhythm and lack of symmetry are paradoxical, but there they are. Both are present to a marked degree. There is always rhythm, but it is the rhythm of segments. Each unit has a rhythm, of its own, but when the whole is assembled it is lacking in symmetry. But easily workable to a Negro who is accustomed to the break in going from one part to another, so that he adjusts himself to the new tempo" (835). *Tell My Horse* demands that its reader adjust to new tempos, all the while searching for the internal rhythm in each of its parts. It compels the reader to accept the paradox, while working to make sense of the whole. Rather than amplifying the troublesome frame to the Vodou ethnography (which consists of Hurston's impressions of travel in Jamaica and Haiti and her description of the Haitian coup and rebellion that incited the U.S. military's takeover of the island in 1915), or minimizing its import in favor of focusing on her representation of Vodou, I want to suggest that the frame's ethnocentric and imperialist politics provide a context for understanding the social and political attitudes that influence the production of anthropological knowledge in the United States.

Haiti in the African American Imagination

Hurston's fieldwork in Haiti captured the attention of her readers because the island's history of anti-colonial insurrection and political turmoil inclined Americans to consider it the proverbial heart of darkness. The international reaction to the slave insurrection (1791–1804) that liberated San Domingo from French colonial rule was swift and brutal, with an almost total isolation of Haiti from global politics.[9] The proliferation of stereotypes about Haitian barbarism can be understood as a discursive response that corresponded to the geopolitics. In the thirties, fiction, travel literature, and film perpetuated a host of negative images:

> Popular books of the day, with such charming titles as *Cannibal Cousins* and *Black Baghdad*, cast the entire nation [Haiti] as a caricature, an impoverished land of throbbing drums ruled by pretentious buffoons and populated by swamp doctors, licentious women, and children bred for the cauldron. . . . There were many of these books, and each one conveyed an important message to the American public—any country where such abominations took place could find its salvation only through military occupation.[10]

As in the U.S. context, Black anthropologists saw their work as responding and providing alternatives to such images of stereotypical Blackness. And yet, Hurston's treatment of Haiti differs from Dunham, who followed the conventions of anthropological writing in "Dances of Haiti" (1947), and restricted her personal feelings about the fieldwork experience to her memoir *Island Possessed* (1969). In contrast, Hurston attempts to weave both "scientific" observation and subjective impressions into a single narrative. Perhaps the greatest difference is that *Tell My Horse* appears to be designed to perpetuate the stereotypes held by the majority of Americans and to provide a rationale for American neo-colonialism by depicting an island full of savagery and barbarism.

For example, in the section entitled "Politics and Personalities of Haiti," Hurston describes the coup d'état that precipitated the U.S. intervention in 1915 with lurid descriptions of violence committed by men against other men, creating a sensationalistic tale filled with melodramatic subheadings ("The Voice in the Night," "The Bloody River," "The Crescendo Cry," and so forth), spilled blood, severed limbs, burning skies, and cries of outrage (65–72). Her description reinforces Haiti's reputation as a place of Black rage and violence, suggesting that there is little that is new and unexpected to learn about the island. Hurston concludes her description of the bloody coup by suggesting that the United States' reign over the island, its demonstration of military prowess, will establish order and calm to an out-of-control region: "the smoke from the funnels of the *U.S.S. Washington* was a black plume with a white hope. . . . It was the end of the revolution and the beginning of peace" (72).[11] Unlike many of her contemporaries such as James Weldon Johnson who, in his capacity as head of the NAACP visited Haiti several times during the invasion and criticized U.S. action there, Hurston never explicitly condemned American imperialism in Haiti.[12] Rather, any critique is expressed by other characters in the book, with Hurston's tongue firmly in cheek, such as in the example of the "black Marine," a Haitian "sergeant of the Garde d'Haiti," who proves his likeness to the American Marines with whom he once served by swaggering about his property exclaiming, "Jesus Christ! God Damn! I kill something" (136–37).

Jacqueline Shea Murphy argues that Hurston's account of Haitian politics is written with an irony that is meant to be transparent.[13] Murphy suggests that the chapter's title, "Rebirth of a Nation," alludes to D. W. Griffith's film *Birth of a Nation*, which celebrates the genesis of the Ku Klux Klan during the Reconstruction era.[14] By gesturing toward Griffith's film, she argues, Hurston masks her criticism of the White supremacy that buttressed the U.S. occupation of Haiti behind an irony that makes her rhetoric palatable to the American public, and thus more marketable. Hurston explicitly challenged European and American imperialism elsewhere, notably in the chapters from her autobiography *Dust Tracks on a Road* that were excised by her editors when it was first published.[15] In "Seeing the World as It Is," one of the expurgated chapters, Hurston wrote about American hypocrisy vis-à-vis democracy, manifest in its blindness to its own imperialist bullying around the globe: "We, too, consider machine gun bullets good laxatives for heathens who get constipated with toxic ideas about a country of their own. If the patient dies from the treatment, it was not because the medicine was not good" (791).[16] If this is Hurston at her sharpest, most acerbic and direct, *Tell My Horse* reveals her at the opposite extreme, dissembling, signifying, using irony and duplicity, and making it virtually impossible to pinpoint with precision her real views on Caribbean societies or international politics. Yet, if we read Hurston's critique of Jamaican and Haitian cultures as ironic, as *knowingly* one-sided, then it may be possible to redirect her social critique back toward a society that she thought unable or unwilling to see its own flaws after they have been projected onto another.

Recognizing the connection between imperialism and anthropological ventures does not result in an automatic integration of the themes and impressions conveyed by the different parts of the narratives. Hurston continues to follow the model of narrative dissonance. For example, after providing this backdrop of violence, she undercuts the image of Haitian savagery by treating Vodou as an ancient and organized religion, as opposed to a collection of superstitions. She compels her readers to see Vodou practitioners, and

Haitians in general, as complex people with a structured and sophisticated social network and worldview. Recognizing the West's condescension toward Vodou, Hurston stresses its sacred content while foregrounding women's centrality to its religious networks.

Perhaps it was Hurston's outsiderness—her marginalization as a Black female anthropologist, or her experiences of transgressing conventional gender roles while in the field—that enabled her to perceive the gendered dynamics of Anglo-American and African American engagements with Haitian culture.[17] Like Dunham, she counters stereotypes of barbarism and idealized images of male rebels by narrating Haiti as a feminized space, embodied by the Vodou Mambo who passes African culture on to the uninitiated. She introduces her first encounter with worshippers of Vodou, in the section entitled "Voodoo in Haiti," with a creation story that declares that Vodou is as ancient as the beginning of the world: "'What is the truth?' Dr. Holly asked me, and knowing that I could not answer him. He answered himself through a Voodoo ceremony in which the Mambo, that is the priestess, richly dressed is asked this question ritualistically. She replies by throwing back her veil and revealing her sex organs. The ceremony means that this is the infinite, the ultimate truth. There is no mystery beyond the mysterious source of life."[18] Hurston represents Haitian women as representing the source of knowledge, truth, and life; and yet the image is troubling because it simultaneously depicts Black femininity as sexually available. This image does nothing to disrupt the pattern that Michael Dash identifies in *Haiti and the United States* of Haiti being coded "negative or feminine and marginalized in a symbolic order devised by the United States." "From the nineteenth century," Dash notes, "what beckons or revolts Americans is Haiti's impenetrable mystery, its strangeness, its unpredictable 'Otherness.'"[19] This moment admittedly traffics in stereotype, yet it is also one of many occasions in Hurston's text that prompts the reader to reflect on the relationships among moments of revelation or dissembling, and the discomfort caused by those occasions. In more ways than one, this introduction to Vodou beliefs and worldviews inspires the reader to look at and reflect on the travel narrative and historiography that Hurston uses to contextualize her fieldwork in Haiti. Most obviously, the focus on female values and power provides a counterpoint to a narration that up to this point has emphasized the masculine origins of political violence and social conflict.

Admittedly the image of the Mambo (priestess) butts up against stereotype, but it also introduces a belief system that equates women with the sacred and natural world, providing one avenue for empowerment that is otherwise unavailable to them. The authority and respect accorded to women in Vodou circles contrasts with their demeaning circumstances in other areas of life. In addition to recognizing women's empowerment in their religious communities, Hurston validates Vodou as a cultural and belief system with "deep meanings" (114). Turning her attention to the pantheon of gods or *lwa*, for example, she described their physical attributes and temperaments; the syncretic associations with Catholic saints; and what the *lwa* represent (Damballah's association with the beautiful in nature, for instance). With that kind of deliberate analysis, Hurston validates the sophistication of Vodou culture. How, then, do we account for her reinscription of the binaries between the West and the "primitive Other" conveyed by the stereotypes discussed above?

Ifeoma Nwankwo has argued that Hurston's narrative "provides an example of the shades of ethnocentrism that have continued to haunt transnational engagements between black peoples" (74).[20] Yet looking at other parts of this unwieldy narrative begs the following series of questions: Does Hurston take up the ethnocentric perspective to appease reader expectations? Does she assume it due to a reflexive response to the strange and unfamiliar? Why was she able to see meaning (as opposed to chaos) in Haitian peasant culture and religious ritual? Why is she unable to wholly incorporate the values of this belief system, even when she clearly recognizes its profundity? The answers to these questions are varying and changeable, offering a composite portrait of the narrator-anthropologist that is unstable and makes precarious any attempt on the part of the reader to find absolute truth or conclusive knowledge in her narrative. And, if I have not been explicit enough, I need to emphasize that this inconclusivity is exactly Hurston's point in her representation of the anthropological endeavor. "What is the truth?" the Western reader enquires, and the answer is a mystery that Hurston cannot fully or accurately articulate.

Imperial Ethnography and the Ironic Subtext

Critics often focus their readings on that aspect of the book they consider most valuable or problematic. Hazel Carby describes the political commentary as "reactionary, blindly patriotic, and consequently superficial."[21] Many critics concur with Ishmael Reed's assessment that Hurston's treatment of Vodou is her "greatest accomplishment . . . in revealing the profound beauty and appeal of a faith older than Christianity, Buddhism, and Islam."[22] Robert Hemenway compares *Tell My Horse*'s "naive" political analysis negatively to the "vivid and exciting" Vodou section.[23] The consensus seems to be that the superficiality of her political and social analysis is superseded by the care and complexity with which she approaches the subject of Vodou.[24]

Yet while it would seem appropriate to conclude, as so many other critics do, that Hurston's political analysis is superficial and her analysis of Vodou is complex, another interpretation is possible and is even invited by the earliest pages of the text in which Hurston signifies on her own intentions. In the first chapter, Hurston provides a journalistic account of Jamaican politics and society, putting particular emphasis on what she views as an excessive amount of internalized racism. I will discuss this commentary at further length later in this chapter, but for now I focus on the rather abrupt conclusion to the chapter in which Hurston declares that "a new day is in sight for Jamaica" because the people have begun to appreciate their songs, stories, proverbs, and dances (9). In particular, Hurston notes, Jamaican proverbs are "rich in philosophy, irony and humor" (9). She goes on to cite twelve proverbs, including the following:

1. Rockatone at ribber bottom no know sun hot. (The person in easy circumstances cannot appreciate the sufferings of the poor.)
3. Sharp spur mek maugre horse cut caper. (The pinch of circumstances forces people to do what they thought impossible.)
5. Table napkin want to turn table cloth. (Referring to social climbing.)
6. Bull horn nebber too heavy for him head. (We always see ourselves in a favorable light.)
7. Cock roach nebber in de right befo' fowl. (The oppressor always justifies his oppression of the weak.)
8. If you want fo' lick old woman pot, you scratch him back. (The masculine is always used for female. Use flattery and you will succeed.) (9)

The proverbs, presented as a random list of humorously philosophical sayings, are also an exercise in the kind of self-referential, reflexive writing that Clifford identifies in modern ethnography. Traces of critical and ironic commentary can be found in the proverbs, from a warning to her American audience to keep from casting other cultures in an unfavorable light at the expense of losing sight of its own social and political failings, to personal references to her own social striving and the ends to which she will go in order to attain the upward mobility she sought, such as flattery and, one can presume, the authorship of a unashamedly imperialistic narrative of the Caribbean. Deborah Gordon argues that the effect of such rhetorical moves is to suggest that "ethnocentricism is not something that the ethnographer simply puts in her/his field diary in order to record more objectively what (s)he observes, but is part of the construction of relations in the field. . . . Hurston offers a vision of fieldwork in which the limits as well as possibilities of cross-cultural understanding are explicitly displayed" (156). Not only does Hurston put her own ethnocentrism on display, she also signifies on its origins, gesturing toward a complex web of motivations that contributed to her particular perspective on Haiti.

Hurston's assertions of American superiority are laced with implicit criticism of that nation's ideological foundation, thereby subverting the very opposition she goes to such pains to erect. For example, when she denounces racism and sexism she places these offensive attitudes solely within the province of the islands. In so doing she underscores a purported difference between American and Caribbean attitudes, and positions American society as the more sophisticated and enlightened of the two nations. In "The Rooster's Nest," for example, Hurston describes Jamaica as "the land where the rooster lays an egg"; in other words, it is an unnatural place (6). She noted that although in the 1930s it was 2 percent White and 98 percent people of color, everyone tried to "talk English, act English and look English." Hurston mocks mulatto Jamaicans who overly identify with and revere their White ancestors, labeling them "census whites," who are "black by birth but white by proclamation" (7). She contrasts the Jamaicans' colonized mentality to the supposed good sense of American Blacks:

Perhaps the Jamaican mixed bloods are logical and right, perhaps the only answer to the question of what is to become of the negro in the Western world is that he must be absorbed by the whites. Frederick Douglass thought so. If he was right, then the strategy of the American Negro is all wrong, that is, the attempt to achieve a position equal to the white population in every way but each race to maintain its separate identity. Perhaps we should strike our camps and make use of the cover of night and execute a masterly retreat under white skins. (7)

Hurston's commentary resonates on multiple levels. When she considers the possibility that "perhaps Jamaicans are logical and right," she clearly means that they are wrong in fetishizing Whiteness. But any familiarity with Hurston's oeuvre clearly shows that she did not truly believe that African Americans rose above such self-negating beliefs.[25] This passage avoids acknowledging the existence of colonisms within Black communities, in preference for espousing a New Negro ideology that weds social equality to race conciousness. Consequently, it allays White Americans' fears of miscegenation while simultaneously positioning the U.S. as a morally superior place because of its purported lack of racial insecurity and confusion. Again, Hurston's other writings (like *Their Eyes Were Watching God* and *Jonah's Gourd Vine*) repeatedly turn to the theme of miscegenation, if only to underscore its occurrence as a fundamental fact of Black people's personal histories. But here, her refusal to dwell on this fact makes the passage virtually duplicitous.

Hurston's representation of Jamaican gender dynamics is as ironic as her discussion of its racial politics. Critics who privilege her foundational importance to Black feminism often look to her analysis of gender for signs of the critically subversive perspective that is lacking in other parts of her social critique. Rachel Stein argues, for example, that Hurston focuses on how ideological constructions of Black, and particularly Black female, subhumanity contribute to Caribbean racial and sexual inequalities. She concludes, "Voodoo presents an alternative spiritual model that reframes the binary hierarchies operating within the denigration of black women as nature incarnate. Through rituals that locate the sacred within nature and within female sexuality, Voodoo challenges the degradation of black women as donkeys."[26] Stein's analysis of Hurston's critique of patriarchal and colonial domination is astute, but it does not dwell on the effect of Hurston's curious silence on American racial and gender inequities.

Hurston invites such comparisons by setting Jamaican and American attitudes against each other. She tells, for example, the story of a young Jamaican man whose sexism, she claims to be representative of the island: "He let it be known that he thought that women who went in for careers were just so much wasted material. American women, he contended, were destroyed by their brains" (16). In contrast to this young Jamaican's assertion of male privilege and intellectual superiority, Hurston writes of American men's more enlightened and solicitous attitudes toward women:

The majority of men in all the states are pretty much agreed that just for being born a girl-baby you ought to have laws and privileges and pay and perquisites. And so far as being allowed to voice opinions is concerned, why, they consider that you are born with the law in your mouth, and that is not a bad arrangement either. . . . But now Miss America, World's champion woman, you take your promenading self down into the cobalt blue waters of the Caribbean and see what happens. You meet a lot of darkish men who make vociferous love to you, but otherwise pay you no mind. (57)

This passage could be read as a straightforward proclamation of American women's privilege in a society that recognizes their civil rights; but in tone and content it borders on the edge of parody, alluding as it does to a bourgeois tradition of putting women on display, while limiting their autonomy and agency. Even if one takes this reference to "Miss America" as straightforward, she is presumably White and bears little resemblance to the Black women whom Hurston so eloquently describes in *Their Eyes Were Watching God* as being treated like "de mule uh de world," hardly the type of woman born with the "law in [her] mouth."[27] Hurston renders the woman as mule metaphor literal in her description of Jamaican women laborers, whom she describes as able to ". . . do the same labors as a man or a mule and nobody thinks anything about it."[28] This is an image of racial, class, and gender inequalities that bears more resemblance to the (Black) American woman that Hurston represents in other narratives, like *Their Eyes*. Even as she satisfies her audience's presumptions of Western civility and non-Western backwardness, she continually invites her audience to read between the lines, sometimes *too* subtly some might argue. By refusing to meet her audience's every demand for transparency, she makes use of the selective silence and contextualized use of language that Visweswaran identifies as one of the tools of feminist ethnography.[29]

One can find the kind of binaristic thinking exemplified by the above examples even in the sections of the book that have been praised as instances of Hurston's empathetic involvement in Haitian culture.[30] For example, Hurston distances herself from the very Vodou ritual in which she participates by slipping from first-person narration to a third-person voice that strives for scholarly detachment. This is a deliberate strategy that she uses at particularly meaningful moments. For example, she writes, "The spirit enters the head of a person. He is possessed of this spirit and sometimes he *or* she is troubled by it because the possession comes at times and places that are, perhaps embarrassing" (173). The tendency of Westerners to demonize spirit possession compels her to write about the experience as if she were viewing it from outside, while remaining in full possession of her own sense of self, even though she actually, actively, underwent an initiation.

Hurston also signals her outsiderness by repeatedly expressing uneasiness with Haitians' ritual use of animals. Because animal sacrifice is an integral part of Vodou, the worshippers express no moral qualms over the practice. Yet she, while supportive of Vodou beliefs, cannot suppress her shock and disgust over what she claims to be an unsavory aspect of the religion. She recounts one ceremony in which she watches the sacrifice to Ogun of a red cock which she has befriended: "I felt I knew that rooster because another had attacked him while he was tethered there and while he showed plenty of courage, being tied by the leg hindered his movements, and I had driven off his assailant. I looked into his round brown eye in the hounfort and looked away" (160). Hurston's emphasis on her discomfort with animal sacrifice places her squarely within a tradition of American commentators on Vodou who emphasize the more lurid elements of the rituals as proof of the islanders' barbarity. Journalist Amy Wilentz notes that "when shooting a voodoo ceremony, for instance, foreign photographers often choose to capture the dying animal, his blood gushing—the lesson: how cruel the heathens are, how untouched by suffering."[31] Hurston's uneasiness reassures her American readers who might identify her too closely with the Haitians and their alleged barbarism that she is on their side.

At the same time that Hurston reinforces certain binaries, her representation of ethnocentricism as "part of the construction of relations in the field" creates an opportunity for critical engagement with the text that resists simple polarities (Gordon 156). Barbara Johnson describes how Hurston constructs binaries and boundaries, only to deconstruct them: "Hurston's work itself was constantly dramatizing and undercutting just such inside/outside oppositions, transforming the plane geometry of physical space into the complex transactions of discursive exchange. In other words, Hurston could be read not just as an *example* of the 'noncanonical' writer but as a commentator on the dynamics of any encounter between an inside and an outside, any attempt to make a statement about difference."[32] Johnson's assertion illuminates the radical potential embodied by Hurston's dramatization of inside/outside and either/or oppositions; namely, her invitation to conceive of spatial (and geographic and national) difference as indicative of social and political relations articulated, indeed even constituted, through linguistic and representational practices. Thus, while Hurston seems bound by convention to highlight the extreme and exotic, and to position it at an axis far from her own, American location, her narrative constantly threatens to erupt from under her, warping that plane geometry of physical space into something more complex, multilayered, and multifaceted.

Hurston's juxtaposition of various genres (travelogue, journalism, and ethnography) and different points of view in one narrative compels her reader to interpret declarations of truth and authenticity that are continually being destabilized. The act of reading this text proves as daunting as Hurston must have found the act of "reading" Haitian culture. Acts of cultural translation and interpretation are often thought of as particularly difficult in Haiti because its social and cultural mores often seem incomprehensible to foreigners. Wilentz explains the difficulty of grasping the inner life of the country.

She writes of contemporary Haiti, but the same could be true of the West's (mis)understanding of the island in Hurston's day. Wilentz writes, "until you've been there for a while, and learned something of the grammar of Haiti's reality. You have to want to figure the place out on its own terms and in its own language. Otherwise, it's all just weird voodoo, lowercase. For almost two centuries, Americans have visited Haiti and come back with only that in their heads, and in their writing: weird voodoo" (6). The "weird voodoo" that Wilentz refers to has little resemblance to the sacred and secret rituals of Vodou, a fact of which Hurston was very aware. Thus while passages such as the one involving the sacrificed rooster demonstrate her indulgence in a certain measure of writing about "weird voodoo," most of the narrative illustrates her attempts to faithfully and respectfully convey the tenets of what she believed to be a sacred religious practice.

Speaking Truth to Power: Irony, Ambiguity, and Expressions of Resistance

The preceding discussion has highlighted the challenges Hurston faced as she attempted to write an anthropological narrative that would satisfy her academic audience and funding source, as well as a larger American readership, while at the same time expressing her anti-colonial views. Her discussion of Gede, the peasant god of life and death centers on the themes of self-expression, and color and class conflict, issues that she wanted to explore in the broader context of U.S.-Haitian relations. According to Hurston, "tell my horse" are the words spoken by Gede when he mounts an initiate. He is a carnivalesque god and when possessed by him, peasants may shout epithets at wealthy mulattoes and Whites, and berate and shame their employers. Although conventional belief has it that, when undergoing ritual possession, devotees have no control over their will, Hurston's translation of Gede's words suggest otherwise. She writes that when Gede speaks through a possessed individual, he prefaces all statements with the phrase, "*Parlay Cheval Ou*," which translated literally from *Kreyol* means "tell *your* horse." Hurston's translation of the phrase as "tell *my* horse" reaffirms the perception that the god is in complete control of the human's will and "the person mounted does nothing of his own accord" (221). A literal translation of the statement would confuse the issue, throwing into doubt the speaker, and therefore the agent of the action. Hurston recognizes the ambiguity of the phrase, even as her interpretation erases it. She notes that although conventional wisdom has it that possessed people have no free will, Gede's rebelliousness in this oppressive society compels some to feign possession by him. She states, "one is forced to believe that some of the valuable commentators are 'mounted' by the spirit and that others are feigning possession in order to express their resentment general and particular" (221). Hurston's interpretation of the cultural act (as opposed to her linguistic translation) highlights social and global inequalities and expressions of resistance. Just as she begins the narrative by signifying her own untrustworthiness as a narrator of the kind of "truth" her audiences expected, so does she suggest that her own informants possess fluid subjectivities that refuse the reader assurance of authentic and accurate reportage that would allow him or her to understand this other culture in absolutist terms.

Hurston's treatment of the figure of Gede underscores that writing ethnography requires acts of translation that demand that the anthropologist produce and then make sense of foreign cultures and societies.[33] This requires multiple levels of translation, first by informants for the anthropologist, who then continues the process for her readers.[34] Hurston typically considers the ideal position for the cultural interpreter to be both inside and outside the culture, looking for guidance from individuals who have traveled either literally or figuratively far enough away from their native culture to provide the kind of insight and analysis that she thought was made possible by those who rode the line between familiarity and detachment. These individuals, not surprisingly, are the ones who most closely resemble Hurston herself. For example, when inquiring into the actions of Haiti's infamous, cannibalistic *sectes rouges*, she runs into a wall of silence and repression, until one afternoon when in a tourist bar she meets, "a man who is a Haitian and also not a Haitian [who] said something that suddenly connected all of these happenings and gave them a meaning beside" (206). This individual is intimate enough with the culture to understand and interpret the signs, symbols, and silences that Hurston encounters; yet he is also detached enough from the social taboos to speak of the unmentionable.

Hurston's preferred informant is an ex-American naval officer named Reser, to whom she devotes an entire chapter. Reser's Whiteness must have been irresistible to Hurston as it turns the notion of native informant in this predominantly Black nation on its head. That irony, coupled with Reser's apparent ability to combine opposing cultural influences made him a compelling subject for her. She writes:

I wanted to know all I could about this educated, widely traveled man, this ex-navy man who could so completely find his soul and his peace in the African rituals of Haiti. I have seen him in the grip of the African loa (spirits) known as possession: that is, the spirits have entered his head and driven his consciousness out. I have seen him reeling as if he were drunk under the spirit possession like any Haitian peasant and I was trying to reconcile the well-read man of science with the credulous man of emotions. (252)

Hurston praises him as a rational man who is also emotional, a learned man who "goes native"—in other words, a hybrid individual mingling the aspects of the self-possessed, rational Westerner with the "primitivism" of the Haitian peasant. Hurston represents Reser as embodying some sort of ideal in that he not only occupies but also embodies a "cultural border zone," the conceptually interesting outcome of military and political encounters between two cultures.[35] Yet evidence exists that she understood the concept of going native in more pragmatic and more critical ways than this description would suggest. For example, Hurston's own decision to "go native" was more a product of financial and material circumstance than a methodological choice. Writing to Ruth Benedict about her desire to do more fieldwork in the Bahamas and Haiti, and lobbying for Benedict to help her find funding, she wrote, "I could do it very cheaply as living conditions there are easy if one goes native as I certainly would do. $500 or less would be enough for transportation and six months work" (Kaplan 252). These references to going native resonate with Marianna Torgovnick's assertion that ethnographers "document the intimate life of primitive peoples so that we can learn the truth about us—safely, as observers."[36] By "going native," Hurston and Reser mediate between the Western and "primitive" societies, purportedly bringing the West in closer contact with its mystical, natural, libidinous, and free self. This process is undercut, however, if the ethnographer, or her informant, fails at the attempt to credibly occupy the "skin" of the native. Perhaps, for this reason, Hurston chose to omit the fact that Reser was a fraud, a military man and pharmacist playing at psychiatry, as well as at native practices. Katherine Dunham reports in her memoir that Reser was an alcoholic who often feigned possession for the *frisson* of "going native." Hurston eliminates these damning details, yet undercuts Reser's authority in more suggestive ways, undermining whatever authority might be granted him on the basis of his race or national identity.

Hurston's representation of Reser begins to shift in a scene that is exclusively about "background information" and conveys next to nothing about the content of the Haitian folklore that he conveys to her. Reser begins to entertain Hurston with "hillbilly" folktales from the Ozarks. Heard above and around his tale are the voices of several patients who chime in with stories of their own:

Dr. Reser's quotations from the folk lore of the Ozarks, and perhaps our merriment attracted them. Another patient came up and began to babble the Haitian folk tales about Brother Bouki and Ti Malice. . . . "Dr. Reser! Dr. Reser!" The Syrian attracts attention to himself. "They have horse racing in Palestine. The horses have contracts in Jewish and Arabic and English and the Jewish horse must be second. It's political." The man who recited Fontaine pointed his stagnant eyes on the porch and babbled on as if he raced with the man who was talking about Ti Malice and Bouki, but he had a weaker voice. So we heard very distinctly: "Of Course, Bouki was very angry with Ti Malice for what he had done and Ti Malice was afraid, so he ran away very fast until he came to a fence. The fence had a hole in it, but the hole was not very big, but Malice tried to go through—" . . .

"Are they annoying you?" Dr. Reser asked me. "They never worry me at all." (254)

The scene in the asylum can be read as a critique of the colonizer's vision of domination. Michel Foucault's analysis of madness is relevant to our understanding of Reser's asylum, for he documents the historical function of asylums to ease the threats of contamination and contagion. Foucault recounts, "if a doctor was summoned, if he was asked to observe, it was because people were afraid—afraid of the strange chemistry that seethed behind the walls of confinement, afraid of the powers forming there that threatened to propagate."[37] On the one hand, Reser controls the patients, suggesting the possibility of containing the "chaotic" Blackness of both the asylum and the island. On the other hand, his story is just one element in the babble of storytelling. His voice, at this point, has no more authority and makes no more sense than those of the insane. Hurston's depiction of the asylum's inhabitants corresponds with traditional Western depictions of the mad and diseased by locating the undesirable in the bodies of the marginalized, such as people of color, homosexuals, and women.[38] However, the seemingly untainted White male body of Dr. Reser is compromised by the tenuousness of his claims to difference from the mad.

Moreover, all of the stories resonate with one another. The struggle for power and dominance are the central themes of both the Syrian's seemingly nonsensical complaints about the hierarchical ordering of Jewish horses over Arab ones and the other patient's recitation of a trickster tale (Bouki and Malice's relationship is defined by their attempts to best each other). These themes get played out in the relations between patients and doctor, who jockey to speak above one another. Read in this way, this passage is less about the benign and ordering presence of White culture in a chaotic Black setting and speaks more pointedly to the complexities of discursive and social exchange within multicultural and cross-cultural settings. This description of the episode can be understood as a reimagining of the 1934 National Folk

Festival, held in St. Louis, where "Hurston's [theater] troupe performed along with various other shows of 'authentic' music and dance presented by: lumberjacks, Indians, Spanish Americans, Appalachian fiddlers, cowboys, 'mountain musicians,' French Creole singers and dancers, harp players, square dancers, New England 'sea chantey' singers, 'Ozark legend' storytellers, singers from the Old Sailors' home of Staten Island, Vermont balladeers, Carolina 'country courtship' performers, and Mormons" (Kaplan 170). The Festival was conceived of as a project in patriotism and national identity building. Hurston's reenactment in Haiti emphasizes the power of some nations to contain and silence others, as opposed to a democratic pluralism performed at the Folk Festival, which assumed an equal cultural playing field. Cross-cultural encounters, this passage suggests, frequently are the source and site of cross-cultural conflict, symbolized by each individual jockeying for position, striving to be heard and acknowledged.[39]

Conclusion

Boasian anthropology, charged with the mission of providing evidence for theories of cultural relativism, presumably shared the ideals of the folk festival, broadening ideas of American citizenship to encompass a more pluralistic society. Hurston's ethnography would have been expected to contribute to a storehouse of emerging scholarship about the cultural contributions of diverse societies. Rather than uncritically celebrating an apolitical idea of diversity, however, she chose the more difficult goal of illustrating how culture is produced and performed through a process of contact and exchange between societies that have uneven and unequal amounts of influence and power. Despite its dissonance, the sense that this narrative's parts do not hold together very well, Hurston proves herself willing to construct an unflattering self-portrait in order to explore the contingency of knowledge and the partiality of identity, in order, as Meehan puts it, to "decolonize ethnography." When she expresses an anti-colonial position, more often than not she does so obliquely or through ironic silences that run the risk of remaining unseen by the reader.

Regardless of one's interpretation of the politics of *Tell My Horse*, the narrative calls into question the assumption of some theorists of migration, ethnography, cosmopolitanism, and the Black Atlantic, who strongly suggest that the act of migration enables individuals to see and act beyond their particular localized interests.[40] This text illuminates how easy it is for travelers to carry their "localized interests" with them on their cosmopolitan journeys into foreign settings.[41] It reveals how much cultural "baggage" in the way of ideology, bias, and preconceptions, ethnographers carried with them into the field; and intentionally or not it challenges the reader to see anthropology as caught up in an imperialist project of defining and containing the other. After reading *Tell My Horse*, one suspects that Haiti remains inscrutable and mysterious to the reader, and yet Hurston captures the truth of colonial power and global hierarchies by allowing her narrative to openly flaunt its multiple, conflicted, and dissonant perspectives.

Chapter 8

Their Eyes Were Watching God *and the Vodou Intertext*

After Zora Neale Hurston spent time immersed in Haitian society and Vodou culture, she recognized that African Americans and Haitians
shared similar conflicts and concerns, but the ethnographic format denied
her the opportunity to explore these commonalities. In fact, she appeared to
believe that the genre demanded that she expand and exploit the perception
of differences between American and Caribbean societies. Yet paradoxically,
her sojourn in Haiti inspired Hurston to write *Their Eyes Were Watching God*
(1937) in a creative outpouring that took only seven weeks, and came on the
heels of a failed love affair. *Their Eyes* is a lyrical novel whose "ethnographic
content" is rendered solely in terms of symbols. One could even call *Their
Eyes* an anti-ethnographic narrative, refusing the mission of translation and
transmission, at the same time that its meaning is utterly dependent on the
folkloric materials Hurston collected while conducting fieldwork. While the
history of these texts suggests that, for Hurston, folklore and fiction converge
in Haiti, few critics have adequately explored that juncture.

Most acknowledge Hurston's interest in Haitian Vodou, but their analyses of the impact of this belief system on her work frequently do not extend
beyond perfunctory glosses. A notable exception is Ellease Southerland's
essay, "The Influence of Voodoo on the Fiction of Zora Neale Hurston," published in the 1979 collection, *Sturdy Black Bridges*.[1] Southerland's article
makes an important contribution to readings of Hurston's integration of
folklore and fiction. The essay discusses the appearance and significance of
various "voodoo" signs, symbols, and rituals in Hurston's fiction; and more
specific to this paper, it identified the use of religious symbolism in *Their
Eyes Were Watching God* very early in the history of the novel's criticism. But
Southerland does not cite her sources for certain "voodoo" spells, or for the
significance of various numbers and colors that appear repeatedly in
Hurston's fiction. Her analysis also ignores the cultural distinctions among
Haitian, Louisiana, and other kinds of voodoo and hoodoo.[2] These aspects of

the essay contribute to the failure, or refusal, of succeeding generations of literary critics to further examine the cultural influences that Southerland found in Hurston's literature.[3] The value of focusing on Hurston's incorporation of Vodou ethnography in her literature lies in its illuminating her exploration of female empowerment and African American cultural identity.

In this chapter, I focus specifically on Hurston's use of Haitian Vodou imagery in *Their Eyes Were Watching God*, and I argue that the folklore enables her confrontation of various kinds of social and personal transformation. Her use of Vodou imagery enables her to analyze the relationship among migration, culture, and identity that lies at the heart of the African Diaspora. In contrast to those critics who read Hurston's use of folk culture as a sign of nostalgia, I view it as her means of comprehending transformation, as *the* vehicle used by Black communities to contend with their ever-changing conditions. Within traditional cultural forms lie a structure that encourages and enables dynamic change. This understanding allows us to read Hurston's reluctance to abandon African American folk traditions not as a rejection of modernity, but rather, as a means for her to acknowledge modernity.

I concern myself here specifically with Vodou because *Their Eyes Were Watching God* alludes to similarities between the protagonist, Janie Killicks Starks Woods, and the Vodou goddess, Ezili. Janie's physical appearance, her romantic relationships, and her interactions with the Eatonville community mirror in a multitude of ways the characteristics of that spirit (*lwa*). These allusions are so embedded into the foundation of the narrative that they are virtually invisible, compelling us to ask what it was about Hurston's experiences in Haiti that compelled her to relate Vodou to her characters. Perhaps her instincts as a folklorist and writer led her to a cultural experience in which the self-expression of a displaced people comes to the fore. Perhaps because she was raised in the self-contained all-Black community of Eatonville, Florida, she looked to a belief system that addressed Black people's capacity for self-determination. Hurston found in Haitian Vodou a syncretic cultural production that spoke to both of those interests and more. Her anthropological research revealed that the ways in which Haitian people worked out their political, social, and psychic conditions in the spiritual plane resonated with the concerns and experiences of African Americans in the United States. Because the Vodou gods' and goddesses' appearances and actions speak to the concerns and experiences of their worshippers, one finds that Vodou alludes to the heroic and the rebellious; reflects mundane jealousies, desires, and hierarchies; illustrates the ravages of slavery on a collective consciousness; and provides a means of self-expression for that same collective.

Hurston was very aware of Haiti's symbolic status for African Americans; references to its significance are scattered throughout the text. For example, Joe Starks dreams of a place where he can be a "big voice" and settles on Eatonville because "de white folks had all de sayso where he come from and everywhere else, exceptin' dis place dat colored folks was buildin' theirselves."[4] This reference to a place where Black people live independent of White authority finds its parallel in post-revolution Haiti, the first Black independent republic in the Western hemisphere, and it underscores the revolutionary notion of a town in the United States built and run by Black people. Nanny makes a similar allusion to the Black republic and the collective desire for autonomy and empowerment. She dreams of "some place way off in de ocean where de black man is in power," obliquely referring to Haiti's significance as a place where the potential for Black autonomy has been realized (14).

Nanny's musings also address a desire for female empowerment; for it is in that "place way off in de ocean" that she also imagines that a Black woman might not have to be "de mule uh de world" (14). Anthropologist Kathy McCarthy Brown writes in *Mama Lola* about the possibilities for empowerment afforded to Haitian women by Vodou:

The adaptability of Vodou over time, and its responsiveness to other cultures and religions; the fact that it has no canon, creed, or pope; the multiplicity of its spirits; and the intimate detail in which those spirits reflect the lives of the faithful—all these characteristics make women's lives visible within Vodou in ways they are not in other religious traditions, including those of the African homeland. This visibility can give women a way of working realistically and creatively with the forces that define and confine them.[5]

Through the use of a Vodou subtext, Hurston comments on and rebels against the forces that "define and confine" Black women as sexual beings, work horses, and mothers. She also uses Vodou philosophy to shed light on the characters' views on poverty, class community, and displacement. Building on the work of those critics who investigate the political implications of Hurston's cultural work, I argue that her use of Vodou imagery provides her with a vehicle for political engagement and social commentary.

Folklore, Literature, and the Lure of the Primitive

In order to fully comprehend the significance of the text's Vodou imagery, it is crucial to understand the context in which Hurston wrote. I believe she submerged the Vodou images in the novel beneath more accessible folk images of the South in a dual effort to conform to and resist popular demands for the primitive. Unlike the performance of the dozens, the telling of folk tales, and other aspects of African American folk culture which the reader can easily identify and separate from the plot, Hurston's use of Vodou is not as easily discerned. Its presence in the text has no stylistic markers, nor can we categorize the Vodou elements as merely ornaments for the central narrative.[6]

As one of the stars of the Harlem Renaissance, courted and funded by White benefactors, Hurston juggled her literary aspirations with the often racist expectations of her patron and audience. For example, her patron, Mrs. Rufus Osgood Mason, was a generous benefactor, but "as perhaps with all patrons, . . . she expected some return on her money. In Hurston's case it was a report on the aboriginal sincerity of rural southern black folk . . . Her black guests were either primitive, or they were not being themselves."[7] Many of Hurston's critics viewed this external pressure as a handicap to her literary production. H. Nigel Thomas, for example, counts Hurston as one of a school of writers (including Charles Chesnutt and Paul Lawrence Dunbar) who could not meet the challenge of simultaneously satisfying the demand for "minstrel-type buffoonery" and "ensuring that [s]he did not compromise the dignity of the black race."[8] Thomas mistakes Hurston's humor for buffoonery, and fails to recognize the dignity of her lowly characters. Furthermore, his dismissal of her work arises from the notion that a successful narrative seamlessly blends folklore with fiction. Thomas marks the 1930s as, in general, a time in which African American writers mastered the art of incorporating those elements of folklore that were necessary to their fiction, without pandering to the audience's "baser instincts" or hindering their art. From the thirties on, Black writers produced literature in which "rituals are not allowed to remain a thing apart or as caricatured quaint antics; instead they are integral aspects of the characters' struggle to survive" (Thomas 175). According to Thomas, Hurston is an exception to this rule, but he fails to acknowledge that Hurston's attempts to set apart and highlight some elements of the folklore (like the stories told by the townsfolk) may be deliberate. Rather than judging the obvious seams between the novel's third-person, standard English narration and its first-person, African American vernacular as a sign of Hurston's failure as a writer, it is possible to view it as an emotionally powerful juxtaposition of two very different kinds of language, something akin to W. E. B. Du Bois's union of European verse and African American vernacular sorrow songs in *The Souls of Black Folk*. Furthermore, like many other critics, Thomas does not recognize that she makes Ezili, a figure from Caribbean folklore and ritual, a central, yet nearly invisible, aspect in Janie's struggle for survival. Hurston achieves a doubled triumph over those in her audience who demanded primitive images. First, by setting apart the African American folklore within the central narrative, she makes an overtly political case for the recognition of the literary possibilities of folklore. Second, her use of Vodou achieves the harmonious blending of folklore and fiction that Thomas holds as a standard of successful creative expression.

During the twenties and thirties, the widespread desire for the primitive extended beyond a demand for minstrel stereotypes of "happy darkies" into the world of the exotic primitive. These demands dovetailed with Renaissance writers' struggles to define what was unique to African American culture. One way they did so was by attempting to articulate and define Blacks' African heritage. But when imagining African culture's relevance to African American culture and identity, Hurston and her contemporaries often used stereotypical images of beating drums and the jungle, feeding American society's perceptions of Africa as a savage, primal, and uncivilized place. Hemenway writes:

Such tom-tom beats were almost a cliché in Harlem Renaissance writing, and both blacks and whites became enmeshed in the cult of exotic primitivism. For the whites it was the idea that Harlem was an uptown jungle, a safari for the price of cab fare, with cabarets decorated in jungle motifs. They went to Harlem to see the natural rhythm and uninhibited grace of America's link with the heart of darkness. For the black artists it was a much more serious concern, an attempt to establish a working relationship with what Locke called in *The New Negro* the "ancestral" past. (75)

Harlem Renaissance writers' uses of African images frequently held a dual significance as expressions of a serious attempt to articulate the relevance of an African past to African Americans' futures, and as a base appeal to racist demands for exotic entertainment. Hurston's literary forays into Blacks' ancestral past often made use of the clichés mentioned above. In *Jonah's Gourd Vine*, for instance, and in her 1928 essay "How It Feels to Be Colored Me," she makes prodigious use of the metaphor of the drums to invoke an ancient African heritage as the foundation of African American identity.

One could view Hurston's turn to Vodou as another example of her exploitation of the primitive because, historically, representations of "voodoo" in the U.S. have been rife with such clichés. For example, Eugene O'Neill's *The Emperor Jones* contains numerous stereotypes in its depiction of Brutus Jones, the noble savage, such as the tom-toms beating incessantly in the background to foreshadow evil, and the natives using black magic to depose their emperor.[9] However, Hurston's weaving of Vodou imagery in *Their Eyes* completely evades such predictable stereotypes, delving instead into the complexities of the belief system, the culture from which it springs, and the ways in which those complexities address African American (not to mention Caribbean) social and political concerns. The Vodou subtext represents a facet of the primitive that exceeds the scope of the plantation and jungle stereotypes that dominated the Harlem Renaissance era. It links the Southern folk with a Black Atlantic experience rooted in slavery, armed revolution, and African spirituality.

Vodou Imagery and Female Agency

The primary Vodou element in this novel is the implied presence of the goddess Ezili. Hurston infuses Janie with the characteristics of two aspects of this spirit: Ezili Freda, the mulatta goddess of love and Ezili Dantò, the black goddess who is associated with maternal rage. These two spirits display attributes that are completely in opposition. Freda is of an elite class; she is a mulatta, self-possessed, and materialistic. Dantò is working-class, Black, and associated with motherhood. These contradictory qualities reside in one spirit, and in the case of the novel, they also lie in one body—Janie's. The tensions that stem from these oppositions reflect the conditions and desires of African Americans; and while they cannot always be assimilated or resolved, they frequently result in cultural and individual expressiveness that is dynamic and powerful. Therefore, Hurston uses Vodou imagery, in particular the image of Ezili, in order to participate in a dialogue on the present circumstances and future possibilities of African American culture.

Just as all Vodou ceremonies begin with songs, dances, and prayers in honor of Legba, the novel starts with an implicit invocation of him. Janie calls forth the power of Legba, the keeper of the crossroads, which is the gateway between the spiritual and material worlds, as she searches "as much of the world as she could from the top of the front steps" (11). And when she walks "down to the front gate"—the symbolic crossroads—"and [leans] over to gaze up and down the road" (11), her air of expectation invokes the potential embodied by Legba. In *Tell My Horse*, Hurston calls Legba the "opener of gates"; he symbolizes opportunity.[10] As Janie stands at the gate, "looking, waiting, breathing short with impatience. Waiting for the world to be made," she feels acutely this sense of opportunity (11).

This invocation of Legba, a Black Atlantic god, takes place in a text marked by its multiple references to the Christian God, most notably in its title. During the storm that erupts near the end of the narrative, the folks stranded on the muck stare into the darkness, putting themselves at the mercy of a Christian God. But throughout the narrative, as they gaze upon Janie's body, they have also been looking to a New World goddess rooted in African spirituality. Rachel Blau DuPlessis notes that "there are a number of substitutions for God made in this book, usually in the form of big talkers— 'Mouth Almighty' of the rural folk, and 'I God' for Joe Stark's comic blasphemous condensation of political and economic power."[11] The temporal powers of Jody and the gossiping Eatonville folk give scant competition to the all-encompassing power of God to whom Janie, Tea Cake, and their friends silently appeal as they wait for the storm to arrive. But the novel refers in passing only to these false gods, and to the ultimate authority, the God who controls the potentially devastating forces of nature. This God often seems like an allegory for racist White society, and is Ezili's primary challenger in the competition for the characters' allegiance.

Janie resembles Ezili Freda physically. In *Voodoo in Haiti*, anthropologist Alfred Métraux describes Freda, the goddess of love, as "a pretty Antillean half-caste . . . a personification of feminine grace and beauty. She has all the characteristics of a pretty mulatto: she is coquettish, sensual, pleasure-loving and extravagant."[12] Freda can make any man she chooses her husband, a characteristic that finds its parallel in Janie's search for a suitable mate. Janie dresses in blue, Freda's favorite color (2).[13] The description of Janie's return to Eatonville echoes Métraux's description of Ezili's entrance into a Vodou temple. Hurston writes, "The men noticed her firm buttocks like she had grape fruits in her hip pockets; the great rope of black hair swinging to her waist and unraveling in the wind like a plume; then her pugnacious breasts trying to bore holes in her shirt. They, the men, were saving with the mind what they lost with the eye" (2). In comparison, Métraux writes: "At last, in the full glory of her seductiveness, with hair unbound to make her look like a long-haired half-caste, Ezili makes her entrance to the peristyle. She walks slowly, swinging her hips, throwing saucy, ogling looks at the men or pausing for a kiss or a caress" (111). Janie's long hair and sensuality mark her as the object of sexual desire. Although, unlike Ezili Freda, Janie does not actively solicit male attention, Freda's desire for sensuality and love blooms in Janie as she muses under the pear tree in her grandmother's garden. And finally, the celebration of love and sexuality symbolized by Freda culminates in Janie and Tea Cake's playful, loving relationship.

The text celebrates female sexuality with its sensuous prose and positioning of Janie's quest for love at its center. By linking Janie's sexuality with Freda's, Hurston radicalizes it by associating it with the ritual of possession in which a god mounts an initiate. The goddess is said to "ride" her horse. The implicit sexuality in this terminology is self-evident and Ezili's desire for numerous "husbands" is well documented in the anthropological literature. The image of a woman, either human or spirit, "mounting" a man proves significant because it implies the woman's control over her own sexuality and over the man's pleasure as well. For Hurston, representing a woman's sexuality in full bloom is not just affirmative, it is revolutionary.

But Freda's presence also represents a desire for wealth and status, which eventually leads to conflict for Janie. After joining in a loveless marriage with Logan Killicks, Janie tells her grandmother, "Ah wants things sweet wid mah marriage lak when you sit under a pear tree and think, Ah . . ." (23). Janie's desire for "things sweet" corresponds with the mythology surrounding Ezili Freda, who also desires sweets.[14] Janie eventually satisfies that desire when she marries a man with a sweet sounding name, Tea Cake, but that only occurs when she shucks off her grandmother's belief that a secure, middle-class home should takes precedence over romantic love. Nanny responds to Janie's rejection of the economically stable and physically unattractive Logan Killicks in the following way: "If you don't want him, you sho oughta. Heah you is wid de onliest organ in town, among colored folks, in yo' parlor. Got a house bought and paid for and sixty acres uh land right on de big road and . . . Lawd have mussy! Dat's de very prong all us black women gits hung on Dis love!" (22). The similarities between Janie and Freda go only so far because, ultimately, Janie rejects the aristocratic ideal that Freda embodies (represented by her love of jewelry, brushes and combs, the valorization of her light skin and long hair, and her preference for French over *Kreyol*, the language of the lower classes in Haiti). She laments to Pheoby the fact that "Jody classed me off," and rejoices when she finds in Tea Cake not only romantic love, but also the connection with the folk from which she has so often been discouraged. Janie finds no satisfaction in Logan Killicks' possessions, resents the fact that Jody sits her on the front porch like "a pretty doll-baby" (28), and rejoices when Tea Cake asks her to work in the muck with all the "common" folk.

Although Janie resents being "classed off," most of the other characters crave and envy the status that comes with having material possessions and a light-skinned wife. They worship and desire the materialistic and elitist lifestyle represented by the mulatta Freda, which eventually proves their downfall. While most of the folk share these desires, Mrs. Turner, Janie's "visiting friend" in the muck, proves the most egregious example of this mindset because her worship of Janie's mixed race features borders on self-hatred. Mrs. Turner "didn't cling to Janie Woods the woman. She paid homage to Janie's Caucasian characteristics as such":

Once having set up her idols and built altars to them it was inevitable that she would worship there. It was inevitable that she should accept any inconsistency and cruelty from her deity as all good worshippers do from theirs. All gods who receive homage are cruel. All gods dispense suffering without reason. Otherwise they would not be worshipped. Through indiscriminate suffering men know fear and fear is the most divine emotion. It is the stones for altars and the beginning of wisdom. Half gods are worshipped in wine and flowers. Real gods require blood. (138–39)

Mrs. Turner worships Janie's Caucasian features like an initiate worships the *lwa*—with blood sacrifices (interpreted in Turner's case to be her renunciation of "blood" ties to the other Blacks in her community) and an awareness that the gods can sometimes be arbitrary in their cruelty. This critique of Mrs. Turner's misplaced faith in whiteness is not a condemnation of Vodou, however. Rather, it is an honest assessment of the religion's tendency to respond to and reflect all of its worshippers' desires, including those that may be self-destructive. While the other characters are not as virulent in their internalized racism as Mrs. Turner, Nanny, Logan, Jody, the townsfolk, and even Tea Cake show signs of being color struck and materialistic. Thus, the text's condemnation of Mrs. Turner implicitly extends to a critique of other characters who share her views. Ironically, Hurston minimized the fact that African Americans shared attitudes of internalized racism with the Haitians and Jamaicans that she described in *Tell My Horse*. Despite the popular tendency to worship that which Ezili Freda represents, Janie eventually rejects the elitist trappings that characterize the *lwa* and embraces the working-class, folk identity of Ezili Dantò. When she returns to Eatonville, the women remark on the changes in her appearance. "What she doin' coming back here in dem overhalls?—What dat ole forty year ole 'oman doin' wid her hair swingin' down her back lak some young gal?" (2). While their vituperative comments reflect their envy of Janie's appearance and wealth, the changes in her appearance reflect a profound change in Janie's self-perception and a departure from the iconography of Ezili Freda.[15] The references to Janie's "overhalls" and age place her in the province of Ezili Dantò, the Petwo spirit, at the same time that her long hair and sensuality continue to align her with Freda. This passage resonates on multiple levels, positioning Janie as two kinds of women: one who benefits from and reaffirms gender, class, and color biases (signified by Freda), and one who is noted for her willingness to work and for her maturity (signified by Dantò).

McCarthy Brown describes Ezili Dantò as an independent woman with an unconventional sexuality. She has "dark black skin," and is "not too proud to work" (229). Although the fair-complexioned, relatively well-off Janie must convince Tea Cake that she is not above working in the fields with the other migrant laborers, she soon proves to be an enthusiastic worker. Dantò's black skin mirrors the blackness of the muck and that of the people in whom Janie finds fulfillment. Unlike the light-skinned Mrs. Turner who says she "can't stand black niggers" (135), or the mulatta Ezili Freda who detests those with black skin, Janie loves Tea Cake, his dark skin, and the affirmative connection with her community that blackness represents.

But Dantò also has the power to destroy, which earns her the reputation of being "red-eyed," or evil. Hurston calls her "the terrible Erzulie, ge-rouge . . . an older woman and terrible to look upon" (*Tell My Horse* 123).[16] That destructive force makes itself known during the hurricane, which erupts in order to convey Dantò's displeasure. This spirit, who represents working-class values and an assertive Blackness, violently objects to the African Americans' deference to White cultural, racial, and economic supremacy at the expense of their own autonomy. The danger of such attitudes becomes clear when the folk remain in the path of the storm, despite the warning signs they receive, because they are making "seven and eight dollars a day picking beans." In contrast to the Native Americans who know how to read the signs that nature gives them—"Saw-grass bloom. Hurricane coming," they say as they flee the Everglades—the African Americans ignore the warnings (146). They stay where they are because "De white folks ain't gone nowhere. Dey oughta know if it's dangerous" (148). This implicit trust in White people's authority proves their downfall and results in the deaths of scores of people. Tea Cake's "possession" by the rabid dog that bites him is the most graphic example of the consequences suffered by Black folks who blindly worship White-ness. His deference to the authority of the White landowners puts him at a risk similar to the Vodou worshippers of Petwo spirits.

Vodou stands in this novel as a reminder of Black independence and expressiveness, and Dantò demands payment when proper attention is not paid to these principles. Janie's deferral to Tea Cake, who insists that they follow the example of the White landowners, runs against her own instincts. Her acquiescence to his will mirrors the African American community's subordination to White authority and underscores the notion that their flaw is in the refusal to read the situation and interpret its meaning for themselves. When we first meet the young Janie, we learn that she can communicate with nature and understand its signs: "Janie had spent most of the day under a blossoming pear tree in the back-yard. She had been spending every minute that she could steal from her chores under that tree for the last three days. That was to say, ever since the first tiny bloom had opened. It had *called* her to come and gaze on a mystery. . . . She had been *summoned* to behold a revelation" (11, emphasis added). Janie's ability to "read" nature's signs mirrors that of the Native Americans who warn her and her friends to leave before the hurricane strikes. But her unwillingness to heed her own internal barometer results in a terrible price paid to nature's forces. Karla Holloway writes in *The Character of the Word*, "Nature has bowed to human forces throughout the novel. Here she shows that she is a power that can control, as well as be controlled. Perhaps her fury is a lesson for Janie, who has been linked with natural imagery throughout the story and who needs to learn the potential strength of her own independence."[17] All of the folks living in the Everglades, and not just Janie, need to learn to honor their independence.

Ezili Dantò makes her presence known at this point in the narrative. She is connected with water; a gentle rainfall signals her presence and a deluge signals her rage.[18] The hurricane is described as a terrifying and cosmic force that extracts the blood sacrifice that "real gods" demand: "Ten feet higher and as far as they could see the muttering wall advanced before the braced-up waters like a road crusher on a cosmic scale. The monstropolous beast had left his bed. The two hundred miles an hour wind had loosed his chains" (153). Dantò's rage erupts as a violent reminder to the folk that their passive faith in Euro-Americans, or Christianity, to determine their fate is misguided. The events leading up to the hurricane illustrate vividly the need for self-determination in the collective Black consciousness. This lesson comes too late for Tea Cake to learn, but his death is an example for other individuals. Likewise, Janie suffers for her passivity not only in losing Tea Cake, but also in having to act as the agent of his death.

Ezili Dantò's brutal insistence that the folk maintain their independence contradicts Christian doctrine, which traditionally advocated submission to authority.[19] The passiveness of the folk as they wait for the onslaught to begin underscores Christianity's traditional call for submissiveness: "They sat in company with the others in other shanties, their eyes straining against crude walls and their souls asking if He meant to measure their puny might against His. They seemed to be staring at the dark, but their eyes were watching God" (151). In contrast to this situation, which forces the folk to assume a posture of defeat, Hurston saw Vodou as facilitating a peasant self-expression that often subverted authority. Her account in *Tell My Horse* of the events that take place when Gede, the peasant god of death, mounts an individual, highlights the potential threat in the Vodou tradition to upend hierarchies and disrupt social order. When Gede speaks through the possessed, political, economic, and social injustices come under attack in way that could never be possible in Haitian society under ordinary circumstances. If an individual pretends to be possessed by the *lwa*, in effect putting on a mask of Gede, that attack becomes even more threatening than one from a possessed individual because it is a willful expression of anger, disgust, or defiance.

In Gede's burlesque antics, we find the most striking, but not the only, example of peasant self-expression threatening the stability of a social order. While possession by Gede results in the subversion of class hierarchies, the presence of Ezili Freda and Dantò illustrates the ways in which class identity and female agency are expressed in Haitian society (and, by extension, within Eatonville society as well). Vodou's implicit stress on self-expression echoes the novel's more explicit celebration of Black expressiveness through the storytelling that takes place. Storytelling and, by extension, other forms of self-expression have the capacity to liberate Janie from the many constraints placed on her. Powerful truths about life and love exist in Janie's story, which she recounts to her friend Pheoby while they sit on the back porch of her house. Janie's story takes on a mythic dimension and her words transcend even the limitations of her own life. Mary Helen Washington aptly describes those limitations:

One can hardly make ... an unequivocal claim for Janie's heroic posture in *Their Eyes*. . . . Her friendship with Pheoby, occurring apart from the community, encapsulates Janie and Pheoby in a private dyad that insulates Janie from the jealousy of other women. Like the other women in the town, she is barred from participation in the culture's oral tradition. When the voice of the black oral tradition is summoned in *Their Eyes*, it is not used to represent the collective black community, but to invoke and valorize the voice of the black *male* community.[20]

While I concur that the novel primarily celebrates the Black male oral tradition, I would reassert the significance of the frame story told by Janie to Pheoby. The frame story takes on the power and status of myth, which Leslie Desmangles describes as possessing "a paradoxical capacity to express complex truths in everyday language, to use common words and familiar objects to reveal what is most sacred in life."[21] Janie's gender and race certainly circumscribe her experiences, but her story speaks to the potential she carries within. Desmangles notes that "myths are . . . powerful vehicles which can transcend the limitations of profane existence" (61). While Janie may not fully realize her voice and agency in the time frame of the narrative, her mythic tale underscores the potential which exists within all Black women. Janie entrusts Pheoby with the responsibility of passing on her story and "de understandin" that goes along with it: "You can tell 'em what Ah say if you wants to. Dat's just de same as me 'cause mah tongue is in mah friend's mouf" (6). With this exhortation, the promise arises that a ritualized sharing of stories and experiences between women will develop. Pheoby will recount Janie's tale, but she will also revise it as she grows and experiences new things. She may inspire future listeners, just as Janie has inspired her. Janie's experience, her story, functions as myth for the folk, teaching them the value of self-expression and the necessity for self-determination.

Critical Schools: Tradition and Transformation

Hurston's incorporation into her novel of a religious tradition that she viewed as ancient and African does not preclude the text's relevance to the condition of modern African Americans. The Vodou intertext in *Their Eyes* actually enabled Hurston to grapple with issues that preoccupied Black intellectuals in the 1920s and 1930s, such as class, gender, interracial, and intraracial conflicts. Critical responses to the text failed to perceive, however, its immediate relevance to current events and modern political thought. Because Hurston positioned herself as an authority on Black culture in her lifetime, she practically instigated others to attack her representations of Black people and Black culture for their lack of authenticity or legitimacy. Alain Locke chastised Hurston in his annual literature review for *Opportunity* magazine for creating "those pseudo-primitives whom the reading public still loves to laugh with, weep over, and envy."[22] More biting than Locke's review was the critique by Richard Wright, who wrote that the novel "carries no theme, no message, no thought," and functioned only to satisfy the tastes of a White audience for the simple and exotic primitive.[23] Locke and Wright registered their conviction that Hurston's characters are too cartoonish, simple, and docile to be real.

They expressed their displeasure with Hurston's portrayal of local color during a time in which Northern Black newspapers regularly instructed those in their readership who were newly arrived from the South on proper etiquette in public places. Their discomfort with her portrayal of folk characters echoed the sensitivity of many African American intellectuals to the public's perception of Black culture. In his introduction to *New Essays on "Their Eyes Were Watching God*," Michael Awkward notes, "Sensitive to the need to improve white America's perception of Afro-Americans, some powerful black intellectuals, including Locke and W. E. B. Du Bois, believing that literature represented the most effective means by which to begin to dispel racist notions that black Americans were morally and cognitively subhuman, insisted that Afro-American writers were obligated to present Afro-Americans in the most favorable—and flattering—light possible" (10). Although Wright was subjected to similar criticisms upon the publication of *Native Son*, his review of *Their Eyes* reflects a touchiness regarding the proper strategy for depicting the African American lower classes. Although Locke and Wright couch their criticism in the rhetoric of authenticity, they seem to object more strenuously to Hurston's seemingly apolitical depiction of poor, uneducated Blacks to a presumably racist White audience.

Hurston's reputation has benefited from a surge in scholarly interest since the publication in the early 1970s of Alice Walker's essay, "Looking for Zora."[24] To this day, however, some critics retain a residual discomfort with her often flamboyant and controversial statements about Black culture. For example, Paul Gilroy asserts that Hurston's romanticization of "the folk" and idealization of rural, Southern culture prevent her from acknowledging African American cultural transformation. Gilroy's critique of Hurston assumes that the desire to preserve a sense of tradition automatically marks one as antagonistic to change. But Hurston proves herself a keen participant in the ongoing dialogues about social and cultural change within Black communities in the United States, which preoccupied her contemporaries during and after the Harlem Renaissance. Contrary to Gilroy's assessment, Hurston was absolutely interested in exploring the extent and effect of cultural transformation within African American communities; and Vodou was the primary avenue for accomplishing this exploration.

To illustrate his point, Gilroy teases out a compelling analysis of Hurston's contempt for the operatic performances of spirituals by the Fisk Jubilee Singers, focusing on her theories of authenticity and Black culture: "For Hurston, the success of the Fisk choir represented the triumph of musicians' tricks over the vital, untrained, angular spirit of the rural folk who 'care nothing about pitch' and 'are bound by no rules.' . . . She attacked the choir's performances as inauthentic."[25] He goes on to say, "I would emphasize that as far as this chapter is concerned, whether Hurston was right or wrong about the Fisk Singers is not the primary question. The issue which interests me more than her correctness is her strongly felt need to draw a line around what is and isn't authentically, genuinely, and really black" (92). The implied criticism in Gilroy's observation is that by insisting on an authentic way of singing the spirituals, Hurston resists an inevitable and dynamic change that is an inherent part of the Black Atlantic experience. In order to make this point, he understates the desire for upward class mobility that motivated individuals like the Fisk Singers to elevate a lowly folk art into "high" culture. I think it important, however, to focus on the reasons for her objections to what she considered the loss of integrity in a Black cultural production. Hurston's criticism was directed primarily toward the group's attempts to transform a rough, improvisational musical form born of illiterate Blacks into an operatic, and therefore more "cultured," form of music.[26] Her refusal to see the operatic performances of spirituals as authentic stems from her resistance to an aesthetic which continued to view poor Black culture as inferior, even as it attempted to rehabilitate and transform that culture for a wider audience.

While Hurston grappled with the significance and consequences of transformed cultural experiences, she was not willing to define a "New Negro" who was completely ignorant of, or free from, the influences of the past. Karla Holloway notes, "Hurston's was an ancient spirit in an age that demanded modernism, that called the Negro 'new' and expected that Negro to be male" (17). In my reading, Hurston's is not an ancient spirit. In fact she is fully engaged in questions of modernity and progress, yet her conception of the new refused to cede the loss or repression of African cultural fragments. Her objection to the choir's innovations was not so much that they diluted the music's Blackness with their injection of class and educational privilege; rather, she objected to the compromise, or abandonment, of the principles on which the music was based.

In an essay entitled, "Spirituals and Neo-Spirituals," Hurston describes such unique characteristics of Negro singing as "jagged harmony," disharmony, shifting keys, "broken time," and improvisation (80–81).[27] She was very much aware that most of these musical characteristics were African in origin. Eric Sundquist's comparison of Black English and Black music proves illuminating in understanding the rationale behind Hurston's objections. He asserts that the perceived strangeness of the language and the music (which we could also call African-ness) often led to anxiety in and ridicule from the dominant culture: "For whites' complaints about the ineffability of black dialect, which led in turn to the grotesque caricatures of minstrelsy and some plantation romance, repeated comparable observations by musicologists . . . that the intonations of the black spiritual were difficult to transcribe."[28] The elements of the spirituals that seem wrong to the ear trained in Western music (like the polyrhythms and blue notes which Hurston called broken time and disharmony) are the very elements that Hurston sought to preserve. Her critique of the Fisk Jubilee Singers was directed as much at the westernization of the spirituals *at the expense* of their African elements as it was toward the elegant concert halls and bourgeois performers and audience members. Hurston expressed her rejection of White cultural supremacy through her insistence on an authentic mode of performance, which Gilroy reads as a rejection of modernity. While some might argue that westernization is an inevitable and not necessarily negative cultural transformation, to do so without reservation is problematic if it does not challenge the then widely held assumption that European characteristics were superior to, more sophisticated, and more developed than African traits.

Unlike Gilroy, Hazel Carby acknowledges Hurston's investment in deflating class-driven pretensions, but like Gilroy, she finds Hurston too quick to delineate who the folk might be, as if such a homogenous group identity ever existed. In "The Politics of Fiction, Anthropology, and the Folk: Zora Neale Hurston," Carby notes that Hurston avoids any mention of the newly emergent Northern, urban Black and chooses to focus on an almost mythical South:

Hurston was concerned to establish authenticity in the representation of popular forms of folk culture and to expose the disregard for the aesthetics of that culture through inappropriate forms of representation. She had no problem in using the term 'the people' to register that she knew just who they were. But critics are incorrect to think that Hurston reconciled 'high' and 'low' forms of cultural production. Hurston's criticisms were not reserved for the elitist manner in which she thought the authentic culture of the people was reproduced. The people she wanted to represent she defined as a rural folk, and she measured them and their cultural forms against an urban, mass culture.[29] (75)

Carby concludes that Hurston displaces the migration of Blacks to the urban North with a nostalgic discourse about the rural South, resisting the cultural transformation that resulted from that migration. Like Gilroy, Carby stresses the need to recognize the transformation of Black culture and warns against the impulse to romanticize a homogenous experience. Carby's critique, like Gilroy's, is facilitated by Hurston's many reflections on the genuine and authentic in Black culture.[30] But Hurston's polemics do not preclude an active engagement in her literature with African American social and cultural change.

While Carby astutely observes that, in *Their Eyes*, Janie reverses the direction of most Black migrants, moving deeper South rather than North, she does not investigate the reasons for and implications of this movement.[31] She notes that Hurston situates "the southern, rural folk and patterns of migration in relation to the Caribbean rather than the northern states," viewing that migration ever southward as yet another displacement (82). Hurston's evocation of the Caribbean through Vodou, however, allows her to grapple with many of the issues being debated in cosmopolitan, intellectual circles during the Harlem Renaissance.[32] Carla Kaplan argues that critics who situate the novel within an "undetermined/undeterminable past" fail to recognize that by the end the novel's scenes take place precisely during the commencement of the Harlem Renaissance, 1921 or 1922.[33] Focusing on the novel's rural setting is a problem, Kaplan argues, because it deflects attention from the fact that Hurston's "treatment of desire and voice responds to that movement's most central debates" (122).

In *Their Eyes*, Hurston comments on issues of class, gender, sexuality, and cultural identity primarily through her use of Vodou imagery. The novel takes up many of the same issues being debated by her contemporaries during the twenties and thirties. For example, Harlem was frequently celebrated as unique because it was a gathering place for diverse people of the African Diaspora. Alain Locke writes in "The New Negro":

Here in Manhattan is not merely the largest Negro community in the world, but the first concentration in history of so many diverse elements of Negro life. It has attracted the African, the West Indian, the Negro American; has brought together the Negro of the north and the Negro of the south; the man from the city and the man from the town and village; the peasant, the student, the business man, the professional man, artist, poet, musician, adventurer and worker, preacher and criminal, exploiter and social outcast. Each group has come with its own separate motives and for its own special ends, but their greatest experience has been the finding of one another. (6)

In asserting that "their greatest experience has been the finding of one another," Locke minimizes any social or cultural tensions that may have existed between the different groups gathered in Harlem and celebrates Harlem as a center of African Diasporic culture. This emerging and changing culture, noted for its diversity, is but one of the social transformations Carby suggests Hurston could have recognized.

Locke's optimism actually was shared by Hurston, and is implicitly echoed in an easily overlooked passage in the novel. In it she describes how the Bahamians and Black Americans working in the Everglades overcome their initial trepidation over each other's foreignness by dancing together. The Bahamians "quit hiding out to hold their dances when they found that their American friends didn't laugh at them as they feared. Many of the Americans learned to jump and liked it as much as the 'Saws.' So they began to hold dances night after night in the quarters, usually behind Tea Cake's house" (146). The relative ease with which these groups overcome their differences suggests that national and ethnic identification can be blurred with a greater awareness and cultivation of cultural similarities, and a greater tolerance of and interest in cultural difference. So, in the midst of their dances, we cannot distinguish between American and Bahamian as they make "living, sculptural, grotesques in the dance" (147). This reference to "sculptural grotesques," African sculptures brought to life, evokes the dancers' shared ancestry. One might question the assumption voiced in this passage that cultural, political, and economic differences can be easily eradicated by social interaction. Nonetheless, while critics like Carby and Gilroy are justified in drawing our attention to Hurston's tendencies toward nostalgic romanticization, I argue that the allusions to Vodou reveal her to possess a more complex vision of Black Atlantic cultures. Her immersion in tradition, specifically Haitian Vodou tradition, opens the novel up to politicized readings of contemporary African American racial, gender, and class politics.

Just as Locke saw the social and political potential of Harlem because it was a site of "group expression and self-determination," Hurston saw that same potential in Haitian Vodou. The elements of the text that Carby identifies as displacements to the South and to the Caribbean actually allow Hurston to explore, through metaphor and symbolism, the social and political concerns of African Americans in the North, South, and throughout the Caribbean. Hurston was not solely interested in elevating African American folk culture; she was also invested in collecting and recreating through fiction what Black people had to say about themselves. Haitian Vodou provided Hurston with the ideal vehicle to voice African Diasporic people's (especially women's) views on their social status and unique experiences, demonstrating that ancient tradition can effectively shape our comprehension of modern cultures that are constantly evolving. This perhaps explains why she broke temporarily from her field notes and fieldwork to write a fictional work that refuses the ethnographic eye and privileges the Black speaking subject's voice. This shift in focus offers a radically different per-spective on knowledge production that needs to be read in conjunction with Hurston's ethnographic narratives. In other words, just as we need to know the ethnographic literature to more accurately read and interpret *Their Eyes'* symbolism, so do we need to know her fiction to more accurately read Hurston's ethnography.

Chapter 9
Afterword

By focusing on five authors who portray different sites that represented to them African American culture, I have elucidated the ways that the ethnographic imagination informs New Negro literature, including the introduction of a set of figurative devices derived from anthropology (the construction of the field and the territorialization of culture, the ethnographic eye, and the participant-observer, for example). I have also examined how their identification with dual sites of identification, "native" and ethnographer (in some cases the assumption of such a guise is more figurative than literal), resulted in the emergence of a literary preoccupation with ways of seeing, knowing, and representing African American culture. This is not to say that such questions had never been asked before the modernization and institutionalization of anthropology; rather, I argue that the active exchange of ideas between Black intellectuals and modern anthropologists in the early part of the twentieth century played a significant role in the cast and tenor of such discussions. Ultimately, thinking about ethnography (or about themselves as ethnographers) underscores for Renaissance writers their own positions in relation to the cultures that they represent *in* writing and *as* teachers, scholars, and politicians. The ethnographer-academic, in other words, assumes a symbolic role in Black literatures beginning in and extending beyond the Renaissance period, representing hegemonic culture.

A group of texts has emerged in the twentieth century that repeatedly returns to such figures of cross-cultural transit. From Alice Walker's reworking of Du Boisian paradigms of culture-work and racial uplift in *Meridian*, to Sherley Anne Williams and Toni Morrison's depictions of the dehumanizing views and actions of the "schoolteacher" figure in *Dessa Rose and Beloved*, to Paule Marshall and Gloria Naylor's fictional rejection of the ethnographer as an adequate bridge between dominant culture and African American communities in *Chosen Place, Timeless People*, and *Mama Day*, the figures for crossing cultures and the methods of knowing and understanding difference established during the modernist era continue to exert their influence.

Still other books ask if individuals can only "find" (authentic) Black culture in the South, or in other geographically bounded locations. The territorialization of culture, often linked to its aestheticization, lies in opposition to a view of culture as process and as relational. This dichotomy is explored in contemporary narratives, such as Paule Marshall's *Praisesong for the Widow*, Toni Morrison's *Tar Baby* and *Song of Solomon*, and Gloria Naylor's *Mama Day*. In *Mama Day*, the ethnographer enters a space that he conceptualizes as "the field," only to learn that it refuses to be managed. Attempting to write a scholarly monograph, this ethnographer arrives with the expectation that he will foreground his observation and analysis of folk customs. The novel turns this assumption on its head, however, by recentering the folks' perspective on the ethnographer, whom we also learn is the offspring of one of the island's inhabitants. We discover that "Reema's boy" was born in Willow Springs, was educated on the mainland, and "came hauling himself back from one of those fancy colleges mainside, dragging his notebooks and tape recorder and a funny way of curling up his lip and clicking his teeth."[1] This (not-quite) outsider strikes a discordant note in this setting because of his inability to listen carefully to what the "folk" find meaningful about their own lives. He is too preoccupied, in other words, with constructing them as primitive other to consider them equal participants in the discursive exchange.

Reema's Boy represents the figure of the African American, adrift from home and longing to remember and preserve it; he also stands in for dominant cultural assumptions of the superiority of cosmopolitan subjects, metropolitan spaces, and institutionalized knowledge. The ethnographer thus stands as a cautionary figure for the novel's main characters, George and Cocoa, who also want to reclaim and reconstruct their origins, as well as being a figure of cross-cultural exchange. By highlighting the experiences of individuals who, in contrast to the ethnographer, either possess or seek to acquire a more meaningful and equitable relationship with the people whom they view as the keepers of their cultural heritage, and by problematizing both the notion of cultural essence and the dynamics of cultural change, Naylor considers the possibility of an African American identity rooted in a communal identity, yet not restricted to a particular geographical location or homogenous idea of blackness.[2]

What I argue in regards to Naylor's text I would extend to a larger segment of African American literature, namely that it takes up a particular tradition of querying the limits and possibilities of representing African American culture. This is a tradition that is indebted at least in part to the prominence of anthropology in the New Negro imagination, and early twentieth-century ventures into the ethnographic field *continue* to have a deep influence on the writings of contemporary African American novelists. Wrestling with and against the constraints of representing "the race," contemporary writers widen the possibilities of transcultural movement and communication, for they can imagine worlds in which black cultures travel temporally and spatially, and black subjects move across a variety of terrains. In the post-Renaissance era, Black writers have found new and creative ways to critique the dominance of Western hegemony. At the same time, contemporary Black writers rely on a store of images, characters, legends, and stories embedded in African American folklore. These are cultural materials that have flooded through the gates opened by Renaissance writers willing to contend with the complexities of the ethnographic imagination.

Notes

Chapter 1

1. Zora Neale Hurston, *Mules and Men* (Bloomington: Indiana University Press, 1935) 4–5.

2. For this reason, I hesitate to fully embrace Kamala Visweswaran's provocative contention that experimental ethnography's concern with the construction of subjectivities would be better served if it were to allow for an "alternate ethnographic canon" consisting of other forms of writing such as novels, short stories, diaries, or autobiography. Perhaps we can read such texts as "expressive of culture," but shouldering the responsibility of representing a personal or fictional narrative as representative of a group experience forecloses the possibilities of individual self-expression and literary creativity. See Kamala Visweswaran, *Fictions of Feminist Ethnography* (Minneapolis: University of Minnesota Press, 1994) 32–33.

3. I am indebted to Fred Moten, who, during a talk at Rutgers University's Black Atlantic Seminar at the Center for Historical Analysis, brought this dimension of Hurston's work to my attention and first illuminated the point through the analogy to Wittgenstein's duck-rabbit. See Ludwig Wittgenstein, *The Philosophical Investigations*, ed. G. E. M. Anscombe (London: Blackwell Publishers, 2001).

4. Houston Baker, *Modernism and the Harlem Renaissance* (Chicago: University of Chicago Press, 1989).

5. Mitchell Breitwieser, "*The Great Gatsby*: Grief, Jazz and the Eye-Witness," *Arizona Quarterly: A Journal of American Literature, Culture and Theory* 7, no. 3 (1991): 17–70.

6 F. Scott Fitzgerald, *The Great Gatsby* (New York: Bantam, 1974) 70.

7. Zora Neale Hurston, *Dust Tracks on a Road* (London: Virago, 1986) 177.

8. Joanne Passaro " 'You Can't Take the Subway to the Field!': 'Village' Epistemologies in the Global Village," in *Anthropological Locations: Boundaries and Grounds of a Field Science*, ed. Akhil Gupta and James Ferguson (Berkeley: University of California Press, 1997) 152.

9. Carla Kaplan, ed., *Zora Neale Hurston: A Life in Letters* (New York: Anchor, 2003) 114.

10. Robert Hemenway, Introduction, in *Mules and Men* by Zora Neale Hurston (Bloomington: Indiana University Press, 1978) xxiii.

11. Shamoon Zamir, *Dark Voices: W. E. B. Du Bois and American Thought 1888–1903* (Chicago: University of Chicago Press, 1995) 8.

12. This is a point that Marc Manganaro makes in examining the intersections

of literature and anthropology (Marc Manganaro, *Culture, 1922: The Emergence of a Concept* [Princeton: Princeton University Press, 2002]). In *Culture, 1922*, he writes that "whereas Eliot, with *The Waste Land*, gained the stage as a main player of literary modernism through his articulation of the fragmentation of culture, Malinowski, on the other hand, established his credentials in *Argonauts of the Western Pacific* by articulating culture as whole. In this regard, following Clifford's line, Malinowski limited his articulation of cultural fragmentation to his diary" (69–70). The difference in the writing of New Negro modernists, I would argue, is that expressions of culture as whole and cultural fragmentation exist in exquisite tension within individual texts conceived with a public readership in mind.

13. Manganaro, in his discussion of modern anthropological definitions of culture writes that Malinowski argued "for a new economy of anthropological method based upon the close participant observation of a single people in a single place in order to arrive at what makes that particular culture cohere or 'function'" (*Culture, 1922* 5). Malinowski's 1922 *Argonauts of the Western Pacific* (Prospect Heights, Ill.: Waveland Press, 1984) is the first, and paradigmatic, example of a narrative employing this method.

14. Gabbin cites a 1974 article by Genevieve Ekaete in which Brown's remarks are recorded. For an extended discussion of Brown's views on the Renaissance, see Genevieve Ekaete, "Sterling Brown: A Living Legend," *New Directions: The Howard University Magazine* 1 (1974): 5–11, and Joanne V. Gabbin, *Sterling A. Brown: Building the Black Aesthetic Tradition* (Westport, Conn.: Greenwood Press, 1985) 199.

15. Olaudah Equiano's *The Interesting Narrative of the Life of Olaudah Equiano or Gustavus Vassa, The African* (New York: W. W. Norton, 2000) and Alex Haley's *Roots* (New York: Doubleday, 1976) offer the most obvious examples of such approaches because both authors relied on travel and/or ethnographic narratives to lend verity to their accounts of West African village life. Yet while these two authors intentionally blur the boundaries between personal and historic accounts, it is not uncommon for naïve readers to come to narratives written by people of color—including those that are clearly fictional—with the expectation of finding representations of "authentic" experience.

16. Kaplan 122–23.

17. Manganaro describes Hurston's body of work as more "hybridic" than that of her cohort of Boas students—"embodying and arguing a conception of both text and culture as less whole and more ragged" (11).

18. This is the subject of fairly recent critical inquiry. See, for example, Ruth Behar and Deborah Gordon, *Women Writing Culture* (Berkeley: University of California Press, 1995) and Visweswaran, *Fictions of Feminist Ethnography*.

19 Marshall Hyatt marks the early part of the century as anthropology's "classical period" because of a number of notable changes to the discipline. He notes that Franz Boas directed the course of the discipline's professionalization by training graduate students in anthropological methods, guiding the creation of psychology and anthropology departments at Columbia University, and helping to establish the American Anthropological Association (Marshall Hyatt, *Franz Boas: Social Activist* [New York: Greenwood Press, 1990] 48–54).

20. Each of Talal Asad, *Anthropology and the Colonial Encounter* (London: Ithaca

Press, 1973), Mary Louise Pratt, *Imperial Eyes: Travel Writing and Transculturation* (New York: Routledge, 1992), and Edward Said, *Culture and Imperialism* (New York: Vintage, 1994) explores the connections between colonialist discursive practices and modern anthropology. Deborah Gordon ("The Politics of Ethnographic Authority: Race and Writing in the Ethnography of Margaret Mead and Zora Neale Hurston," in *Modernist Anthropology: From Fieldwork to Text*, ed. Marc Manganaro [Princeton: Princeton University Press, 1990] 146–62) makes the astute observation that "Anthropology's very existence as a profession was complexly linked to colonialism, yet the pose of ethnographers was as if they were the first Westerners to encounter the colonies" (153). In other words, the separation of the anthropologist from the colonial encounter is an artificial one.

21. Joyce Aschenbrenner credits George Stocking with identifying Bronislaw Malinowski as establishing the precedent of identifying cultural translation as the mythic charter of anthropology. See Joyce Aschenbrenner, "Katherine Dunham: Anthropologist, Artist, Humanist," in *African-American Pioneers in Anthropology*, ed. Ira E. Harrison and Faye V. Harrison (Chicago: University of Illinois Press, 1999) 142.

22 See James Clifford, "Power and Dialogue in Ethnography: Marcel Griaule's Initiation," in *The Predicament of Culture: Twentieth-Century Ethnography, Literature, and Art* (Cambridge: Harvard University Press, 1988) for an analysis of a parallel moment in post-World War I France. His discussion of how the ethnographers' documentation of cultural difference and collection of cultural artifacts functioned to satisfy Europeans' passion for things African also pertains to the climate in the United States during the same historical period.

23. David Levering Lewis, *W. E. B. Du Bois: A Biography of a Race 1868–1919* (New York: Henry Holt and Company, 1993) 276.

24. Hurston wrote to Langston Hughes on April 30, 1929, "I want to leave no loop-holes for the scientific crown to rend and tear us," but nevertheless, rend and tear they did. See Kaplan (165–68) for a discussion of a particularly galling incident in which the Rosenwald foundation decreased the amount of an award it had granted to Hurston, despite her years of experience as an ethnographer and multiple publications, for fear of her lack of discipline and commitment to producing "serious scholarship."

25. W. E. B. Du Bois, *The Souls of Black Folk* (New York: The Library of America, 1986) 457.

26. Vernon Williams, *Rethinking Race: Franz Boas and His Contemporaries* (Lexington: University Press of Kentucky, 1996) 16.

27. William S. Willis, Jr., "Skeletons in the Anthropological Closet," in *Reinventing Anthropology*, ed. D. Hymes (New York: Pantheon, 1972) 121–52, adds in his biting indictment of anthropological discourse that even the "scientific antiracism" practiced by Boas and his followers shared with the "scientific racism" practiced by E. B. Tylor and other Victorian anthropologists the expectation that their work would contribute to the improvement of White societies. The guise of scientific neutrality, Willis argues, masked these aims while also providing a rationale for the anthropologists' refusal to participate in or advocate for socioeconomic reform. See Willis especially 129–41.

28. Mary Louise Pratt, "Fieldwork in Common Places," in *Writing Culture: The*

Poetics and Politics of Ethnography, ed. James Clifford and George E. Marcus (Berkeley: University of California Press, 1986) 32.

29. Gloria Anzaldua, *Borderlands/La Frontera: The New Mestiza* (San Francisco: Spinsters/Aunt Lute, 1987) 37.

30. In "Ethnography as Politics," in *Decolonizing Anthropology: Moving Further Toward an Anthropology for Liberation*, ed. Faye V. Harrison (Washington, D.C.: Association of Black Anthropologists, American Anthropological Association, 1991) 88–109, Faye V. Harrison asserts, "Few would argue . . . that anthropology is a politically neutral quest for objective knowledge and truth about the human condition" because the discipline and the politics of neo-colonialism and imperialism are too closely intertwined. Arguing that an "anthropology of liberation" can only be based on a practitioner's deliberate choice to work against social and economic injustice, Harrison writes that the most constructive alternatives have been conceived and produced by Blacks who challenge the discipline's Eurocentric and colonial aspects by producing "native or indigenous anthropology." The inclusion of "native" perspectives on First and Third World societies is a necessary step toward the decolonization of anthropology (88).

31. The virtual anthropologist, Weston argues, always lacks an authentic other unless she speaks as an authentic other, in which case she loses the authority to be an authentic anthropologist. Yet, Weston argues, the virtual anthropologist's hybridity may also offer the best vantage point from which to critique and complicate the anthropological venture because she constantly wrestles with the terms that are used to define her (Kath Weston, "The Virtual Anthropologist," in *Anthropological Locations* 163–84).

32. Weston argues that the Virtual Anthropologist is a hybrid, characterized not by the mixture of two distinct attributes but by a compound reaction that "transforms the whole into something different from either of its two parts." She adds, "whether or not the Native Ethnographer embraces the categories that define her, she is not a split subject, but a hybrid who collapses the subject/object distinction" (168).

33. The possible exceptions may be Du Bois and Hurston, whose influence on sociology and anthropology, respectively, is more widely recognized. Yet their institutional reputations have only recently begun to be established within their respective fields. Because Hurston never terminated her studies with an anthropology degree, her legitimacy rests on the innovativeness of her work, which anticipates the postmodern turn of contemporary anthropology. On the other hand, Dan Green and Edwin Driver in *W. E. B. Du Bois: On Sociology and the Black Community* (Chicago: University of Chicago Press, 1978) 39, argue that Du Bois's legacy should have been recognized long before the 1970s, when he began to receive his due, because of "his work during the years 1896–1910, when sociology was being established as an academic discipline. He established a department of sociology at Atlanta University, created a laboratory of sociology, instituted a program of systematic research, founded and conducted regular sociological conferences on research, founded two journals (*Crisis* and *Phylon: A Journal of Race Relations*)," and his list of achievements and contributions to the field continues.

34. In "Ethnography, Thievery, and Cultural Identity: A Rereading of Michel Leiris's *L'Afrique Fantome*," *Publications of the Modern Language Association* 112, no. 2 (1997): 229–42, Ruth Larson argues that French ethnography of the 1920s and 1930s

"practices a sensitivity to native cultures and to the difficulties inhering in any project to represent them" and that this practice echoes the postmodern era's "crisis of representation" (229). Because of the complexities of describing cultures that they identify with and are removed from, Du Bois's, Johnson's, Brown's, Dunham's, and Hurston's texts resemble French ethnography of the 1920s and 1930s in their sensitivity to the difficulties of representing "other" cultures.

35. Alain Locke, "The New Negro," in *The New Negro*, ed. Alain Locke (1925; reprint New York: Atheneum, 1992) 3–16.

36 Walter Jackson, "Melville Herskovits and the Search for Afro-American Culture," in *Malinowski, Rivers, Benedict and Others: Essays on Culture and Personality*, ed. George Stocking (Madison: University of Wisconsin Press, 1986) 95–126.

37. Faye V. Harrison, "Ethnography as Politics" 88.

38. Clifford, *Predicament of Culture* 104.

39. See Manganaro, *Culture, 1922* 66–73.

40. Manganaro makes a similar observation about the difference between Ruth Benedict and Zora Neale Hurston's ethnographies. He writes, "Benedict's stance throughout *Patterns [of Culture]* is one of distance, the comparative anthropologist-God paring [her fingernails]: there is no mention in *Patterns* of fieldwork trouble, nor is there much of a sense of the ethnographer's 'being there,' despite Goetz's claim. . . . Hurston's persona Zora, on the other hand, is there in one's face, often invisible *only* in the sense of being indistinguishable from the rural madding crowd of welding into the black folk culture" (*Culture, 1922* 176).

Chapter 2

1. Herbert Hovenkamp, "Social Science and Segregation Before *Brown*," *Duke Law Journal* 1985, no. 3/4 (June-September 1985): 637.

2. Perceived racial differences were viewed to be so profound that these" hereditary determinists" believed that race mixing was hazardous because it could "slow the evolutionary progress of the more advanced race" and lead to the reproduction of unhealthy children (Hovenkamp 635–36).

3. Tylor articulated his theories in *The Origins of Culture*, vol. 1 (1871; repr., New York: Harper and Row, 1958).

4. Daryl Michael Scott, *Contempt and Pity: Social Policy and the Image of the Damaged Black Psyche, 1880–1996* (Chapel Hill: University of North Carolina Press, 1997) argues that the history of social science has been one that reinforces the image of Black pathology, resulting in responses that are opposing yet related, harboring either contempt or pity. In his book, which examines the history of the social sciences from 1880 to 1996, Scott argues, "damage imagery has been the product of liberals and conservatives, of racists and antiracists. Often playing on white contempt toward blacks, racial conservatives have sought to use findings of black pathology to justify exclusionary policies and to explain the dire conditions under which many black people live. Often seeking to mobilize white pity, racial liberals have used damage imagery primarily to justify policies of inclusion and rehabilitation" (xi). In contrast to

Scott who might argue that all social science discourse is fundamentally racist, Hovenkamp argues that "the real beginning of the end of racist anthropology" occurred in late 1920s when Melville Herskovits's *The American Negro* "discredited many long-held scientific ideas about the physical and mental characteristics of the black American." Hovenkamp concludes "environmentalism encouraged—even demanded—integration" because it suggested that Black inequality could only be redressed by giving African Americans the same opportunities in education and economic opportunities (670–72).

5. Donald Waters, "The Hampton Folklore Society and its Collection of Black American Folklore: An Introduction," in *Strange Ways and Sweet Dreams: Afro-American Folklore from the Hampton Institute* (Boston: G. K. Hall & Co., 1983) 1–128. For a more complete discussion of the Hampton Idea, see Waters 17–22.

6. Waters describes the HFS membership as comprising "ordinary black teachers and students, prominent Negro businessmen, present and future leaders of the black community, and white teachers both of humble origins and of distinguished family backgrounds" (52).

7. Michael Elliot, "Ethnography, Reform, and the Problem of the Real: James Mooney's *Ghost-Dance Religion*," *American Quarterly* 50, no. 2 (1998): 201–33 discusses how ethnography and ideologies of assimilation were wedded in U.S. treatment and reform of Native Americans. In many ways these attempts to bring received notions of civilization and progress to Native peoples paralleled Hampton Institute's pedagogical aims; not surprisingly Native Americans, as well as African Americans, matriculated at Hampton.

8. Lee Baker, "Research, Reform and Racial Uplift: The Mission of the Hampton Folklore Society 1893–1899," in *Excluded Ancestors, Inventible Traditions: Essays Toward a More Inclusive History of Anthropology*, vol. 9, ed. Richard Handler (Madison: University of Wisconsin Press, 2000) 43.

9. Baker suggests that folklore could contribute to a kind of rhetorical "before and after" portrait. In Bacon's December 1893 call to form the Hampton Folk-Lore Society, he argues she "seems to suggest that her proposed folklore society might be the last opportunity of Hampton educators to record the 'ignorant people,' before the impact of common schools eclipsed the remaining folk culture. Armed with a record of African American folklore that was no longer practiced, the educators at Hampton would be able to reproduce the popular before and after images used to raise money for their Indian program" ("Research" 56).

10. Reprinted in Waters 150. Originally published in *Southern Workman* 22, no. 12 (December 1893): 180–81.

11. In a more moderate tone, Booker T. Washington (*Up from Slavery*, ed. William Andrews [New York: W. W. Norton, 1996]) also declared, "The students were making progress in learning books and in developing their minds; but it became apparent at once that, if we were to make any permanent impression upon those who had come to us for training, we must do something besides teach them mere books. The students had come from homes where they had had no opportunities for lessons which would teach them how to care for their bodies" (60).

12. See also K. K. Gaines, *Uplifting the Race: Black Leadership, Politics, and Culture in the Twentieth Century* (Chapel Hill: University of North Carolina Press, 1996).

13. It is not surprising to learn that, as Baker informs us, Moton and Davis "made a significant departure from the espionage and exorcism outlined by Armstrong and adapted by Bacon." Moton, for example, viewed folklore and its collection as an opportunity to challenge the contemptuous treatment of African American folksongs and stories by the minstrel industry (Baker, "Research" 58–59).

14. Cooper made these remarks at the same inaugural 1894 folklore conference of the HFS at which William Wells Newell, president of the American Folklore Society, gave his keynote address. Her paper was subsequently published in *Southern Workman* 23 (1894): 5, and reprinted in Waters 190–92.

15. As evidence of this fundamental divergence of philosophies, Waters describes the response of Samuel Chapman Armstrong, the founder of the Hampton Institute, to an 1884 article in which Shaler argued for a genetic link between intelligence and race. Armstrong argued in a rebuttal to Shaler that, based on his observation of hundreds of Hampton students, some of whom gained admission to elite institutions of higher education such as Harvard and Yale, intellectual development varied within the race, and that mental capacity did not correspond to the darkness or lightness of one's complexion. Both Shaler and Armstrong observed differences in the intellectual achievements of Blacks and Whites, but where Shaler attributed those differences to a question of mental capacity; Armstrong proposed that the problem was rooted in the experience of slavery, which deprived Blacks of the opportunity to attend to their abilities (Waters 13–15). Waters describes the "Hampton Idea's" fundamental difference with Shaler's theories in *Strange Ways and Sweet Dreams* 17–22.

16. Boas had just migrated to New York in 1887.

17. The first president of the American Folklore Society was Francis J. Child, a professor of English at Harvard University and authority on English and Scottish ballads; but AFLS founder Newell sought to define folklore as a science, distinguishable from literature. Consequently, after Child stepped down following a one-year term, Newell sought Franz Boas and other anthropologists out in order to establish the organization's scientific credentials (Waters 61).

18. Waters notes that Alice Bacon was Newell's main contact. Through his correspondence with her, he encouraged the group to strive for scientific rigor and to function as more than just a social club (36–37).

19. It is important to note that Newell included ethnicity in the category of "race," and so spoke without hesitation about similarities among the English, French, German, and Negro "races."

20. An exchange between Bacon and Newell over the HFS's procurement of recording equipment lends insight into the significance of this technological intervention. In "Work and Methods of the Hampton Folklore Society," a paper presented in 1897 and published in the *Journal of American Folk-Lore* in 1898, Bacon described the "difficulty of transcribing a 'weird melody chanted at baptism' or a 'complicated negro religious ritual'" (quoted in Baker 65–66). She concluded with an appeal to the AFLS for a graphophone in order to record the songs and other folklore that HFS members were committed to collecting. The need for a technological means of capturing the folklore and folksongs *in situe* suggest that the folklorists' attempts at cultural preservation necessitated that the actual "object" be put on display. Reenactment, which they recognized could only be an approximation, was not suitable for their ends; and so

Newell worked hard, albeit unsuccessfully, to provide Bacon with the equipment she requested.

21. Baker, "Research," 66.

22. Anthropologists in the nineteenth and early decades of the twentieth century tended to focus on Native American cultures more than others. Antecedents to the ethnologists' focus on African Americans include not only the Hampton Folklore Society but also two folklore collections: the popularized *Uncle Remus: His Songs and His Sayings* (1880) and *Slave Songs of the United States* (1867).

23. Waters discusses the Institute's pedagogical concern with "character" (20). Baker argues the work of folklorists of the 1890s differed from that of folklorists of the twenties. New Negro intellectuals "were succeeding in empowering new understandings of black culture, in part by using folklore to *embrace* their African heritage" ("Research" 44, emphasis added).

24. In a 1945 address to the American Folklore Society, departing president Melville Herskovits ("Folklore after a Hundred Years; A Problem in Redefinition," *The Journal of American Folklore* 59, no. 232 [April–June 1946]: 89–100) described the shifts in definitions of folklore that took place over the preceding one hundred years. He states, "In the field of folklore, we now recognize that 'superstition' is a segment of custom, and as such is a sociological, an historical, a psychological, an ethnographic phenomenon; and that the study of such materials calls for techniques that we, as folklorists, have not taken time to develop. If we refuse to consider 'the folk' as quaint, or backward, or ignorant, but use the term to designate any people or any class in any society that as a group exhibit identifiably distinctive modes of life; if we then concentrate our efforts on the study of their literary expression, folklore becomes a field concerned with realities of life and not with the relics of a dead past" (99).

25. Lee Baker, *From Savage to Negro: Anthropology and the Construction of Race, 1896–1954* (Berkeley: University of California Press, 1998) 166–67.

26. Desley Deacon observes that New York's geographical layout made it more amenable than more spread-out cities like Chicago to nurturing the development of communities that broke with convention and attempted to remake the world on more tolerant and democratic grounds. "As novelist Edna Ferber observed, Chicago never developed a lasting bohemia because it took so long to travel from one part of the city to another. Greenwich Village, by contrast, provided cheap accommodation and eateries close to the settlements, publishing houses, and ethnic communities that provided work, subject matter, and the stimulus of imported ideas and cultural practices (Desley Deacon, *Elsie Clews Parson: Inventing Modern Life* [Chicago: University of Chicago Press, 1997] 112).

27. The intersection of social policies and legal codes with anthropological theories has been well documented by scholars. See, for example, Baker, *From Savage to Negro*; Hovenkamp, "Science and Segregation Before *Brown*"; Walter Jackson, *Gunnar Myrdal and America's Conscience: Social Engineering and Racial Liberalism* (Chapel Hill: University of North Carolina Press, 1990); and Scott, *Contempt and Pity*.

28. Boas completed a doctorate in physics with a minor in geography in 1871. After completing his doctorate, Boas participated in a geographic expedition to the Cumberland sound in Baffinland, Greenland in 1883. There he encountered a community of Eskimos that transformed him and influenced the shape of his career by

illuminating for him the ways that environment "affect[s] the institutions, beliefs, rituals, and social rules of a society." He went on a second field trip in 1886 to the Pacific Northwest where he studied members of the Bella Coolla. After this trip, he went to New York instead of returning to Germany and joined the editorial staff of *Science*. He then joined the faculty of Clark University in Worcester, Mass., working there from 1889 to 1892, when he resigned to work on the World Columbian Exposition with F. W. Putnam (Baker, *Savage* 101).

29. The term is Lee Baker's.

30. See Gelya Frank, "Jews, Multiculturalism, and Boasian Anthropology," *American Anthropologist* 99, no. 4 (December 1997): 731–45 for an examination of the significance of the prevalence of Jewish intellectuals in the early years of Boasian anthropology.

31. Franz Boas, "Human Faculty as Determined by Race," in *A Franz Boas Reader: The Shaping of American Anthropology, 1883–1911*, ed. George W. Stocking, Jr. (Chicago: University of Chicago Press, 1974) 221–42.

32. Franz Boas, "The Real Race Problem," *Crisis Magazine* 1, no. 5 (1910): 22–25.

33. Franz Boas, "The Negro and the Demands of Modern Life: Ethnic and Anatomical Considerations," *Charities: A Review of Local and General Philanthropy* 15, no. 1 (1905): 86–88.

34. Boas consistently joined his critique of scientific racism with a rejection of Western colonial practice. For example, in this essay, Boas asserts, "Native industries and native art disappear with incredible rapidity wherever the European and American trader steps. This is largely due to the fact that an hour or two of service makes it possible to acquire efficient tools and utensils, which are only too willingly substituted for the less effective though artistic products of native industry, which it may require days or months to make. Owing to the ease with which cheap foreign goods are acquired, the whole basis of the economic life of primitive peoples breaks down" (Franz Boas, "Industries of the African Negroes," *Southern Workman* 38 [1909]: 221).

35. Williams, *Rethinking Race* 29.

36. W. E. B. Du Bois, *Black Folks Then and Now: An Essay in the History and Sociology of the Negro Race* (New York: Henry Holt & Co., 1940) vii.

37. George Hutchinson, *The Harlem Renaissance in Black and White* (Cambridge: Harvard University Press, 1995) 62.

38. Hutchinson's focus on intellectual exchanges that take place in "intentionally egalitarian interracial efforts, intimacies and commitments," because, he suggests, previous scholars have overemphasized the conflicts that arose over the control over the production of knowledge and culture (27). See especially chapter 3. Hutchinson's emphasis on the mutual exchange of ideas challenges typical accounts of interracial relations during this period, such as Nathan Irvin Huggins's and David Levering Lewis's, that paint a picture of unequal exchange and co-optation by Whites. Two examples best illustrate this more typical interpretation of interracial relations in this period. In "Paul Robeson and the Problem of Modernism," in *Rhapsodies in Black*, ed. Richard J. Powell (Berkeley: University of California Press, 1997), Jeffrey C. Stewart offers an example of the struggle for editorial control: "Du Bois and Johnson . . . edited the magazines *The Crisis* and *Opportunity*, respectively, which published most of Harlem's poetry, fiction and visual illustration, but they operated at the behest of

largely white organizations with whom both editors had problematic relationships. . . . A system of white vetting of black intellectuals and artists ensured that when the writers or actors veered too far outside of the parameters of white modernist enthusiasm, the black recipients of white patronage often found themselves abandoned" (93). In a similar vein, in *Harlem Renaissance* (London: Oxford University Press, 1973), Nathan Irvin Huggins describes Langston Hughes' struggles for authorial control when he worked under the financial patronage of an elderly Park Avenue matron: "Hughes felt pushed to produce, even when he did not feel like writing. 'I didn't realize that she was old and wanted quickly to see my books come into being before she had to go away'" (134). After writing a poem that parodied the social disparities of Black and White New York, Hughes recognized he had disappointed his patron's expectations that he would only write about the primitive mysticism and soulful harmony of the Negro. He wrote, "I knew that my friend and benefactor was not happy, for months now, I had written nothing beautiful" (134–35). Despite the evidence that Black/White relations were vexed, even while productive, Hutchinson's claim that Black and White intellectuals sought out communities of like-minded individuals that transcended racial differences is indisputable and his claim for Boas's influence is one shared by many scholars including Williams, *Rethinking Race*; Mark Helbling, *Harlem Renaissance: The One and the Many* (Westport, Conn.: Greenwood Press, 1999); Stewart, "Paul Robeson and the Problem of Modernism" 92–101; Manganaro, *Culture, 1922*; Arnold Rampersad, Introduction, in *The New Negro*, ed. Alain Locke (1925; reprint New York: Atheneum, 1992) ix–xxiii; Huggins, *Harlem Renaissance*; Hutchinson, *The Harlem Renaissance in Black and White*; and David Levering Lewis, *When Harlem Was in Vogue* (New York: Penguin, 1997).

39. George Stocking, "The Critique of Racial Formation," *Race, Culture and Evolution: Essays in the History of Anthropology* (New York: Free Press, 1968).

40. Hutchinson writes, "The myth of American national identity as a unitary, self-contained sphere was never so open to question, which in itself helps explain the intensity of concern over what American national consciousness should be" (11). For a fuller discussion of the culture concept, see Hutchinson 62–77.

41. In *Invisible Genealogies: A History of Americanist Anthropology* (Lincoln: University of Nebraska Press, 2001), Regna Darnell argues that these are common features of Boasian anthropology, contradicting contemporary discussions of anthropology that propose an absolute break by contemporary anthropologists from modern anthropology developed by Boas and his students (1–30). Hutchinson concurs, arguing for example that reflexivity was a characteristic of Boas's work, and that he thought about anthropology's complicity in racist and imperialist practices. Boas recognized, Hutchinson asserts, "that all of us are trapped by the customs and habits (including mental ones) of our cultural environment. Science itself is always prone to entrapment by convention" (71–72).

42. See *The New Negro* 3–18.

43. Letter dated March 29, 1927, in *Zora Neale Hurston: A Life in Letters*, ed. Carla Kaplan (New York: Doubleday, 2003) 97.

44. Manganaro cites James Clifford, "On Ethnographic Allegory," *Writing Culture: the Poetics and Politics of Ethnography*, ed. James Clifford and George E. Marcus (Berkeley: University of California Press, 1986) 112 and Bruce Robbins, *Secular*

Vocations: Intellectuals, Professionalism, Culture (London: Verso, 1993) 173 as emphasizing that the profession has an investment in sustaining and creating this ever-present disappearance because it gives the discipline a reason for being (*Culture, 1922* 2).

45. Baker names a number of factors in Boas's and the AFLS's renewed interest in Negro folklore in the twenties including Boas's censure by the American Anthropological Association in 1919 in response to an antiwar letter that he published in *The Nation* accusing several scientists of working as spies; his collaboration with Elsie Clews Parsons, who demonstrated an enthusiasm for Negro folklore; the rise of African Americans' interest in folklore; and his need to collect physical data on Black people, which he thought would be facilitated by the inclusion of Black researchers in his projects (*From Savage to Negro* 148–50).

46. Among the many books and theatrical productions reviewed by Locke, in addition to Cunard's anthology, were Langston Hughes, *The Ways of White Folks* and Asadata Dafora's *Kykunkor or The Witch Doctor*. See Alain Locke, "The Eleventh Hour of Nordicism: A Retrospective Review of the Literature of the Negro for 1934," *Opportunity* 13, no. 1 (January 1935): 8–12, reprinted in *The Critics and the Harlem Renaissance*, ed. Cary D. Wintz (New York: Garland Publishing, 1996) 281.

47. This article appraises sociological and anthropological works by E. F. Frazier, Charles S. Johnson, Robert E. Park, and James Weldon Johnson among others. See Alain Locke, "The Eleventh Hour of Nordicism," *Opportunity* 13, no. 2 (February 1935): 46–48, 59, reprinted in *The Critics and the Harlem Renaissance* 283.

48. Baker describes the pool of anthropological resources from which the New Negro drew: "Cultural patterns, specific historical reconstructions, geographic diffusion of rites and rituals, evidence of African survivals and of ancient African civilizations—all became anthropological grist used to produce new interpretations of culture by those New Negroes articulating the heritage project" ("Research" 73).

49. Arthur Huff Fauset, "American Negro Folk Literature," in *The New Negro* 242.

50. Cited in Baker, "Research" 74. The article originally appeared in *Journal of American Folk-Lore* 14, no. 52 (1901): 1–11.

51. Deacon describes Boas's students and collaborators as being less averse than he to controversy and more inclined to take up the social and disciplinary battles with which his ideas engaged. For example, she describes feminist and public intellectual Elsie Clews Parsons as "an avowed propagandist," who was interested in anthropology "as a practical guide to action." Parsons's scholarly work blended sociology, ethnology, and psychology, an approach that would have seemed out of place in the *American Anthropologist* or the *Journal of American Folklore*: "Psychology and social reform were treated with suspicion by anthropologists, despite the fact that Boas had been advocating for years an understanding of the native mind, and that his whole program for reform of the discipline was based on a fierce desire for social justice" (148–49). Deacon also describes anthropology's transformation being "carried out by Boas's graduate students rather than by Boas himself" (98). In "Melville Herskovits and the Search for Afro-American Culture," Walter Jackson traces a similar divergence in other prominent Boas-trained anthropologists in his history of Melville Herskovits's influence on the emergence of Afro-American studies. Herskovits occasionally found himself at odds with social scientists, like Margaret Mead, Ruth Benedict, Charles Johnson, and

Franklin Frazier, either because they found fault with his refusal to consider the social implications of his research on African "survivals" in Afro-American culture; or because he disagreed with their attempts to combine scientific research with social engineering.

52. This shift in Black intellectuals' uses of Boasian concepts is interesting. Where, during the twenties, New Negro intellectuals favored Boas's theories of cultural relativism because they supported racial equality, during the thirties sociologists like E. Franklin Frazier and Charles Johnson challenged the idea that African Americans were racially inferior by arguing for Black people's assimilability into normative American culture. Thus, they "discarded [Boas's] research on culture because it implied that Negroes could not easily assimilate." Baker includes a compelling discussion of this very point in "Research."

53. See Douglas Cole, *Franz Boas: The Early Years, 1858–1906* (Seattle: University of Washington Press, 1999) for a fuller discussion of the secularization of Germany's Jews, especially 7–16.

54. Baker cites both Harrison and Diggs as demonstrating that Du Bois's method and theoretical point of view were foundational in the transformation of the discourse on race and culture from ideas informed by Social Darwinism to notions premised on racial equality and cultural diversity. Baker notes, "What is at stake is who ultimately gets 'credit' for the profound shift in the social sciences. Although Du Bois's work in *The Philadelphia Negro* and his Atlanta University studies were innovative, they did not have the same direct influence, credibility, and prestige as did studies by White scholars who explored social relations in urban arenas" (*From Savage to Negro* 115).

55. W. E. B. Du Bois, "The Conservation of Races," *Du Bois: Writings*, ed. Nathan Huggins (New York: Literary Classics of the United States, 1986) 815–26. Originally printed in American Negro Academy, *Occasional Papers*, no. 2, 1897.

56. Du Bois observed, "Many criteria of race differences have in the past been proposed, as color, hair, cranial measurements and language. And manifestly, in each of these respects, human beings differ widely." Nonetheless, he concluded, "so far as purely physical characteristics are concerned, the differences between men do not explain all the differences of their history. It declares, as Darwin himself said, that great as is the physical unlikeness of the various races of men their likenesses are greater, and upon this rests the whole scientific doctrine of Human Brotherhood" (815–16).

57. As significant as the differences between these two figures are, their similarities are also provocative. Like Boas, Du Bois had trained in the German traditions of empirical research, and both men had firsthand experiences with discrimination. Baker ponders the effect of the racial politics of academic influence in *From Savage to Negro* 107–10.

Chapter 3

1. Lewis 170–72.

2. In *Dark Voices: W. E. B. Du Bois and American Thought 1888–1903* (Chicago:

University of Chicago Press, 1995), Shamoon Zamir cites the American Social Science Association as an example of the "older, more reform-oriented and less professionalized social science" practiced in the nineteenth century (68–81).

3. Visweswaran reflects on the possibilities of turning the anthropological gaze inward, figured through the idea of "homework" in contrast to fieldwork. In so doing, she suggests that one can view sociology as "Anthropology at home," a view made acceptable once the move to decolonize anthropology was made after the 1960s (101).

4. Lewis 91–92.

5. Ironically, Du Bois also took classes with Nathaniel Southgate Shaler at Harvard, the geologist whose challenge to put the Negro problem under scientific scrutiny led to the formation of the Hampton Folklore Society in 1868. Shaler's offensive racial ideologies did not prevent him from expelling from his classroom a White Southerner who refused to sit next to Du Bois (Lewis 80).

6. In discussing the impact of Schmoller and Wagner, two professors of political economy, on Du Bois, Lewis tells us, "Schmoller, whose subsequent disparaging of the value-free, 'transcendentalist and purely formal ethic' of Weberian sociology would be notable, pounded home in his lectures that sociology was 'as much a realistic science to me as economics.' Du Bois was by intellectual temperament profoundly susceptible to a belief in universals (and, in fact, to all manner of Hegelian excesses), and much restraint was provided by Schmoller's seminar in political economy and Wagner's lecture course in the same subject" (142). Green and Driver offer a concise and thorough synopsis of Du Bois's education in sociology and the influence of his mentors.

7. Du Bois published *The Quest of the Silver Fleece* in 1911 and *Dark Princess* in 1928. My intention is not to argue that he abandoned academia in favor of literature, or activism, but to emphasize the ongoing, dialogic exchange among all these discursive forms over the course of his career. Vernon Williams writes, "W. E. B. Du Bois—because of the tremendous tension between his elitist and scientific values and his desire to find a solution to the problem of ethnic solidarity among his oppressed brethren—from 1897 to 1915, vacillated between racial chauvinism in reference to the cultural background of African Americans and scientism in reference to their socioeconomic status" (2). By "racial chauvinism" Williams alludes to references to African cultural achievement, which he views as originating in Boas's attempts to discredit myths of Euro-American superiority by calling attention to African Americans' "glorious" African ancestry.

8. Wilson Moses, "The Poetics of Ethiopianism: W. E. B. Du Bois and Literary Black Nationalism," in *Critical Essays on W. E. B. Du Bois*, ed. W. L. Andrews (Boston: G. K. Hall, 1985) 92–106.

9. Du Bois concluded "one could not be a calm, cool, and detached scientist while Negroes were lynched, murdered and starved" (Lewis 226).

10. Robert Stepto, "The Quest of the Weary Traveler: W. E. B. Du Bois's *The Souls of Black Folk*," in *Critical Essays on W. E. B. Du Bois* 148.

11. Houston A. Baker, "The Black Man of Culture: W. E. B. Du Bois and *The Souls of Black Folk*," in *Critical Essays on W. E. B. Du Bois* 136.

12. Du Bois's experimentation with more emotional and polemical writing did not begin with the publication of *Souls*. Many of the essays in this collection were

published earlier and some were written simultaneously with the more academic works with which he began his career. When "Strivings of the Negro People" was first published by *Atlantic Monthly* in 1897, for example, it surprised the magazine's readership with its passionate engagement with some of the most controversial issues having to do with African Americans of the day. Lewis writes, " 'Strivings of the Negro People' was startlingly personal. It abandoned the controlled prose of *The Suppression of the African Slave Trade* and *The Philadelphia Negro* (in progress) for the indignation of the English 12 writings and the lyricism of the student notebooks" (Lewis 199).

13. W. E. B. Du Bois, *The Souls of Black Folk* (New York: The Library of America, 1986).

14. Henry Louis Gates and Cornel West, *The Future of the Race* (New York: Vintage Books, 1996) 115.

15. Attempts such as this, at psychologizing, are much shorter and less sustained than those in *Souls*. "The Black North in 1901" seems to anticipate and rehearse in brief a rhetorical style that Du Bois will come to master two years later.

16. Houston Baker, *Turning South Again: Re-thinking Modernism/Re-reading Booker T.* (Durham: Duke University Press, 2001) 53.

17. Houston Baker cites this passage as one example of Du Bois's elitism: "While elevating the black intellectual, Du Bois perhaps depressed the masses too far. Throughout *The Souls of Black Folk*, one finds invidious distinctions between the man of culture and all black people who inhabit the realms 'beneath' him. One finds the author speaking of the 'black lowly,' 'Sambo,' the 'black peasantry,' and the 'black crowd gaudy and dirty.' These terms might have acted only as heuristic epithets reinforcing Du Bois's argument, but he made it indubitably clear that he believed the man of culture was qualitatively better than the next man" ("The Black Man of Culture" 133–34). Too often the "man of culture" is identified with urban cosmopolitanism and uncouth boorishness with the rural South. Yet Du Bois did treat the subject of African American homogeneity and heterogeneity with complexity. For example, he assumed that the talented tenth would rise from, hence were a part of, the crowd of ordinary working people.

He also recognized that migratory patterns made comparable the lower classes in city and country, but he also expressed a wariness that Whites' increased exposure to Black communities in the North would result in their inability to perceive difference within those communities. He wrote in "The Negroes of Farmville" of unsavory characters that marred the reputations of Black communities. "In all, there would appear to be about 45 or 50 families of negroes who are below the line of ordinary respectability, living in loose sexual relationship, responsible for most of the illegitimate children, chief supporters of the two liquor shops, and furnishing a half-dozen street walkers and numerous gamblers and rowdies. *It is the emigration of this class of people to the larger cities that has recently brought to notice the large number of negro criminals* and the development of a distinct criminal class among them" (Green and Driver 193, emphasis added). What in the countryside is a small and marginalized population becomes a larger, more visible and more ominous threat in cities when different groups coalesce into a larger whole. The threat is that the criminal minority will be taken by the majority culture as representative of the race.

18. Hazel Carby, *Race Men* (Cambridge: Harvard University Press, 1998) 45.

19. Renato Rosaldo, *Culture and Truth: The Remaking of Social Analysis* (Boston: Beacon Press, 1989) 204.

20. Stepto, "The Quest of the Weary Traveler" 149–50.

21. In "Du Bois's 'Of the Coming of John,' Toomer's 'Kabnis,' and the Dilemma of Self-Representation," in *The Souls of Black Folk: One Hundred Years Later*, ed. Dolan Hubbard (Columbia: University of Missouri Press, 2003) 130–60, Chester Fontenot emphasizes the fact that Du Bois, like Jean Toomer, had to travel away from his northern home in order to discover, construct, and assign meaning to his racial identity. "Both Du Bois and Toomer, however, though physically distant from the actual existence of black people, find that in the South, they first locate what Donald Gibson calls their 'bodies,' their social essence. In a sense, both writers locate the 'black essence" through what Paul Gilroy calls 'routes,' not 'roots.' That is to say, they both find that geographical routes, the black South, allow them to represent African Americans accurately" (134).

22. "The New Negro in Literature (1925–1955)," in *A Son's Return: Selected Essays of Sterling A. Brown* (Boston: Northeastern University Press, 1996) 185.

23. Akhil Gupta and James Ferguson discuss the symbolic and epistemological significance of "the field" in *Anthropological Locations: Boundaries and Grounds of a Field Science* (Berkeley: University of California Press, 1997). They argue that the field is especially significant for anthropologists who rely, more than other social scientists on participant-observation methods.

24. Marc Manganaro argues that without the contributions of Tylor, Boas and "a host of other formative modern social scientists . . . it would not have been possible to conceive of culture "as 'geographically' based, that is, readable in terms of its ties to a plot of earth; and finally, that it needs to be contemplated in a minimal compass known as the 'local'" (19).

25. "One might say that *being framed* for the black American is being indexed by—and sometimes *in*—the South. This is so primarily because at the moment of joy marked by the Emancipation Proclamation, more than four million of the United States's five-million-plus black Americans were enslaved residents of the American South. And as the nineteenth century came to a close, over 90 percent of black Americans still resided in the South. . . . Mental attitudes and habits of mind, soul rhythms, ethical assessments, intellectual judgments, somatic adaptations, nocturnal anxieties, academic ideologies of black being in American are most profoundly imbricated with 'the mind'—and here one must surely add the very bodies and demographics—of the South" (Baker, *Turning South* 18).

26. Pierre Nora, "Between Memory and History: Les Lieux des Memoires," in *History and Memory in African American Culture*, ed. Fabre and O'Meally (New York: Oxford University Press, 1994).

27. Farah Jasmine Griffin, *Who Set You Flowin'?: The African-American Migration Narrative* (New York: Oxford University Press, 1995) 142–83.

28. For a fuller discussion of this idea, see Daphne Lamothe, "Bridging Routes and Roots in Gloria Naylor's *Mama Day*," *African American Review* 39, nos. 1–2 (2005): 155–69.

29. See Corey D. B. Walker, "Modernity in Black: du Bois and the (Re)Construction of Black Identity in *The Souls of Black Folk*," *Philosophia Africana* 7, no. 1 (2004):

83–93 for a discussion of Du Bois's negotiation of the objectifying power of the sociological gaze.

30. Du Bois's thesis vis-à-vis the "Sorrow Songs" is a potent example of George Hutchinson's assertion that Renaissance writers contributed to a new American discourse cultural pluralism by redefining the Negro contribution to American identity. Du Bois argues that "the Negro folk-song—the rhythmic cry of the slave—stands today not simply as the sole American music, but as the most beautiful expression of human experience born this side the seas" (536–37).

31. In *The Literary Legacy of W. E. B. Du Bois* (White Plains, N.Y.: Kraus International Publications, 1989), Herbert Aptheker emphasizes that as early as *The Philadelphia Negro*, Du Bois seeks to represent the "full humanity" of the Negro people: "Du Bois' [sic] rejection of the idea of the inferiority of his people permeates the volume; his insistence on their full humanity and the logical conclusion therefrom—namely, their being entitled to all the dignities and rights of citizens of the United States— appears in the footnote on the first page. . . . The volume as a whole rejects the then very commonplace idea that poor people are poor because they are 'poor'—i.e., not good. . . . his whole emphasis is upon the social and economic and political sources of their impoverishment" (35–36).

32. My thoughts on this subject have been shaped by the work of Brent Edwards on the intersection of musical and literary expression.

33. This chapter is the only one that offers a song verse as an epigraph, the culmination of Du Bois's efforts to establish the spirituals as "the articulate message of the slave to the world" (538).

34. Sandra Adell, *Double-Consciousness/Double Bind: Theoretical Issues in Twentieth-Century Black Literature* (Chicago: University of Illinois Press, 1994) 27.

35. Hazel Carby argues against the idea of linguistic insufficiency and instead points to Du Bois's preference for discursive substitution. She writes, "I would argue that despite the absence of lyrics, the way in which Du Bois uses his own essays functions as a *substitute* for these missing lyrics. Indeed, I believe that the text of each chapter has a specific performative role: each is a composition of improvised lyrics upon the musical fragments that precede them. Du Bois does not reflect directly upon the lyrics of the sorrow songs prior to his conclusion precisely because he intends that his chapters be regarded as new lyrics, new improvisations" (*Race Men* 88).

36. Christopher Brooks in "The 'Musical' Souls of Black Folk: Can a Double Consciousness Be Heard?" in *The Souls of Black Folk: One Hundred Years Later* 269–83 correctly notes that Western conventions of musical notation failed to adequately represent African musical forms. "Several of the collectors (such as Allen, in the preface to *Slave Songs*) had, after all, mentioned the inability of Western musical notation to capture, in transcription, the melodies of many songs, much less the stylized African vocalities such as falsetto, moans, screams, raspy voice, and yodels. These musical notations, therefore, represent a 'faint shadow of the original' " (274). Thus, even if readers can read the bars of music in the chapters' epigraphs, we can rightly conclude that they would not be exposed to an authentic representation of the spirituals. Yet Brooks maintains that Du Bois might counter this argument with the assertion that the essence or soul of the slave songs remained.

37. Although the reviewer considers Du Bois's effectiveness in cultivating the emotions and imagination of "his people" as evidence that Blacks should have access to higher education, Du Bois's rhetoric does not seem to disturb his binaristic thinking, which relegates Blacks to the emotional end of the spectrum and Whites on the rational end (Anonymous review of *The Souls of Black Folk* in *Critical Essays on W. E. B. Du Bois* 31).

38. See Zamir 81–93 for a discussion of the various philosophical and intellectual traditions in which Du Bois was trained and his construction of a scientific method from those traditions.

39. Zamir argues that "most accounts of Du Bois's life that have focused on his political and academic career have marginalized *Souls* at the cost of simplifying the range of doubt and self-interrogation in his early life" (10).

40. Ross Posnock, *Color and Culture: Black Writers and the Making of the Modern Intellectual* (Cambridge: Harvard University Press, 1998) 16.

41. Posnock attempts to resolve this paradox by reasoning that "One reason the cosmopolitanism found in, say, Du Bois and Locke has never been appreciated is that they defamiliarize the word, turning it from its typical connotations of an apolitical leisure class with 'essentially a tourist's view of the world.' . . . Above all, for Du Bois and Locke cosmopolitanism means that 'culture has no color' " (10). While this interpretation is certainly accurate, it does not displace or explain away the implied class biases that I find so vexing.

42. Gayatri Spivak, "Can the Subaltern Speak?" in *The Post-Colonial Studies Reader*, ed. B. Ashcroft, G. Griffiths, and H. Tiffin (London: Routledge Press, 1995) 24–28.

Chapter 4

1. James Weldon Johnson, *The Autobiography of an Ex-Colored Man* (New York: Penguin, 1990).

2. Hutchinson remarks that participant-observation grew into the dominant method of inquiry because Boas recognized full participation in another culture as the most suitable way for the anthropologist to correct his ethnocentrism.

3. James Weldon Johnson, *Along This Way: The Autobiography of James Weldon Johnson* (New York: Da Capo Press, 1933) 326.

4. In "Passing as Autobiography: James Weldon Johnson's *The Autobiography of an Ex-Colored Man*," *African American Review* 30, no. 1 (1996): 17–33, Donald Goellnicht discusses how historically African American autobiographies "became ethnography, a genre designed to educate white America about its 'exotic' and unknown 'other.' "

5. See Robert E. Fleming, "Irony as a Key to Johnson's *The Autobiography of an Ex-Coloured Man*," *American Literature* 43 (1971): 83–96 and Joseph T. Skerrett, Jr., "Irony and Symbolic Action in James Weldon Johnson's *The Autobiography of an Ex-Coloured Man*," *American Quarterly* 32, no. 5 (Winter 1980): 540–58.

6. Valerie Smith argues that the narrator's sociological commentary is more

reliable than the psychological. His self-assessment is marked, she argues, by evasions, omissions, and circularity: "In short, as long as the ex-colored man can remain at a distance from what he describes, he can articulate it clearly. Once his analyses impinge on his own relation to his racial identity, however, he is unable to sustain his acuity" (Valerie Smith, *Self-Discovery and Authority in Afro-American Narrative* [Cambridge: Harvard University Press, 1987] 60–61). Robert Fleming sees the narrative as a more convincing psychological portrait than sociological one: "*The Autobiography* is not so much a panoramic novel presenting race relations throughout America as it is a deeply ironic character study of a marginal man who narrates the story of his own life without fully realizing the significance of what he tells his readers" (83). These are just two representative examples of the ways that critics try to identify something consistently true in this narrative, whether or not the narrator intentionally generates it. My point, however, is that truth about the narrator or the societies he encounters is always elusive, and more readily discernible is the work that goes in his making of particular narratives or fictions about self and others.

7. James Clifford, *Writing Culture: The Poetics and Politics of Ethnography* (Berkeley: University of California Press, 1986) 6.

8. Robert Fleming makes a similar point, first stating that the book is about emotional and psychological responses (85) and then attributing the protagonist's sociological analysis to his never feeling part of the Black race (91).

9. Jean Toomer, *Cane* (New York: Liveright, 1993) 1

10. The ethnographer subject with which I concern myself resembles the literary figure Farah Jasmine Griffin, drawing from the work of sociologists Georg Simmel and Robert Park, has labeled "the stranger." For Griffin, the stranger appears in migration narratives that work for a more "objective" approach. The stranger offers a new worldview, and is "in a dialectical relationship with the ancestor," the figure that represents traditional wisdom and the renewal associated with an affirmative home (6–8). Although Griffin locates "the stranger" as a contemporary literary trope, the figure can be found in early twentieth-century works as well. One could add the narrator of Jean Toomer's *Cane* and various characters in Langston Hughes' collection of short stories, *The Souls of White Folk*, to a long list of contemporary fiction that includes depictions of searching outsiders including, Alice Walker's *Meridian*, Toni Morrison's *Tar Baby*, Paule Marshall's *Praisesong for the Widow*, and Gloria Naylor's *Mama Day*.

11. William Andrews declares that in order to "rejoin the life and culture of black folk," the narrator will have to carefully reevaluate his priorities. He ". . . will have to shift the focus of his attention from himself to 'those I consider my people' if his art is 'to voice all the joys and sorrow, the hopes and ambitions, of the American Negro, in classical musical form'" (*The Autobiography of an Ex-Colored Man* xxiv).

12. J. Martin Favor argues that the narrator's mother emphasizes "the patrilineal and class-based over the matrilineal and race-based in helping her son construct his sense of self" (*Authentic Blackness: The Folk in the New Negro Renaissance* [Durham: Duke University Press, 1999]).

13. The Ex-Colored Man's analysis echoes that of Du Bois in "Of the Sons of Masters and Man," in *Souls*. In that essay Du Bois describes a professional and middle class of Blacks post-emancipation that grew in the midst of rigid and strict segre-

gation. Of this class, he writes, "... it is usually true that the very representatives of the two races, who for mutual benefit and the welfare of the land ought to be in complete understanding and sympathy, are so far strangers that one side thinks all whites are narrow and prejudiced, and the other thinks educated Negroes dangerous and insolent" (W. E. B. Du Bois, *The Souls of Black Folk* [New York: The Library of America, 1986] 334).

14. Eric Sundquist, *The Hammers of Creation: Folk Culture in Modern African-American Fiction* (Athens: University of Georgia Press, 1992) 12.

15. According to Sundquist, he "arrives in Macon, . . . like a European explorer in colonial Africa" (12). And Donald Petesch observes: "It is as 'white folks' that the protagonist seems to move among other blacks. It is appropriate that he moves into the 'interior' as a collector of folk music. His stance is distanced; he is the anthropologist, the observer, and the observer could as easily be white." See Donald A. Petesch, *A Spy in the Enemy's Country: The Emergence of Modern Black Literature* (Iowa City: University of Iowa Press, 1989) 154.

16. In "Of Souls and Pottage: James Weldon Johnson's *The Autobiography of an Ex-Colored Man*," *CLA Journal* 23, no. 1 (September 1979): 60–70, Maurice O'Sullivan asserts that, "the narrator's methods of bringing honour and glory always involve a bleaching out of what is black. This process and his dreams are nowhere so evident as in his music" (68). But Kathleen Pfeiffer astutely counters with the argument that he "also blackens what is white by simultaneously refusing to accept classical music as classical music. Many critics and readers of *The Autobiography*, like O'Sullivan, give too much weight to the moments when the narrator resists full participation in black culture, without crediting the degree to which they are juxtaposed against resistance to white culture" (Kathleen Pfeiffer, "Individualism, Success, and American Identity in *The Autobiography of an Ex-Colored Man*," *African American Review* 30, no. 3 [1996]: 410).

17. Pisiak's analysis of class dynamics here becomes relevant because she argues that his reference to the richness of works which "no one had yet touched" is "not a racist comment implying that a white man needs to anglicize and sanction the music by rewriting it, for the narrator is living as a black man at this time. It is, instead, an indictment of the lower classes and their simple, crude art forms; an individual of a certain level of class, intelligence, and talent, it implies, needs to authorize the material (presumably by being the first person to write it down)" (92). Pisiak's reference to the significance of being able to write down the music underscores the importance of literacy in enabling members of the elite like the Ex-Colored Man (and Johnson and Du Bois) to overcome the limitations society places on African Americans (Roxanna Pisiak, "Irony and Subversion in James Weldon Johnson's *The Autobiography of an Ex-Colored Man*," *Studies in American Fiction* 21, no. 1 [Spring, 1993]: 83–96).

18. In "James Weldon Johnson and the Autobiography of an Ex-Colored Musician," *American Literature* 72, no. 2 (June 2000): 249–74, Christina Ruotolo states, "Standing in the way of a truly cross-cultural musical expression, Johnson implies, are obstacles not only of racism but also of an American 'culture industry' that reifies racial difference as it depends on the repeatability, marketability, and novelty of its products, separates performer and audience into commodity and consumer, and erases the social history of musical styles and forms" (267–68).

19. Pisiak is one of the few critics to focus with any depth on the class identification of the narrator in the *Autobiography*. Pisiak notes, for example, that the narrator's childhood memories emphasize class over race: "There is no distinction between black and white well-dressed boys here; the emphasis would appear to be on class rather than race. The narrator spends his childhood in a comfortable home, his mother dresses him well, and she carefully chooses his companions for him. This early exposure to physical (and fiscal) comfort never decreases; in fact it develops into a 'necessity' of his adult life" (86). Pisiak goes on to argue that the protagonist displays more class than racial prejudice (91). Her focus on the importance of class in this novel is crucial, for it points to one of the primary motivations of the Ex-Colored Man for passing as White. I would also argue that the class distinction that the narrator draws between himself and lower-class Blacks enables his assumption of the role of detached social analyst.

20. Pfeiffer refers to critics such as O'Sullivan, who argues that the narrator "acts solely for himself. He is a rebel violating the most sacred taboos of his time, but a rebel who sees himself as more confidence man than revolutionary" (62). O'Sullivan's suggestion that the narrator should want to be a revolutionary gives credence to Pfeiffer's assessment that critics have put forth a "racially correct" way of reading this novel. But at the same time, she tries to inject his act with a rebelliousness in the service of a different cause: "The Ex-Colored Man's 'passing' thus offers a problematic but potentially legitimate expression of American individualism which simultaneously refutes 'one-dropism' and critiques the U.S.'s consciously constructed ideology of racial difference" (405). I believe that while the narrator's existence certainly subverts any attempts to maintain a rigid code of racial difference, he actually *does* little or nothing to critique or challenge that code.

21. O'Sullivan argues that "[t]he most notable image of the narrator's irresolution is his passing, which is not taken as a willed, conscious act but accepted as the inevitable result of not acting" (66). I hold, however, that to remain silent is a conscious act.

22. Hazel Carby is only one of many scholars who remark on Du Bois's sacrifice of individual desires in order to promote the cause of his race. She begins her critical text, *Race Men*, with this description of the great leader: "In a grand Victorian gesture of self-sacrifice, W. E. B. Du Bois, then a young man in the formative years of his intellectual development, determined to subordinate his individual desires and ambitions to promote a political project that would benefit the world in general by advancing the particular interests of African American peoples" (9).

Chapter 5

1. Hazel Carby makes a compelling argument for the new complexities that emerged within the race with the growth of Southern migrants to Northern cities. Northern intellectuals, faced with the actual presence of Black migrants from the south, could no longer conceive of themselves so easily as being responsible for representing a monolithic racial community that was united in their shared oppression. Carby notes, "The relation of the black intellectual elite to the majority of black peo-

ple changed drastically as a result of the migration North of Southern Blacks. Before World War I, the overwhelming majority of blacks were in the South, at a vast physical and metaphorical distance from those intellectuals who represented the interests of the race. After the war, black intellectuals had to confront the black masses on the streets of their cities and responded in a variety of ways" (Hazel Carby, *Reconstructing Womanhood* [New York: Oxford, 1989] 164).

2. Kelley's larger point is that a historiography that attends to everyday, unorganized acts of resistance in Black communities reveals that ". . . members of the most oppressed section of the black community always resisted, but often in a manner intended to cover their tracks" (Robin D. G. Kelley, " 'We Are Not What We Seem': Rethinking Black Working-Class Opposition in the Jim Crow South," *The Journal of American History* 80, 1 [1993]: 110).

3. Brown was born in 1901 into Washington, D.C.'s Black middle class. The son of a minister and theologian, he attended Washington's famed Dunbar High School with Jean Toomer, then graduated with degree in English from Williams College and Harvard University.

4. Brown won prizes for an essay on Roland Hayes submitted to *Opportunity* and for "When the Saints Go Ma'ching Home." Countee Cullen included six of his unpublished poems in *Caroling Dusk*, and several of his poems were published in *The Crisis, Opportunity*, and other literary journals. While at Virginia Seminary, he read Claude McKay's *Harlem Shadows* (1922), Jean Toomer's *Cane* (1923), and Langston Hughes's *The Weary Blues* (1926).

5. In *Sterling A. Brown: Building the Black Aesthetic Tradition*, Joanne Gabbin recounts how Brown and his editorial staff supervised and reviewed material about the Negro for state guidebooks. The most notable FWP contributions included *Washington City and Capital*, edited by Roscoe Lewis, to which Brown contributed essays titled "The Negro in Washington" and "The Negro in Virginia." Brown also organized a collection of oral histories by former slaves. Brown was among a handful of African American researchers, including Charles S. Johnson, Ralph Bunche, and E. Franklin Frazier, who contributed monographs to Myrdal's project. Walter Jackson describes the primary question that drove most of these scholars as being whether or not to stress "the Negro's Americanisms." Jackson singles Brown out among all of Myrdal's collaborators as having "the most subtle understanding of Afro-American folklore and the traditions of resistance developed by blacks in the rural south." He concludes, "Unfortunately, this subtlety was lost on Gunnar Myrdal, who never had much of an ear for music and was much more interested in politics than literature" (Jackson, *Gunnar Myrdal* 131–32).

6. David Anderson, "Sterling Brown's Southern Strategy: Poetry as Cultural Evolution in *Southern Road*," *Callaloo* 21, no. 4 (1998): 1023–37.

7. Boas's interventions in museum display practices took place when he worked in Berlin's Royal Ethnographic Museum, before undertaking his fieldwork with the eastern Eskimo from the Northwest Coast of North America and moving to the United States to begin his highly influential tenure in academia. See Ira Jacknis, "Franz Boas and Exhibits: On the Limitations of the Museum Method of Anthropology," *Objects and Others*, ed. George Stocking (Madison: University of Wisconsin Press, 1985) 75.

8. Despite his radical revision of curatorial practices, Boas found that he still had to meet museum attendees' expectations that an exhibition's significance would provide them with a sense of order and accessibility. Thus Jacknis notes that Boas's theory and exhibition practice occasionally conflicted when constraints in resources and audience expectations forced him to move toward a "Masonian" model of evolutionary and typological exhibits; at the same time Mason eventually adopted Boas's practice of tribal and regional arrangements. Significantly, despite these disagreement in methods, both Boas and Mason's theories assumed that ethnography and anthropology played a critical role in articulating a frame through which cultural, geographical and social distinctions were understood, thus naturalizing the struggle for power between Western and non-Western cultures.

9. Zora Neale Hurston, "What White Publishers Won't Print," in *Hurston: Folklore, Memoirs, & Other Writings* (New York: The Library of America, 1995) 950.

10. See Gabbin for a detailed account of Brown's literary influences, especially 25–33.

11. Sterling Brown, "A Son's Return: Oh Didn't He Ramble," *A Son's Return: Selected Essays of Sterling A. Brown*, ed. Mark A. Sanders (Boston: Northeastern University Press, 1996) 15–16.

12. Gabbin, *Sterling A. Brown* 14.

13. "The Negro in the United States has achieved or been placed in a certain artistic niche. When he is thought of artistically, it is as a happy-go-lucky, singing, shuffling, banjo-picking being or as a more or less pathetic figure. The picture of him is in a log cabin amid fields of cotton or along the levees. Negro dialect is naturally and by long association the exact instrument for voicing this phase of Negro life; and by that very exactness it is an instrument with but two full stops, humor and pathos. So even when he confines himself to purely racial themes, the Aframerican poet realizes that there are phases of Negro life in the United States which cannot be treated in the dialect either adequately or artistically" (James Weldon Johnson, "Preface from *The Book of American Negro Poetry* (1922)," in *Voices from the Harlem Renaissance*, ed. Nathan Irvin Huggins [New York: Oxford University Press, 1995] 300).

14. Brown, "Our Literary Audience," in *A Son's Return* 144.

15. James Weldon Johnson, *Southern Road* (New York: Harcourt, Brace and Company, 1932) xiv.

16. Sterling Brown, "Negro Character as Seen by White Authors," in *A Son's Return* 174.

17. Gabbin writes that Brown considered Lindsay's attempt "'phony.'" Though Brown challenged what he considered to be a superficial and condescending treatment of Black themes, he was impressed with 'the marvelous ragtime flin' Lindsay got into his poems, with Lindsay's interest in breaking up the rhythm, and with his free handling of new material" (31).

18. Sterling A. Brown, Arthur P. Davis, and Ulysses Lee, *The Negro Caravan* (New York: Dryden Press, 1941) 831.

19. Sterling A. Brown, "Conference on Character and State of Studies in Folklore," *Journal of American Folklore* 59 (October-December 1946): 506.

20. Sterling Brown, "Negro Folk Expression," in *A Son's Return* 232–42.

21. Sterling Brown, "The New Negro in Literature (1925–1955)," in *A Son's Return* 202.

22. Kelley cites Lipsitz's idea of a "culture of opposition" to argue for historians paying greater attention to the "hidden transcript" that can be discerned in working-class people's everyday, unorganized and covert acts of resistance against racism and class oppression. Both Kelley (" 'We Are Not What We Seem' " 79) and George Lipsitz (*A Life in the Struggle: Ivory Perry and the Culture of Opposition* [Philadelphia: Temple University Press, 1988]) are part of a tradition of cultural historians that identify working Black people's agency in actions that had long been overlooked by traditional scholarship. Farah Jasmine Griffin contends, "It is in the cultural histories, rather than in the sociological texts, that Southern blacks emerge as agents involved in their own destiny. It is the cultural creations of the migrants—particularly letters and blues lyrics—that present the most well-rounded and complex picture of the factors that motivated them to leave" " (Griffin, *Who Set You Flowin'?* 18–19).

23. Kelley argues that the most widely used strategy for resisting workplace injustice was "simply to leave. Central to black working-class infrapolitics was mobility, for it afforded workers relative freedom to escape oppressive living and working conditions and power to negotiate better working conditions" " (95).

24. In "Sterling Brown's Southern Strategy: Poetry as Cultural Evolution in *Southern Road*," *Callaloo* 21, no. 4 (1998): 1023–37, David Anderson's analysis of *Southern Road* underscores still more threats to Black life. These include: social alienation, personal and sexual insecurity, cultural alienation, conspicuous consumption, sexual exploitation, and cultural co-optation.

25. Mark A. Sanders, Foreword, in *A Son's Return* xii.

26. What I am trying to suggest is that Mandy Jane's actions should be understood as an oppositional attempt at redistributing resources. Kelley argues, "Any attempt to understand the relationship between theft and working-class opposition must begin by interrogating the dominant view of 'theft' as deviant, criminal behavior. From the vantage point of workers, as several criminologists have pointed out, theft at the workplace is a strategy to recover unpaid wages or to compensate for low wages and mistreatment" (90).

27. We must acknowledge, however, that Brown consistently locates desires for emancipation in male subjects. Even in this poem, which has a woman as its subject, the female figures exists as a projection of the male consciousness. Luke Johnson "ruminates" on Mandy Johnson's journey and its significance, illuminating *his* frustrations and desires more than hers.

28. Vera Kutzinski, "The Distant Closeness of Dancing Doubles: Sterling Brown and William Carlos Williams," *Black American Literature Forum* 22 (Spring 1982): 21.

29. Griffin provides a detailed and complex account of the multiple reasons that Black migrants gave for leaving the South in *Who Set You Flowin'?* In the chapter " 'Boll Weevil in the Cotton / Devil in the White Man': Reasons for Leaving the South," Griffin examines sociological and journalistic accounts of migrant journeys, as well as the creative work of migrants, cultural histories of their creative output and contemporary literature to explore the broad range of explanations for the decision to leave, the extent to which migrants' agency is stressed, and the attitudes that

migrants held toward the South. See especially 13–24 for a discussion of the historical and social factors that influenced Black migrants and the cultural productions, like the blues, that they created in response.

30. The origins of "Backwater Blues" are unclear. Both Griffin and Angela Davis (*Blues Legacies and Black Feminism* [New York: Vintage, 1999] 108–11) cite Bessie Smith as composing the song after encountering a Southern Black community in the midst of recovering from a 1927 flood of the river, but seasonal rains caused the Mississippi to flood on a regular basis. The source of Brown's attribution of the song to Rainey is unclear, but his poem emphasizes the same dynamics of communal trauma, recovery, and fellowship as Griffin and Davis's accounts of the story (Griffin 21).

31. Griffin 20–21.

32. In the context of discussing women's blues singers' performances of songs about romantic rivalries, Angela Davis describes the paradoxical development of "aesthetic communities": "While women are clearly perceived as antagonists—as potential intruders into others' relationships—they are also viewed as possessing common fears and common interests. They are located both outside and inside a community of women." Davis offers this as one example of individual/communal dynamics expressed in blues songs and blues performances (Davis, *Blues Legacies* 54).

33. Hazel Carby, "'It Jus Be's Dat Way Sometimes': The Sexual Politics of Women's Blues," in *Unequal Sisters: A Multicultural Reader in U.S. Women's History*, ed. Ellen Carol Du Bois and Vicki L. Ruiz (New York: Routledge, 1990). Angela Davis offers a different interpretation of travel imagery in early women's blues lyrics. While acknowledging that women more than men were tied to family responsibilities and domestic labor, limiting their opportunities for travel, she also argues that mobility was an ubiquitous theme in women's blues, as it was in men's blues lyrics: "Gertrude Rainey—the 'Mother of the Blues'—sings about women who were forever walking, running, leaving, catching trains, or sometimes aimlessly rambling" (66). Davis attributes this preoccupation with travel imagery to new social realities with the onset of emancipation. Sexuality and the freedom to travel, Davis argues, were two immediate ways in which the recently freed Blacks could express their new autonomy (66–90).

34. Mark A. Sanders, *Afro-Modernist Aesthetics and the Poetry of Sterling A. Brown* (Athens: University of Georgia Press, 1999) 50.

35. Gabbin quotes Brown as saying, "you got a view of life [in the poetry of Robert Frost and Edwin Arlington Robinson] that was so far from a pastoral view. This was hardship. This was tragedy; but it was not the gentle kind of, I think, condescending attitude to the people that you would find in James Whitcomb Riley, or as far as our people were concerned . . . in Dunbar (in Dunbar's portraits)" (29).

36. Griffin provides a comprehensive reading of depictions of migrants' initial encounter with the city in migration literature. See especially 48–99.

37. Sterling Brown, "Georgia Sketches," *Callaloo* 21, no. 4 (1998): 784.

38. In "A Brown Study: Sterling Brown's Legacy of Compassionate Connections," *Callaloo* 21, no. 4 (1998): 903, Callahan describes "Cabaret" as a virtuosic jazz performance that ironically depicts the degradation of a performance.

39. In "Notes on Deconstructing 'The Folk,'" *American Historical Review* 97, no. 5 (1992): 1400–1408, Robin Kelley uses this definition of (popular) culture as "con-

tested terrain" to describe what characterizes a cultural studies approach to historiography. He cites Stuart Hall Fredric Jameson, Dick Hebdige, Paul Willis, and Lawrence Levine among others as scholars whose contributions helped to define the field. See especially 1400–1401.

Chapter 6

1. In *Writing Chicago: Modernism, Ethnography, and the Novel* (New York: Columbia University Press, 1993), Carla Capetti seconds Hazel Carby's contention in *Reconstructing Womanhood* that the centrality of the Harlem Renaissance in historiographies of the African American tradition of letters "obfuscates rather than explains its relationship to what came before and to what came after" (Capetti 9). In agreement with Carby's claim that literary historians would be better off focusing on the shift in the concerns of African American intellectuals during the twenties, Capetti focuses her analysis on literature's influence on Chicago sociologists who attempted to represent " 'others' *within* the West" (16), as well as sociology's influence on Chicago writers. I view this project as engaged in the same process of examining the intellectual influences and formation of New Negro intellectuals, rather than strictly being a study of a literary movement centered in Harlem specifically.

2. See, for example, Houston Baker, David Levering Lewis, and Nathan Huggins. In the field of anthropology, see Lee Baker, George Marcus, and James Clifford.

3. Cheryl Wall, *Women of the Harlem Renaissance* (Bloomington: Indiana University Press, 1995) xiv.

4. James Haskins, *Katherine Dunham* (New York: Coward, McCann and Geohegan, 1982) 43.

5. Haskins recounts the now famous episode when Dunham appeared before the Scholarship Committee to apply for her grant. After removing her suit and shoes and standing before the astonished committee members, dressed only in a black leotard and tights, Dunham performed some ballet and then her own imitation of an African tribal dance, Dunham then explained her reason for wanting to study the indigenous dances of other cultures. See especially 48–49.

6. At the time sociology and anthropology were housed under the same department at the University of Chicago and their theories and methods were so intertwined that it was difficult to distinguish between the two fields.

7. Jackson, *Gunnar Myrdal* 100–101. See also Kevin A. Yelvington, "The Anthropology of Afro-Latin America and the Caribbean: Diasporic Dimensions," *Annual Review of Anthropology* 30 (2001): 227–60 and Jackson, "Melville Herskovits and the Search for Afro-American Culture" 95–126 for a discussion of Herskovits's centrality in the formation of African American studies. Herskovits's focus on African survivals initiated one persistent line of inquiry in the field; another, opposing line was identified with E. Franklin Frazier, focusing on the extent of cultural assimilation, creolization, and hybridity.

8. See Capetti 182–210 for a discussion of Wright's use of theoretical and methodological tools borrowed from the Chicago School of Sociology.

9. Faye V. Harrison and Ira E. Harrison, *African-American Pioneers in Anthropology* (Chicago: University of Illinois Press, 1999) 19.

10. Clifford and Marcus, eds., *Writing Culture* (2–3).

11. Behar and Gordon, eds., *Women Writing Culture* 4.

12. Kamala Visweswaran defines a feminist ethnography as one that "generates multiple levels of meanings" by situating itself along "lines of difference" (41). Because Hurston's and Dunham's ethnographies reveal and describe "the production of knowledge as situated and relational," we recognize their contributions to a feminist epistemology (42).

13. Dunham's description of her decision to exorcise Habitation Leclerc of the ghosts that haunted its grounds inspire Dayan to focus on the ideological uses of this dichotomy (282). The shadows of the past, represented by the "ghosts" that prevent her from easily occupying the property she purchased, Dayan argues, are at the heart of Dunham's analysis of Haitian society. See Joan Dayan, "Haiti's Unquiet Past: Katherine Dunham, Modern Dancer, and Her Enchanted Island," in *Women at Sea: Travel Writing and the Margins of Caribbean Discourse*, ed. Lizabeth Paravisini-Gebert and Ivette Romero-Cesareo (New York: Palgrave, 2001) 281–91.

14. Katherine Dunham, *Island Possessed* (Chicago: University of Chicago Press, 1969) 63. In *Framing Silence: Revolutionary Novels by Haitian Women* (New Brunswick: Rutgers University Press, 1997), Myriam Chancy discusses Seabrook's *The Magic Island* and his description of the engulfing mambo's womb. Chancy argues that this sexualization of encounters with Haitians stereotypes the island and Haitian women in ways that perpetuate subordination of the culture (55–56). Dunham differentiates herself from Seabrook's sensationalism, but nonetheless is implicated in the colonizer's logic of objectification.

15. Because the term "voodoo" is so embedded in distorting stereotypes of savagery and unreason, I will follow the more accepted practice of referring to "Vodou," a spelling that is more in keeping with practitioners' self-identification. "Vodou" also references the etymology of the word in the Fon language-group in which *Vodun* refers to a "god" or "spirit." See, for example, Metraux 27.

16. Katherine Dunham, ""Dances of Haiti,"" *Acta Anthropologica* 2 (November 1947): 9.

17. Roy Wagner, *The Invention of Culture* (Englewood Cliffs, N.J.: Prentice-Hall, 1975) 6–7.

18. For a fuller treatment of African dance's influence on Williams and his representation of ideal African communities, see John O. Perpener, *African-American Concert Dance: The Harlem Renaissance and Beyond* (Chicago: University of Illinois Press, 2001) 78–100.

19. Ruth Beckford, *Katherine Dunham: A Biography* (New York: Marcel Dekker, 1979) 35.

20. Katherine Dunham, *Recommendation for a Program of Cultural Expansion in Three Areas*, quoted in "Plan for Goré as Residence Academy for West African Cultural Arts," in *Kaiso!*, ed. Clark and Wilkerson (Berkeley: Institute for the Study of Social Change, CCEW Women's Center, 1978) 137.

21. Ramsay Burt, *Alien Bodies: Representations of Modernity, "Race" and Nation in Early Modern Dance* (New York: Routledge, 1998) 2.

22. Claude McKay, "The Harlem Dancer," in *The Book of American Negro Poetry*, ed. James Weldon Johnson (New York: Harcourt Brace Jovanovich, 1922) 169–70.

23. According to dance historians Marshall and Jean Stearns, nine Black shows were mounted between 1921 (beginning with *Shuffle Along*) and 1924 (ending with *Dixie to Broadway*), all of them featuring innovative dance performances. Also during this period, Black dancers such as Josephine Baker, Bill Robinson, and Florence Mills ascended into stardom. See Marshall Stearns and Jean Stearns, *Jazz Dance: The Story of American Vernacular Dance* (New York: Schirmer Books, 1979).

24. Nella Larsen, *Quicksand* (New Brunswick: Rutgers University Press, 1986).

25. Katherine Dunham, ""The Negro Dance,"" in *Negro Caravan* (New York: Dryden Press, 1941) 68–69, reprinted in *Kaiso!*, ed. Clark and Wilkerson 66–74.

26. Zora Neale Hurston, *Their Eyes Were Watching God* (1937; repr. New York: Harper & Row, 1990) 133.

27 Joseph Roach, *Cities of the Dead: Circum-Atlantic Performance* (New York: Columbia University Press, 1996) xi.

28. Dunham's privileging of the indigenous and authentic was not relegated to the early years of her career. After performing in the Festival of Black Arts in Dakar, Senegal in 1966, for example, she stayed on to advise and train Senegal's National Ballet. Dunham found herself opposed to the company's attempts to work with " 'new' creative forms," and she encouraged them to "recreate from their own authentic cultural heritage" (Beckford 62).

29. Katherine Dunham, "Thesis Turned Broadway," *California Arts and Architecture*, 1941, reprinted in *Kaiso!*, ed. Clark and Wilkerson 57.

30. VèVè Clark, "Performing the Memory of Difference in Afro-Caribbean Dance: Katherine Dunham's Choreography, 1938–87," in *History and Memory in African-American Culture*, ed. Genevieve Fabre and Robert O'Meally (New York: Oxford University Press, 1994) 188–204.

31. Kaye Dunn, "*L'Ag'Ya* of Martinique," *Esquire* 12, no. 5 (1939), reprinted in *Kaiso!*, ed. Clark and Wilkerson 47.

32. Roy Thomas, "Focal Rites: New Dance Dominions," in *Kaiso!*, ed. Clark and Wilkerson 114.

33. Pierre Nora, "Between Memory and History: *Les Lieux de Mémoire*," in *History and Memory in African-American Culture*, ed. Genevieve Fabre and Robert O'Meally (New York: Oxford University Press, 1994) 12

34. Frederick L. Orme, "Negro in the Dance: As Katherine Dunham Sees Him," *American Dancer* 11, no. 5 (March 1938): 60–61, reprinted in *Kaiso!*, ed. Clark and Wilkerson 59–62.

35. John Martin, "The Dance: A Negro Art," *New York Times*, reprinted February 25, 1940, in *Kaiso!*, ed. Clark and Wilkerson 63–64.

36. Edward Barry, "Miss Dunham Is Sensation in Haitian Dances," *Chicago Daily Tribune*, June 4, 1937, reprinted in *Kaiso!*, ed. Clarke and Wilkerson 58.

37. It is important to note that African and Caribbean dances, like vernacular and social dances, were all assumed to lack the aesthetic sophistication of high art (synonymous with ballet and modern dance performed by Ruth St. Denis or Martha Graham). In *Modern Bodies: Dance and American Modernism from Martha Graham to Alvin Ailey* (Chapel Hill: University of North Carolina Press, 2002) 65, Julia L.

Foulkes argues that White audiences "rejected Dunham's and [Pearl] Primus's attempts to imbue the popular dances with artistic intention—by choreographing, not improvising, them and by performing the numbers on stage alongside other kinds of choreography" (75).

38. See Perpener for a fuller treatment of the stereotypical views of Black subjectivity that led many mainstream dance critics to deride Black dancers as cultural interlopers, outsiders to European-American traditions like ballet (18–24).

39. In *On the Real Side: Laughing, Lying and Signifying* (New York: Simon and Schuster, 1994), Mel Watkins argues that in the film ""the 'New Negro,' or at least a hip, comic version of that transplanted city dweller, has finally come to the screen" (263–64). Knight underscores that travel is an important motif in the film; the implication being that travel and modernity are closely aligned. See Arthur Knight, *Disintegrating the Musical: Black Performance and American Musical Film* (Durham: Duke University Press, 2002) 155.

Chapter 7

1. Robert Hemenway, *Zora Neale Hurston: A Literary Biography* (Chicago: University of Illinois Press, 1977) 63, 88.

2. Franz Boas, "Human Faculty as Determined by Race," in *A Franz Boas Reader* 225.

3. Zora Neale Hurston, *Dust Tracks on a Road* (London: Virago, 1986) 171.

4. Cited in Hemenway 227.

5. At the invitation of the Julius Rosenwald Foundation, Hurston applied for a grant to pursue her PhD with Boas. At first they offered to award her $3,000 over two years to complete the degree, but they took back the offer within a month (Hemenway 205–12). Hurston expressed her sense of betrayal in a 1936 letter addressed to Melville Herskovits which she wrote while living among the Maroons of Accompong: "Also found that Catherine [sic] Dunham had been here last year carrying out the program that I mapped out for the Rosenwald gang. I can afford to laugh at them, of course, but their littleness is astounding" (Kaplan 386).

6. Meehan notes that Hurston's "gendered and gendering cultural descriptions" are part of her decolonizing practice (246). See Kevin Meehan, "Decolonizing Ethnography: Zora Neale Hurston in the Caribbean," in *Women at Sea: Travel Writing and the Margins of Caribbean Discourse*, ed. Lizabeth Paravisini-Gebert and Ivette Romero-Cesareo (New York: Palgrave, 2001) 245–79.

7. My conceptualization of narrative dissonance is influenced by Edward Pavlic's argument that in *Their Eyes Were Watching God*, Hurston alludes to and invites consideration of Legba, the Vodou god of the crossroads. "For Hurston," he writes, "Esu-Elegba invokes black cultural confrontations with the dissonance at the modernist crossroads" (62). See Edward M. Pavlic, " 'Papa Legba, Ovrier Barriere Por Mois Passer': Esu in *Their Eyes* & Zora Neale Hurston's Diasporic Modernism," *African American Review* 38, no. 1 (2004): 61–85.

8. Zora Neale Hurston, "Characteristics of Negro Expression," in *Hurston: Folk-*

lore, Memoirs, & Other Writings, ed. Cheryl A. Wall (New York: The Library of America, 1995) 830–46.

9. See C. L. R. James, *The Black Jacobins: Toussaint L'Ouverture and the San Domingo Revolution* (New York: Vintage, 1989) for a complete discussion of the slave rebellion, its causes, and repercussions. See also Paul Farmer, *The Uses of Haiti* (Monroe, Maine: Common Courage Press, 2005) for a discussion of how Haitian isolation and demonization that originated in the nineteenth century continues to have implications in transnational politics and economic relations in the contemporary moment.

10. Wade Davis, *The Serpent and the Rainbow* (New York: Simon and Schuster, 1985) 208–9.

11. The U.S. military occupation of Haiti lasted from 1915 to 1934.

12. In his autobiography, *Along This Way* (New York: Da Capo Press, 2000), Johnson criticized the flimsy and insincere reasons given for the U.S. invasion of Haiti: "For the seizure of an independent nation, we offered the stock justifications: protection of American lives and American interests and the establishment and maintenance of internal order. Had all these reasons been well founded, they would not have constituted justification for the complete seizure of a sovereign state at peace with us" (344).

13. Jacqueline Shea Murphy, "'Words Like Bones': Narrative, Performance, and the Reconfiguring of United States Literatures" (dissertation, University of California, Berkeley, 1996).

14. Meehan makes a similar observation, albeit more tentatively (251).

15. The Library of America edition, edited by Cheryl Wall, includes the excised chapters.

16. Zora Neale Hurston, "Seeing the World as It Is," in *Hurston: Folklore, Memoirs, & Other Writings* 782–95.

17. I thank Cheryl Wall for the insight.

18. Zora Neale Hurston, *Tell My Horse: Voodoo and Life in Haiti and Jamaica* (New York: Harper & Row, 1938) 113.

19. J. Michael Dash, *Haiti and the United States: National Stereotypes and the Literary Imagination* (New York: St. Martin's Press, 1988) 2–3.

20. Ifeoma C. K. Nwankwo, "Insider and Outsider, Black and American: Rethinking Zora Neale Hurston's Caribbean Ethnography," *Radical History Review* 87 (2003): 49–77.

21. Hazel Carby, "The Politics of Fiction, Anthropology, and the Folk: Zora Neale Hurston," in *New Essays on* Their Eyes Were Watching God, ed. Michael Awkward (New York: Cambridge University Press, 1990) 71–93.

22. Ishmael Reed, Foreword, *Tell My Horse* xv.

23. Hemenway, *Zora Neale Hurston* 249.

24. Deborah Gordon describes this approach as reading Hurston's book "as an account of Haiti through the meaning of voodoo . . ." (157). See Deborah Gordon, "The Politics of Ethnographic Authority: Race and Writing in the Ethnography of Margaret Mead and Zora Neale Hurston," in *Modernist Anthropology: From Fieldwork to Text*, ed. Marc Manganaro (Princeton: Princeton University Press, 1990).

25. Hurston's depiction of the self-hating Mrs. Turner in *Their Eyes Were*

Watching God is evidence that she recognized African Americans' own problems with colorism. She also won second place in *Opportunity's* literary contest in 1925 for a play, *Color Struck*, indicating her ongoing interest in the topic.

26. Rachel Stein, *Shifting the Ground: American Women Writers' Revision of Nature, Gender, and Race* (Charlottesville: University of Virginia Press, 1997) 54.

27. Hurston, *Their Eyes* 14.

28. "She can do the same labors as a man or a mule and nobody thinks anything about it. In Jamaica it is common sight to see skinny-looking but muscular black women sitting on top of a pile of rocks with a hammer making little ones out of big ones. They look so wretched with their bare black feet all gnarled and distorted from walking barefooted over rocks. The nails on their big toes thickened like a hoof from a life time of knocking against stones" (Hurston, *Tell My Horse* 59).

29. "Experimental ethnography has argued that we play with voicing, but let me suggest that we look not only at language, or how things are said, but also at when and where things are said. The partiality of identity is seen to be inextricable from the contingency of speech. In locating the temporality of speech, we gain another lens on the constitution of subjectivity" (50).

30. Stein astutely argues, "Not only does Voodoo defy Western binary division, it also confounds realist objectivity and conclusive knowability" (68). One would therefore have to conclude that Hurston's attempts to represent her dual roles as dispassionate observer of and adherent to Vodou beliefs would be riven with ambivalence and ambiguity.

31. Wilentz's commentary ("A Place They Call Haiti," in *Haiti: Feeding the Spirit*, ed. Rebecca Busselle [New York: Aperture Foundation, 1992] 6–13) was written almost sixty years after Hurston wrote *Tell My Horse*, yet its relevance remains the same.

32. In "Thresholds of Difference: Structures of Address in Zora Neale Hurston," in *Zora Neale Hurston: Critical Perspectives Past and Present*, ed. Henry Louis Gates, Jr. and K. A. Appiah (New York: Amistad, 1993) 130–40, Johnson deconstructs Hurston's use of inside/outside binaries in *Mules and Men* and "How It Feels to Be Colored Me," but her analysis is equally relevant to *Tell My Horse* (130).

33. In "Hermes' Dilemma: The Masking of Subversion in Ethnographic Description," in *Writing Culture* 51–76, Vincent Crapanzano states, "like translation, ethnography is also a somewhat provisional way of coming to terms with the foreignness of languages–of cultures and societies. The ethnographer does not, however, translate text the way the translator does. He must first produce them" (51).

34. Anthropologist Clifford Geertz writes, "In finished anthropological writings, . . . this fact—that what we call our data are really our own constructions of other people's constructions of what they and their compatriots are up to—is obscured because most of what we need to comprehend a particular event, ritual, custom, idea, or whatever is insinuated as background information before the thing itself is directly examined." Clifford Geertz, *The Interpretation of Cultures* (New York: Beacon Press, 1989) 9.

35. Renato Rosaldo, *Culture and Truth: The Remaking of Social Analysis* (Boston: Beacon Press, 1989) 217.

36. Marianna Torgovnick, *Gone Primitive: Savage Intellects, Modern Lives* (Chicago: University of Chicago, 1990) 8.

37. Michel Foucault, *Madness and Civilization: A History of Insanity in the Age of Reason* (New York: Random House, 1965) 206.

38. Sander L. Gilman, *Disease and Representation: Images of Illness from Madness to AIDS* (Ithaca: Cornell University Press, 1988).

39. Meehan might argue that this is an example of the "constant parade of informants who talk back to the roving narrator" and deprive her the privilege of being the sole locus of authority (256).

40. For example, in *The Black Atlantic* (New York: Oxford University Press, 1995), Paul Gilroy defines the Black Atlantic as a "modern political and cultural formation that can be defined through the desire to transcend structures of the nation-state and the constraints of ethnic and national particularity" (19). See also Pheng Cheah and Bruce Robbins, *Cosmopolitics: Thinking and Feeling Beyond the Nation* (Minneapolis: University of Minnesota Press, 1998) and Ross Posnock, *Color and Culture: Black Writers and the Making of the Modern Intellectual* (Cambridge: Harvard University Press, 2000).

41. There are other reasons for Hurston's marginalization in critical accounts of travel and cosmopolitanism. Posnock argues that since Black intellectuals are "typically depicted as particularists, bent on creating a nationalist, vernacular folk culture of uplift" there has been a "historical blindness" to their cosmopolitan experiences and universalist ideals (7). Yet he is not alone in failing to accord the same status of travel between the U.S. and the Caribbean as that which takes place between the States and Paris (Richard Wright, for instance) or Germany (W. E. B. Du Bois, for example). One can surmise that this bias toward the metropole derives from critics' desire to challenge the "modernist/urban configuration of the 'primitive' object of study as romantic, pure, threatened, archaic, simple, and so forth" (James Clifford, *Routes: Travel and Translation in the Late Twentieth Century* [Cambridge: Harvard University Press, 1997] 21). Hurston's predilection to generalize about "the folk," her participation in an anthropological discourse that privileges "villages" like Eatonville over cities like New York or Berlin, would make her suspect in Posnock's notion of cosmopolitanism, as well as in Paul Gilroy's model of Black Atlantic cosmopolitanism. So would her impulse, again engrained by her anthropological training, to view such locales as "bounded sites" that serves as "mappable centers for the community, and by extension, the culture" (Clifford, *Routes* 21). While these scholars offer a necessary corrective, it seems to me a problematic endeavor when the effect is to recenter Europe or the West. African American experiences of migration have typically been overlooked and undervalued because they contradict stereotypical notions of the provincial Black. Yet at a moment when much scholarly energy is devoted to the recuperation of such experiences, Black women's particular experiences of travel continue to be undervalued.

Chapter 8

1. Ellease Southerland, "The Influence of Voodoo on the Fiction of Zora Neale Hurston," in *Sturdy Black Bridges: Visions of Black Women in Literature*. ed. Roseann P. Bell, Bettye J. Parker, and Beverly Guy-Sheftall (New York: Anchor Books, 1979).

2. Hurston used "voodoo" to refer to the Haitian belief system and "hoodoo" to refer to African American beliefs.

3. There are exceptions, of course, to this critical trend. See Derek Collins, "The Myth and Ritual of Ezili Freda in Hurston's *Their Eyes Were Watching God*," *Western Folklore* 55, no. 2 (1996): 137–54 and Edward M. Pavlic, "'Papa Legba, Ovrier Barriere Por Mois Passer': Esu in *Their Eyes* & Zora Neale Hurston's Diasporic Modernism," *African American Review* 38, no. 1 (2004): 61–85. Collins identifies Hurston's blending of African American and Caribbean folklore in order to argue that the novel should not "be read exclusively or even primarily within the context of American racial and gender politics" (150). Pavlic reads Legba, the master of the crossroads, as a figure of modernist dissonance that resonates with Hurston's exploration of cultural conflicts.

4. Hurston, *Their Eyes Were Watching God* 27.

5. Karen McCarthy Brown, *Mama Lola* (Berkeley: University of California Press, 1991) 221.

6. In *Fiction and Folklore: The Novels of Toni Morrison* (Knoxville: University of Tennessee Press, 1991), Trudier Harris claims that Hurston "excessively packs in folk expressions and beliefs to the extent that the excessively metaphorical folk language becomes an added character, plugging up the cracks between theme and plot, not a smoothly woven, integral part of the whole; language and story seem to have mutually exclusive functions" (6). Although the African American folklore functions separately from, and sometimes competes with, the narrative, the Haitian folklore blends in with and extends the narrative's themes.

7. Hemenway, *Zora Neale Hurston* 107.

8. H. Nigel Thomas, *From Folklore to Fiction: A Study of Folk Heroes and Rituals in the Black American Novel* (New York: Greenwood Press, 1988) 175.

9. Eugene O'Neill, *The Emperor Jones* (New York: Random House, 1921).

10. Hurston's characterization of Legba as the master of potentiality, the "opener of gates," is supported by other sources (Hurston, *Tell My Horse* 115). For example, in *Flash of the Spirit: African and Afro-American Art and Philosophy* (New York: Random House, 1983), Robert Farris Thompson writes that "God granted Eshu [the Yoruba manifestation of Legba] the force to make all things happen and multiply (*ashé*). . . . He is . . . the ultimate master of potentiality" (18–19).

11. References to God and god-like figures abound. In "Power, Judgment, and Narrative in a Work of Zora Neale Hurston: Feminist Cultural Studies," in *New Essays*, ed. Michael Awkward 95–123, Rachel Blau DuPlessis notes that "the absolute beginning of the book begins playing with title materials and meanings by opening issues about words and the Word in relation to gender and racial power. The third paragraph starts with a revisionary articulation of Biblical rhetoric 'So the beginning of this was a woman,' taking the world-creating place of Word or God" (109). In "'The Infinity of Conscious Pain': Zora Neale Hurston and the Black Female Literary Tradition," in *Zora Neale Hurston*, ed. Harold Bloom (New York: Chelsea House Publishers, 1986) 9–17, Lorraine Bethel writes, "Hurston's first description of Nanny in *Their Eyes* establishes her as a representative of the religious experience that stands at the center of Afro-American folk tradition. She is described in terms suggestive of a Christ figure. Janie makes Nanny a wreath of 'palma christi leaves,' and the words 'bore' and 'pierce' used in this passage invoke images of the crucifixion" (13–14). Bar-

bara Johnson and Henry Louis Gates, Jr. note that "Joe Starks . . . fondly and unconsciously refers to himself as 'I-God.' During the lamp-lighting ceremony . . . Joe is represented as the creator (or at least the purchaser) of light" (73). See Barbara Johnson and Henry Louis Gates, Jr., "A Black Idiomatic Free Indirect Discourse," in *Zora Neale Hurston*, ed. Bloom 73–85.

12. Alfred Métraux, *Voodoo in Haiti* (New York: Schocken Books, 1959) 110.

13. "Each *loa* has its representative colour—red for Ogu, white for Damballah, blue for Ezili etc." (Métraux 167).

14. "Ezili being a white *loa* and a 'woman of the world' has a fondness for pale and sugary drinks" (Métraux 176).

15. Janie's donning of the overalls can be read as a moment of transvestisms which disrupts and challenges Eatonville's social order. In *Vested Interests: Cross-Dressing and Cultural Anxiety* (New York: Routledge, 1992), Marjorie Garber argues that "transvestisms was located at the juncture of 'class and gender,' and increasingly through its agency gender and class were revealed to be commutable, if not equivalent. To transgress against one set of boundaries was to call into question the inviolability of both, and the set of social codes—already demonstrably under attack—by which such categories were policed and maintained" (32). The townsfolk react to Janie's transgression of class and gender boundaries, seeing the overalls as a violation of their social codes.

16. While some anthropologists mistakenly represent the Rada and Petwo spirits as symbolizing good and evil (Hurston included), the actual significance of these two Vodou pantheons is more complicated than suggested by this binarism. McCarthy Brown writes: "The Rada spirits are sweet-tempered and dependable; their power resides in their wisdom. . . . They are intimate, familial spirits who are given family titles such as Papa and Kouzen [cousin]. . . . The Petwo spirits, in contrast, are hot-tempered and volatile. They must be handled with care and precision. Debts must be paid and promises kept, or they will badger and harass those who serve them. The power of the Petwo spirits resides in their effectivity, their ability to make things happen" (100–101).

17. Karla Holloway, *The Character of the Word: The Texts of Zora Neale Hurston* (New York: Greenwood Press, 1987) 65.

18. " Dantò's anger can exceed what is required for strict discipline. At times, it explodes from her with an irrational, violent force. Ezili Danté, like Lasyrenn, has connections with water. A gentle rainfall during the festivities at Saut d'Eau, a mountain pilgrimage site for Ezili Dantò (Our Lady of Mount Carmel), is readily interpreted as a sign of her presence; but so is a sudden deluge resulting in mudslides, traffic accidents, and even deaths. . . . Thus Dantò's rage can emerge with the elemental force of a torrential rain, which sweeps away just and unjust alike. This aspect of Ezili Dantò might be described as an infant's eye view of the omnipotent mother" (McCarthy Brown 231).

19. Donald Petesch notes that during the period of enslavement, in sermons and catechisms, "grand moralizing gave way to immediate practical ends: the language of religion became the language of social control." *A Spy in the Enemy's Country: The Emergence of Modern Black Literature* (Iowa City: University of Iowa Press, 1989) 60.

20. The title of Washington's essay is key in signaling that female hero of the

novel is in the process of emerging, but has not yet arrived. See Mary Helen Washington, "'I Love the Way Janie Crawford Left Her Husbands': Emergent Female Hero," in *Zora Neale Hurston: Critical Perspectives*, ed. Gates and Appiah 99.

21. Leslie Desmangles, *The Faces of the Gods: Vodou and Roman Catholicism in Haiti* (Chapel Hill: University of North Carolina Press, 1992) 61.

22. Alain Locke, "Literature By and About the Negro," *Opportunity* 16 (1938): 7–11, reprinted in *Zora Neale Hurston: Critical Perspectives*, ed. Gates and Appiah 18.

23. In that same review Wright deemed the novel to be no better than a minstrel show. See Richard Wright, "Between Laughter and Tears," *New Masses* 5 (October 1937): 22, 25, reprinted in *Zora Neale Hurston: Critical Perspectives*, ed. Gates and Appiah 16–17.

24. Alice Walker, "Looking for Zora," in *I Love Myself When I Am Laughing . . . and Then Again When I Am Looking Mean and Impressive* (New York: The Feminist Press, 1979).

25. Paul Gilroy, *The Black Atlantic: Modernity and Double Consciousness* (Cambridge: Harvard University Press, 1993) 91–92.

26. Arnold Rampersad's assessment of the contributors to *The New Negro*, some of the most influential Black intellectuals of the day, supports my suggestion that the desire to elevate the spirituals to a "higher" art form betrays a belief in the cultural inferiority of African Americans. In the Introduction to *The New Negro*, Rampersad writes, "It is fair to say that, in the face of racial 'science,' most of the contributors to the volume accepted the notion of black racial and cultural inferiority compared to the standards of European civilization. Most also believed, however, that the African race was on the move forward, that politically, economically, and culturally, peoples of African descent around the world were engaged in the first stages of a transformation that would eventually lead to independence from Europe" (xvi). Ironically, most believed that independence from Europe could be achieved only by successfully replicating, with minor adaptations, its cultural, social, and political paradigms.

27. Zora Neale Hurston, "Spirituals and Neo-Spirituals," in *The Sanctified Church: The Folklore Writings of Zora Neale Hurston* (Berkeley: Turtle Island, 1981) 79–84.

28. Sundquist, *The Hammers of Creation* 60.

29. Carby, "The Politics of Fiction" 71–93.

30. For example, in "Spirituals and Neo-Spirituals," Hurston asserts, "There never has been a presentation of genuine Negro spirituals to any audience anywhere. What is being sung by the concert artists and glee clubs are the works of Negro composers or adaptors [sic] *based* on the spirituals" (80).

31. Carby is far from alone in perceiving the novel as being removed from history and reality. Robert Stepto writes, "The narrative takes place in a seemingly ahistorical world: the spanking new all-black town is meticulously bereft of former slave cabins; there are no railroad trains, above or underground, with or without Jim Crow cars; Matt's mule is a bond with and catalyst for distinct tribal memories and rituals, but these do not include the hollow slogan, 'forty acres and a mule'; Janie seeks freedom, selfhood, voice, and 'living' but is hardly guided—or haunted—by Sojourner Truth or Harriet Tubman, let alone Frederick Douglass" (6). What Stepto calls an "ahistorical world," Carby names a displacement. Carby remarks upon the text's

avoidance of the present while Stepto focuses on its avoidance of the past. But just as Hurston implicitly signifies on then contemporary debates and experiences, so does she signify on African American history. For example, while it is true that no character remarks upon the proverbial and unrealized promise of forty acres and a mule, it is no coincidence that Logan Killicks owns not just forty, but *sixty* acres and a mule.

32. Deborah E. McDowell makes a similar point about Hurston's willingness to engage in political dialogue in an essay on *Moses, Man of the Mountain*. In "Lines of Descent/Dissenting Lines," in *Zora Neale Hurston: Critical Perspectives*, ed. Gates and Appiah 230–40, McDowell discusses the ways in which the text's symbolism critiques the United State's rhetoric of liberation and reveals its hypocrisy by implicitly juxtaposing the United States' oppression of African Americans with the ideology of racial purity which fueled Germany's entry into a world war in 1939. McDowell concludes, "All too often Hurston's readers have consigned her to Eatonville and left her there on the porch. . . . Even when readers stretch her province to New Orleans and the Caribbean, the sites of her fieldwork, they often read these migrations as extensions of Eatonville, seen as the repository of black folk culture on which all Hurston's work is dependent. But, reducing Eatonville, and its symbolic geographic coordinates to the repositories of black 'folk' expression that Hurston mined so well 'regionalizes her work and ensures her removal from a more global context of cultural production and exchange" (240).

33. In "The Erotics of Talk: 'That Oldest Human Longing' in *Their Eyes Were Watching God*," *American Literature* 67, no. 1 (March 1995): 115–42, Kaplan's discussion centers on how Hurston's representation of women pose a direct challenge to New Negro politics that emphasized feminine propriety and respectability in the interest of uplift (121–27).

Chapter 9

1. Gloria Naylor, *Mama Day* (New York: Ticknor and Fields, 1988) 7.

2. See Daphne Lamothe, "*Mama Day*: Bridging Roots and Routes," *African American Review* 39, nos. 1–2 (Spring/Summer 2005): 155–69.

Index

Adell, Sandra, 60, 63–64

Afro-Caribbean culture: dance, 132–36; Hurston's studies of, 141–42, 149–52; and Johnson's youth, 74–75. *See also* Haiti; Haitian Vodou; Jamaica; Martinique

"allegory of salvage," 38–39

American Anthropological Association, 193 n.45

American Association of Anthropological Societies, 34

An American Dilemma (Myrdal), 92

American Folklore Society (AFLS), 28–31, 39, 41, 189 n.17, 193 n.45; HFS scholarly delegation at 1894 meeting, 30–31; recording of African American folk songs, 30, 189 n.20

American Museum of Natural History (AMNH), 33

American Negro Academy, 44

Anderson, David, 92, 112, 205 n.24

Andrews, William, 81, 200 n.11

anthropology: "allegory of salvage," 38–39; African American folklore and the JAFL, 39; "applied," 20; Chicago School of Sociology, 115, 117–20, 207 nn.5–6; "classical period" of the discipline, 12, 184 n.19; and colonialism, 12, 184–85 n.20, 186 n.30; Columbia department, 32, 33, 184 n.19, 190 n.26; cultural relativism, 22, 31, 41–42, 158; cultural syncretism, 119; cultural translation, 12, 134–36, 155–58, 185 n.21, 212 nn.33–34; culture concept, 22, 32, 38, 42, 93–95, 114, 183–84 n.12, 192 n.41; culture shock, 123; dance anthropology, 115, 117–18, 122–23, 129–32; development of modern, 21–23, 31–38; early changes to the discipline, 184 n.19; ethnocentrism, 150, 153; feminist ethnography, 18, 120–21, 208 n.12; fieldwork, 9, 19, 118–20, 123–24, 150, 153; French ethnography of the 1920s and

1930s, 186–87 n.34; "going native," 156; the Hampton Folklore Society, 23–32, 188 nn.6–7, 188 n.9; Hurston and the contradictions of the ethnographic perspective, 2–3, 5–9, 18, 142–44, 148, 150, 152–59, 187 n.40; hybrid narratives, 10–12, 17, 48, 163, 183 n.2, 184 n.15; methods, 9–20; movement between cultures, 13–14, 15; museum model, 93–95, 203 n.7, 204 n.8; the "native ethnographer," 2–3, 14–16, 186 nn.30–32; New Negro confrontation with assumptions/objectives, 14–16, 185 n.27, 186 n.30; notion of "the field," 54–56, 197 nn.23–24; and participant-observation, 9, 15–16, 69, 80, 125–26, 184 n.13, 199 n.2; and political neutrality ideal, 20, 186 n.30; possibilities and limitations, 12, 19–20, 183 n.2, 184–85 n.20; and postmodern "crisis of representation," 16, 186–87 n.34; and scientific racism, 13, 21–23, 32–38, 40, 42, 141, 185 n.27, 191 n.34; and sociology discipline, 44–45, 186 n.33, 195 n.3; subject-object dichotomies, 14–16; views of race and cultural assimilation, 42–43, 194 n.52; "virtual anthropologists," 14–15, 186 nn.31–32; women in the field, 33. *See also* Boas, Franz; folklore collection; New Negro ethnographic literature

Anzaldùa, Gloria, 14

Aptheker, Herbert, 198 n.31

Argonauts of the Western Pacific (Malinowski), 20, 183–84 n.12, 184 n.13

Armstrong, Samuel Chapman, 23–24, 25, 31, 189 n.15

Arnold, Mathew, 47

Aschenbrenner, Joyce, 142, 185 n.21

Assen, Abdul, 127

"The Atlanta Conferences" (Du Bois), 55, 65

Atlanta University, 46, 186 n.33

Haiti (*cont.*)
　ism/imperialism, 145–46; as gendered/fem-
　inized space, 147–48; Habitation Leclerc,
　121, 208 n.13; Hurston's *Tell My Horse*,
　144–48; and stereotypes of barbarism/sav-
　agery, 145–48; U.S. imperialism in, 145–46,
　211 n.12
Haiti and the United States (Dash), 147
Haitian Vodou: and animal sacrifice, 152–53;
　critics of Hurston's approach to, 160–61,
　172–78, 214 n.3; Dunham's ethnographies,
　122, 124–28; and female agency, 162, 165–72;
　and female sexuality, 166–67; and Gede,
　154–55, 171; and gender, 147–48, 151–52, 162,
　165–72; and the (hegemonic) gaze, 125–26;
　Hurston's binarism/scholarly detachment,
　152–53, 212 n.30; Hurston's Janie and god-
　dess Ezili, 19, 161, 164, 165–72, 215 n.15, 215
　n.18; Hurston's response to popular de-
　mands for the primitive, 162–65; Hurston's
　Tell My Horse, 146–49, 151–55, 171; Hurston's
　Their Eyes, 19, 160–78, 214 n.3;
　initiation ceremony, 124–25; psychological
　functions of sacred dance (for diasporic
　affinity), 127–28; and resistance, 155, 171;
　and self-expression, 154–55, 171
Haiti ethnographies: and the anthropological
　gaze, 125–27; cultural aspects of Haitian
　dance, 122–23; "Dances of Haiti" (Dunham),
　115, 121–23, 145; Dunham's, 18, 115, 121–27; as
　gendered/feminized space, 121–22, 147–48,
　208 n.14; and Hurston's ethnographic per-
　spective, 152–53, 212 n.30; and Hurston's
　Their Eyes, 18–19, 53, 160–78; *Island Possessed*
　(Dunham), 18, 123–27; liminality and field-
　work, 123–24; and New Negro attitudes to-
　ward Haiti's history, 121, 144–48, 162; and
　participant-observation, 125–26; and popular
　demands for the primitive, 162–65; and
　stereotypes of barbarism/savagery, 145–48;
　Tell My Horse (Hurston), 2, 18, 142–59. *See
　also* Haitian Vodou
Haley, Alex, 184 n.15
Hampton Creative Dance Group, 127
Hampton Folklore Society (HFS): and AFLS
　concept of scientific folklore collection,
　28–31, 39, 41, 189 n.17, 193 n.45; and envi-
　ronmentalist theories of racial difference,
　28, 189 n.15; and folklore collection, 23–32,
　188 nn.6–7, 188 n.9; folklore collection as

science, 28; folklore collection goals, 24–27,
　188 n.9; the "Hampton Idea," 23–32; and
　the JAFL, 39; and Native American culture,
　188 n.7, 190 n.22; and New Negro turn to
　folklore/culture of South, 23–32; scholarly
　delegation at 1894 AFLS meeting, 30–31;
　and Shaler, 23–32, 195 n.5; treated as native
　informants, 30–31; uses to which folklore
　collection could be put, 27–28, 189 n.13,
　190 n.23
Hampton Institute, 23–32, 127
"Harlem Dancer" (McKay), 129–30
Harlem Shadows (McKay), 95, 203 n.4
Harris, Abram L., 98
Harris, Joel Chandler, 24
Harris, Trudier, 214 n.6
Harrison, Faye V., 42, 120, 186 n.30
Harrison, Ira E., 120
Harvard University, 45, 62, 91, 195 n.5
Hemenway, Robert, 8, 143, 148–49, 164
Herskovits, Melville, 31, 33; anthropological
　approach to African culture, 118–19, 193
　n.51, 207 n.7; attack on scientific racism,
　187–88 n.4; and Dunham, 118–19, 124; and
　Hurston, 141, 210 n.5; on shifts in defini-
　tion of folklore, 190 n.24
Holloway, Karla, 170, 174
Hose, Sam, 46
Hovenkamp, Herbert, 187–88 n.4
Howard University, 92, 98
Huggins, Nathan Irvin, 191–92 n.38
Hughes, Langston, 91, 95; on dance and the
　body, 130; and Haiti, 121; Hurston's letters
　to, 7, 10–11, 185 n.24; and patronage, 191–92
　n.38. *See also Ways of White Folk*
Humboldt University, 45
Hurston, Zora Neale, 1–3, 18–19, 141–59,
　160–78; at Barnard College, 1, 141; and the
　Black modernist gaze, 5–9; and Boas, 1, 5,
　31, 38, 141, 142, 143, 210 n.5; critics of narra-
　tive dissonance, 144; critics of political
　analyses, 144, 148–49; critics of representa-
　tion of Black culture, 172–76, 216 n.23, 216
　n.31; culture concept, 7; on dance and
　communal bonds, 131–32; and Dunham,
　141, 142, 145, 147, 210 n.5; and the ethno-
　graphic perspective, 2–3, 5–9, 18, 142–44,
　148, 150, 152–59, 187 n.40; and feminist
　ethnography, 18, 208 n.12; on folklore col-
　lection, 38; and generic hybridity, 10–11,

Acknowledgments

I could not have written this book without the support of my family, friends, and colleagues. This project has been a long time coming, and I would not have been able to realize my ideas without the guidance and inspiration of many people. My first thanks go to the book's initial readers, Mitchell Breitwieser, Katherine Bassard, and VèVè Clark. Their support extended beyond offering constructive criticism on the project to including words of advice, encouragement, and advocacy. Barbara Christian and VèVè Clark were models of rigorous and humanist engagement with black literature; they made their imprint on me as a young scholar, and I hope their spirits live in these pages. I am also especially grateful to friends and colleagues from the University of California, Berkeley, who formed my first intellectual community: Theresa Tensuan, Cynthia Dobbs, Anne Marie Harvey, Juana Rodriguez, Stafford Gregoire, Linda Chandler, Valorie Thomas, Donna Weir, Cynthia Liu, and Harry Lin. Many of them read the earliest versions of this manuscript and offered incisive criticism and encouragement when I most needed it. They all offered friendship and humor and reminded me to center myself through fellowship with others.

My sincere thanks also to Abena Busia, Wesley Brown, and Brent Edwards, who read and commented on my work and offered insight and support at critical moments. I am especially indebted to Cheryl Wall, whose questions were pointed, whose suggestions were generous, and whose work on women of the Harlem Renaissance has been a model of clarity, insight, and precision. I owe a special debt to Herman Bennett, Jennifer Morgan, and Vilna Bashi Treitler for the wisdom and guidance they provided while we all worked to balance the demands of careers in academia and family life. They in their various ways helped me to become a better scholar and mother and to see that these two roles need not compete with or contradict each other. My gratitude also to the English Department Working Group at Rutgers, a community of junior scholars who came together regularly to read and critique each other's work. The group offered a venue for receiving careful and generous readings from colleagues. Chris Chism, Mary Pauline Sheridan-

Rabideau, Edlie Wong, and Stacey Klein provided emotional support, as well as intellectual engagement, and for that I am especially grateful.

At Smith College, I have found my second intellectual home, and I am fortunate to benefit from the collegiality of Paula Giddings, Kevin Quashie, Louis Wilson, Katwiwa Mule, and Anne Ferguson. I share works in progress with a group of brilliant feminist scholars: Jennifer Guglielmo, Ginetta Candelario, Elisabeth Armstrong, Michelle Joffroy, and Adriane Lenz-Smith. They challenge and inspire me and nurture both body and mind. The intelligence and wit of Danielle Elliott and Christina Greer got me through the longest days as the book neared completion. Ayoka Stewart proved invaluable as my research assistant, and Astride Charles's skills as a researcher cannot be rivaled. I also thank Farah Griffin, Valerie Smith, Lee D. Baker, and Joan Dayan for their support of my work. I learned an enormous amount from their scholarship and owe them a debt of gratitude for their generous and constructive criticism of the manuscript.

At Rutgers University, I shared drafts of chapters with the Institute for Research on Women's Faculty Fellows Seminar and with the Center for Historical Analysis's Black Atlantic Seminar. A Mabelle McLeod Lewis Fellowship supported me during the 1995–96 academic year at the University of California, Berkeley. The Department of Afro-American Studies at Smith College granted me resources and leave time to complete the book. I also want to extend my gratitude to Johns Hopkins University Press for permission to use in Chapter 8 material that had originally been published in the journal *Callaloo: A Journal of African and African American Literature.*

I benefited from the expert guidance and scrupulous work of the University of Pennsylvania Press and my editors, Jerome Singermans and Erica Ginsburg. I appreciated and found quite helpful the comments of two anonymous readers. It is a better book as a result of their having read and responded to it in its earlier stages.

Finally, I could not have completed this work without the support of my family. They always remind me to keep my priorities straight and to remember that communion with loved ones is a fundamental human need. They have kept me grounded and made me laugh when I took myself too seriously. They are my haven. I am permanently indebted to my parents, who paved the way with their love, unflagging support, and terribly good sense. Rutherford Wilson's love has helped me to find my way when the road has been rocky. This book has developed in tandem with my two precious daughters, Maya and Kira. I dedicate it to them and want them to know it would not have been possible if they had not blessed me with their presence.